*45989*

947
ABE

Abel, Elie

The shattered bloc

$20.95

| DATE | | | |
|---|---|---|---|
| | | | |
| | | | |
| | | | |
| | | | |
| | | | |
| | | | |
| | | | |
| | | | |
| | | | |
| | | | |
| | | | |
| | | | |

May 1990

© THE BAKER & TAYLOR CO.

# THE
# SHATTERED
# BLOC

# THE
# SHATTERED
# BLOC

—

*Behind the Upheaval in*
*Eastern Europe*

—

ELIE ABEL

HOUGHTON MIFFLIN COMPANY · BOSTON
1990

For information about permission to reproduce selections
from this book, write to Permissions, Houghton Mifflin
Company, 2 Park Street, Boston, Massachusetts 02108.

*Library of Congress Cataloging-in-Publication Data*
Abel, Elie.
The shattered bloc : behind the upheaval in Eastern Europe /
Elie Abel.
p.    cm.
ISBN 0-395-42019-9
1. Europe, Eastern — Politics and government — 1945–   2. Europe,
Eastern — Economic conditions — 1945–   I. Title.
DJK50.A24   1990   89-26821
947 — dc20   CIP

Printed in the United States of America

BVG 10 9 8 7 6 5 4 3 2 1

*For Mark and Suzanne*

# Contents

# EAST BLOC
## COUNTRIES

# PART I

---

# 1

## An Empire in Dissolution

THE ASTONISHING WAVE of revolutions that swept across Central and Eastern Europe in 1989 pronounced the doom of Joseph Stalin's external empire, raising hopes for a rebirth of democracy and the rule of law. As the Cold War passed into history, Communism was in retreat throughout the region.

In the West the age of empire had ended decades earlier. Britain, France, Portugal, Belgium, and the Netherlands gave up their overseas possessions in the aftermath of World War II, yielding power to subject peoples clamoring for independence and the right, as India's Jawaharlal Nehru once put it, to make their own mistakes. Now it was the turn of the Soviet Union.

In the impoverished countries ruled by totalitarians of the left for over four decades, incredible things were happening. The wall that disfigured the border between the two Germanys — and sliced the city of Berlin in two — suddenly became irrelevant as the desperate East German regime punched holes in it to allow free passage in both directions. The hard-line Communist leadership collapsed, creating a political vacuum that sooner or later was likely to be filled by unification with the Federal Republic or some form of confederation. The prospect of a united Germany, some eighty million strong, in the center of Europe rang alarms in Western capitals as well as Moscow.

Czechoslovakia witnessed a similar collapse of the old Stalinist regime, brought down without violence by a coalition of dissident intellectuals and students. For the first time since 1948, Communists were no longer in command as a new government started to dismantle the most repressive features of the old order. In Poland the discredited Communist Party grudgingly accepted a back seat in the new coalition government led by Solidarity, following the near-total repudiation of the party by the voters. Hungary ripped out its barbed wire fence along the Austrian border on the west while preparing for its first totally free election, which the Communists were expected to lose, since 1945. Even in Bulgaria, the rigid Stalinist regime of Todor Zhivkov ended in his ouster after thirty-five years in power.

Romania was the last domino to fall as Nicolae Ceausescu's dictatorship ended in a pre-Christmas spasm of police terror and wholesale bloodshed. It was the only country in the shattered bloc where the pattern of peaceful revolution broke down, as security forces fought the army in the streets of Bucharest, Timisoara, and Arad.

These extraordinary changes exceeded all predictions. The unlikely revolutionaries were no less surprised by their swift successes than the rest of the world. They had started as would-be reformers of a system that was breaking down, though not everywhere or all at once; its failures could no longer be disguised or hidden. The reformers wanted change, the opportunity to increase trade with the West, to restructure their obsolete economies, to restore basic freedoms and, in the words of a Hungarian party member, to "be a part of Europe again." Few expected the totalitarian systems imposed by overwhelming Soviet force in the forties to disintegrate overnight.

That outcome was not preordained. The Soviet Union had

more than enough power, if it came to that, to save Communist rule in the satellite belt. The Kremlin had not flinched at the use of force to crush the East German workers' uprising in 1953. Nikita Khrushchev sent his Red Army tanks roaring into Budapest in 1956, and Leonid Brezhnev did it in Prague in 1968. Mikhail Gorbachev, a reformer himself, understood that the time for a mailed-fist response had passed. He had promised the people of the Soviet Union a new era of democratization, economic efficiency, more openness between rulers and the ruled, and an end of the Cold War by negotiation with the West. He was beset by grave problems at home: an enormous, long-concealed budget deficit, precarious food supplies, low morale, and demands for self-determination in the Baltic republics as well as other regions.

There was also the considerable risk that armed intervention in Eastern Europe would wreck Gorbachev's greatly improved relations with the West, whose help he needed. It would certainly torpedo the arms control negotiations at Geneva and Vienna, nullifying the hope of relief for the overstrained Soviet economy through deep negotiated cuts in military spending. In any event, Gorbachev decided against intervening to slow or stop radical change in Eastern Europe. More than that, he used his influence to speed the process of reform, notably in East Germany, Poland, and Czechoslovakia.

The six countries that lie between the Bug River in the east and the Elbe in the west do not bulk very large on the map of Europe, but the Kremlin had long considered them important out of all proportion to their combined area, population, and natural resources. Initially, they provided a buffer zone to guard the frontiers of European Russia against hypothetical attack from the West. No such attack has ever been launched or seriously threatened. But existence of the bloc, and the Warsaw Pact as its military arm, served other purposes. They kept Germany divided, a major goal of Soviet policy. The permanent presence of 550,000 Soviet troops in the region also served a political purpose, guaranteeing that the subject peoples would not be tempted to break out of the "camp of socialism."

It is not a trivial distinction that Communism came to Central and Eastern Europe by force of alien arms rather than by social revolution. With Hitler's armies in strategic retreat during the final months of World War II, Soviet forces overran, and stayed to occupy, the whole of Poland, Hungary, Bulgaria, Romania, most of Czechoslovakia, and half of Germany. This was Stalin's way of securing the western borders of the Soviet Union against military threats in the future. But security, to Stalin and his successors, had another dimension. It meant total political control of the region, to be exercised through the installation of Soviet-style regimes whose leaders and policies carried the seal of Kremlin approval. In this process the Red Army played an indispensable role. Its presence gave a certain weight of authority to the actions and pronouncements of the new leaders, who lacked the popular support to carry out revolutionary changes on their own.

In the absence of revolution, as Wladyslaw Gomulka conceded in a 1945 speech, only the presence of the Red Army made it possible to begin what he called the "transformation of Polish society." In a midnight conversation with the Yugoslav leader Milovan Djilas, Stalin made no secret of his intentions. "This war," he said, "is not as in the past; whoever occupies a territory also imposes on it his own social system. Everyone imposes his own system as far as his army can reach. It cannot be otherwise."

Many of today's problems are rooted in the immediate postwar period, when this new class of rulers, installed with Moscow's blessing and support, set up virtually identical totalitarian regimes in all six countries of the new Soviet imperium. They called them people's democracies, a double misnomer. Like the old Radical Socialist Party in prewar France, which was famous for being neither radical nor socialist, the people's democracies of Central and Eastern Europe were in no sense democratic, nor did the people have much to say about how they were to be ruled or by whom. What they got instead of elections was a set of single-party dictatorships, answerable in the first instance to Moscow.

With the consolidation of Communist rule in the late 1940s, the Soviet way of doing things became the only way in all six countries, regardless of differing national circumstances. Human rights were grandly proclaimed in official documents, though they were seldom observed. The oppressive weight of bureaucracy hung over the most trivial transactions between citizen and state. Governments busied themselves with tasks better left undone, or better done by others: deciding, for example, what products each factory should produce, in what quantities; fixing the prices of all goods and commodities, regardless of supply or demand; controlling the movements of all citizens within their own countries or across frontiers; dictating what should be taught in the schools; censoring all books, magazines, journals, newspapers, radio, television, stage plays, and motion pictures; clapping dissidents, real or suspected, into jail and not infrequently roughing them up. In the early postwar years, fidelity to the Soviet model also demanded show trials of prominent Communist leaders (Laszlo Rajk in Hungary and Rudolf Slansky in Czechoslovakia, to name two), on patently preposterous charges leading to death sentences.

The pattern varied slightly from country to country, save in two respects: there could be no thought of any Soviet bloc country quitting the Warsaw Pact or abandoning the established, so-called socialist order. A bit of tinkering around the edges of party dogma, a mild flirtation with a hybrid notion called market socialism, might be tolerated in one or two countries, though not before the late 1960s. But the "commanding heights" of the economy, and of society as a whole, had to remain under firm and permanent Communist control.

These restrictions have lost much of their power in the final decade of the century. Poland has a non-Communist prime minister, and Hungary may soon have one. Even the East German Communists, reversing course after forty years of orthodox Stalinist methods, have promised free elections in 1990, unrestricted travel to the West, market-oriented reforms, and freedom of expression. Czechoslovakia is expected to follow suit. The Soviet Union itself, like Eastern Europe, is in the grip of a crisis that is political and moral as well as economic. The old Leninist-Stalinist order appears to be crumbling, and the shape of the new order has yet to be defined.

For the men in power, Gorbachev's "new thinking" was a two-edged sword. It widened their space for independent action, most markedly in Poland and Hungary. But as members of the *nomenklatura,* a highly privileged class, they had a great deal to lose if radical reform created turbulence at home. Few East European leaders, accordingly, had embraced Gorbachev's *perestroika* or *glasnost.* Only Hungary and Poland, at the outset, chose the route of political pluralism and market-driven economic reform. Even in these countries, however, one encounters far more skepticism than in the West about the prospects of Gorbachev's political survival.

The East European Communist leaders have spent most of their lives working inside a system modeled directly on the Soviets'. They understand better than Western politicians how difficult it is to turn that system around, to decentralize the world's most centralized economy, to weed out the lazy, corrupt, and incompetent managers, to establish and enforce rules of public accountability, to shut down state enterprises that cannot survive without enormously wasteful subsidies, to restrain the police and the military, and to waken a spirit of enterprise in a populace that for decades past has looked to the state as employer, landlord, educator, and moral guide. They also know that they are more vulnerable than their counterparts in Moscow. Any Soviet leader can count on a broad layer of patriotic support, notably among ethnic Russians. The remarkable fact about the peoples of Central and Eastern Europe, by contrast, was that tens of millions among them, after more than four decades, remained unreconciled to a system they regarded as alien, to be enforced, when the need arose, by the armed might of the Red Army.

Three times since World War II the Red Army has been called on to defend the Soviet hegemony by force of arms. Each time Moscow sent troops and tanks to rescue Communist regimes from their own people — in East Germany, Hungary, and Czechoslovakia. The huge Soviet troop commitment, in short, while difficult to justify in purely military terms as fear of a third world war receded, remained the ultimate instrument of control over the restless peoples of the empire.

At the annual meeting of the Warsaw Pact ministers in 1989, Gorbachev proclaimed a modified policy of nonintervention. The official communiqué said, "No country has the right to dictate events in another country, to assume the position of judge or arbiter." The document also laid down the principle that "there are no universal models of socialism."

Gorbachev told the leaders of all six nations that they no longer were required to follow the Soviet example in every respect. Their task, he said repeatedly, was to reshape and revive their feeble economies, to make their systems more responsive and above all more efficient, bearing in mind the needs and traditions of their people. The Poles and Hungarians needed no urging to move in that direction. Both countries anticipated and surpassed Gorbachev's reforms in the Soviet Union. But Gorbachev's urgings to speed the reform process met with lip service or dogged resistance in the other Soviet bloc countries until it was too late to save their recalcitrant leaders — Erich Honecker in East Germany, Milos Jakes in Czechoslovakia, Todor Zhivkov in Bulgaria (there is clear evidence that the Kremlin had a hand in their removal) and, finally, Nicolae Ceausescu in Romania.

Although the Warsaw Pact remains intact, the once-seamless political unity of the East bloc will be hard to restore with non-Communists moving into positions of power in several countries. The countries of the shattered bloc, moreover, are increasingly caught up in neighbor-to-neighbor disputes over nationality issues, emigration, and trade.

With bloc unity faltering and ideology losing its force, the external empire has seen a remarkable resurgence of long-suppressed national feelings and traditions, including a revival of churchgoing. What is even more remarkable, the internal Soviet empire of non-Russian peoples is in turmoil as Estonians, Latvians, Lithuanians, Moldavians, Armenians, and other national entities press demands ranging from the right to replace the use of Russian with their own languages to outright independence. Terms like "self-determination" and "national sovereignty" have become part of everyday speech.

Like Charles de Gaulle, whose vision of the future encompassed an unbroken stretch from the Atlantic to the Urals, Gorbachev talks to Western European audiences about "our common European home." When reminded that the phrase, which he had used repeatedly, suggested an effort to counteract the influence of the United States, Gorbachev backtracked. In a subsequent speech he made a point of endorsing active participation in European affairs by the United States and Canada. In Eastern Europe, coffee house talk of making Europe whole again has another meaning. It means tearing down the rusty Iron Curtain, as Hungary has already done; demolishing what remains of the Berlin wall; establishing closer ties of trade, culture, and travel with the prosperous West; and putting an end to one-party rule.

Even the terminology is changing. Diehard Communist officials today are commonly described as "Bolsheviks," and the term "Eastern Europe" has fallen out of favor. Large numbers of Poles, Hungarians, Czechs and Slovaks, Slovenes and Croats object to being labeled East Europeans. They prefer to think of themselves as Central Europeans, who, like Austrians and Germans, share a common civilization with the West. They have in mind shared religious beliefs, Catholic or Protestant, the historical experiences of the Renaissance and the Enlightenment, and the powerful contemporary values they associate with the West: the rule of law, respect for human rights, parliamentary democracy, and thriving economies — all values of which they felt deprived within the boundaries of the Soviet empire.

On the theoretical level, the underlying goal of Gorbachev's program has been described as a return to Leninism after the distortions of the Stalin era have been stripped away and the idealism once associated with the Russian revolution has somehow been recaptured. That is not the goal of most reformers in Eastern Europe. They see little hope of solving their economic and social problems unless the Marxist-Leninist system itself can be dismantled and preserved under glass in a museum. Many think of that system as an unmitigated disaster which has pauperized their peoples and plunged the whole region into a profound and chronic crisis. In fact, the word "crisis" kept recurring with extraordinary frequency in almost every one of dozens of conversations I had during the three months of my latest visit to Eastern Europe.

I met party members who denounced the Soviet model as a demonstrable failure. They praised the dynamism of mar-

ket-driven systems in contrast to the rigid and wasteful command economies they knew so well. Some argued for a complete redefinition of socialism that would ensure social justice,
human rights, and parliamentary democracy. But comparatively few of the people I interviewed advocated a transition to full-scale, unrestrained capitalism. For most, the
United States was not the preferred model. They conceded
that the American economy was admirably productive and
remarkably efficient in allocating resources. But more than
a few were troubled by what they viewed as its essential
heartlessness; they cited our boom-and-bust cycles, recurrent unemployment, the stubborn survival of poverty in the
midst of plenty, and the astronomical cost of medical care.
When I asked them to name countries that had resolved
these problems, Finland, Sweden, and Austria led the list —
all three parliamentary democracies with mixed economies
and generous social services. A Hungarian official remarked that Finland was a more convincing example of socialism at work than was his own country.

The disastrous state of the economy dominated my discussions with government and party officials. A common thread
running through these talks was their concern that continued stagnation could push the countries back to a Third
World level. It seemed to me that debate about whether a
socialist state should allow privately owned pizza parlors,
restaurants, or taxis was an absurd waste of time. Deng
Xiaoping had it about right, a Yugoslav friend suggested,
when he said that it didn't matter whether a cat was black or
white as long as it caught mice. In Budapest, Prague, and
Warsaw, people readily acknowledged that Austria and Finland, both spared the benefits of Soviet-style socialism, had
far outdistanced their own countries. The most admired
foreign leader, according to my informal soundings, was

Margaret Thatcher, not least because she was perceived as having turned Britain away from Socialism.

The Soviet model was not always so unpopular in this part of the world. Forced-draft industrialization did produce rapid growth in the early postwar years. Millions of peasants left the countryside for new jobs in industry, the avenue of upward mobility for themselves and their children. But the rapid growth of the 1950s and 1960s concealed underlying defects of the Stalinist system, which became more apparent as the growth rate slowed. Thomas W. Simons, Jr., a knowledgeable American foreign service officer, put it this way: "Everywhere, in one degree or another, the rigidity and centralization of the Soviet model is increasingly seen as an obstacle to further development. It is a model that in today's conditions tends to produce the wrong goods for the wrong markets, and to educate people for the wrong jobs or for no jobs at all. It is extremely wasteful in the use of human and material resources. It has no reliable self-correcting mechanism. The time of extensive resources to be exploited — of abundant manpower drawn from the peasantry — is gone."

Eastern Europe, moreover, has become a heavy economic burden for the Soviet Union, whose leaders complain that it is being shortchanged in its trade relations with the rest of the bloc. The Stalin era, when Russians felt free to loot the machinery and industrial raw materials of such countries as East Germany and Romania, is long past, though not forgotten. Today there are grievances on both sides. The Soviets supply their resource-poor allies with vast quantities of petroleum, natural gas, iron ore, and other commodities, some of which would command higher prices on the world market. The East Europeans, in exchange, supply machinery, grains, and other foodstuffs, mostly products they cannot easily sell to the West.

The fact that socialism in theory and practice is being reexamined even in the Soviet Union under Gorbachev's guidance has been acutely discomfiting to party conservatives there and elsewhere in the bloc. The new criterion is economic efficiency, not ideological correctness. The effect has been to tell the former satellites that there is no longer a Soviet model to be imitated. This leaves both liberals and conservatives without fixed reference points. Another feature of the new era that pleases the liberals and galls the conservatives in Eastern Europe is the Soviet Union's turn toward harder bargaining with its Warsaw Pact allies than in years past. Moscow now demands goods of higher quality in exchange for the raw materials it supplies. As products of world-class quality in many cases demand imported technology from the West or from Japan, in addition to economic reforms, the new Soviet approach gives its Eastern European suppliers wider latitude in decision making than they were accustomed to as recently as five years ago. Gorbachev and his associates have not, however, defined the outer limits of the new permissiveness.

There is less ambiguity about the hoped-for direction of political change in Eastern Europe. Reformers in the East bloc are pushing for values and institutions long taken for granted in most Western societies. They want trade unions that represent the workers rather than the party in power, newspapers that are free to publish truthful news, an end of censorship, governments freely chosen by the people in multiparty elections, and universities where students and faculty are free to explore an unlimited range of ideas instead of having to parrot Marxist formulations prescribed by the party. That is a tall order, amounting to the repudiation of forty years of unchallenged dogma.

But it is no longer an impossible dream.

# 2

## *Hungary*

### The Collapse of Ideology

HISTORY has not been kind to Hungary. Defeated by Ottoman Turkey in the sixteenth century and subordinated to Habsburg Austria in the eighteenth, Hungarians revolted under the leadership of Louis Kossuth to proclaim an independent republic in 1849. It was quickly suppressed when the tsar of Russia sent imperial troops to help restore monarchical rule. With the collapse of the Austro-Hungarian Empire in 1918, Hungary also lost two thirds of its territory and population for having fought on the wrong side in the Great War. Today Hungarians are on the way toward breaking the bonds of a system imposed by foreign arms at the end of World War II. They fell into the Soviet sphere when the Red Army invaded Hungary in 1944 to drive out the retreating Germans and stayed to help a tiny Communist Party fasten its grip on the diminished nation.

The party in those days claimed all of three thousand members. Its membership rose to 150,000 over the first five months of 1945. Many of the recruits to Communism were plainly motivated by opportunism, a smaller number by conviction. They were a mix of poor peasants attracted by the false promise of land, city workers yearning for a better life, intellectuals, and young people driven by ambition or a desire for social justice too long deferred. There were few hints in the party's early propaganda of the grim totalitarian future just over the horizon, which in 1956 would ignite a thirteen-day uprising that shook the Soviet empire.

Coming to terms with the truth about 1956 has been a long, painful process for the Hungarian people. Its emotional climax came on June 16, 1989, when Imre Nagy, leader of the doomed revolt against Stalinism, though himself a lifelong Communist, received a hero's funeral thirty-one years to the day after his death sentence was carried out and his body thrown into an anonymous grave. It was something less than a state occasion by design of its organizers, Hungary's emerging non-Communist opposition. Although four leading Communists paid tribute to the murdered prime minister by their silent presence, they had been told in advance that they would not be welcome as party representatives. Instead, they were introduced by their government titles to a throng of more than 200,000 in Budapest's Square of Heroes.

The ruling party was still resisting pressure to rehabilitate Nagy and the associates reburied with him. But, step by reluctant step, the divided Communist leadership retreated from the official dogma that Nagy had led a counterrevolution and thus was guilty of treason. Some two weeks before the funeral, a party spokesman declared that the former prime minister had been put to death illegally, a statement that struck ordinary citizens as banal and redundant. "It can already be determined," he said, that Nagy was condemned in "a fabricated political trial" and that his execution was "judicially illegal."

In another concession to the truth, the party allowed the official radio to rebroadcast Nagy's last speech to his countrymen, delivered on November 4, 1956, as Soviet tanks were rolling into Budapest to crush the uprising. Nagy was heard to say again, his voice cracking with emotion: "Today at day-break, Soviet forces started an attack against our capital, obviously with the intention of overthrowing the legal Hungarian democratic government. Our troops are fighting. The government is in its place. I notify the people of our country and the entire world of this fact."

Nagy had been betrayed by the Kremlin. On the morning of November 1, he had received reports, soon confirmed, that the Soviet Union (with eighty thousand troops already on permanent station in Hungary) was pouring fresh troops and tanks across the borders with the Carpatho-Ukraine and Romania. The intelligence could be interpreted only as a clear violation of Nagy's prior agreement, negotiated with Anastas Mikoyan and Mikhail Suslov on behalf of the Moscow leadership, that the Soviet Union would withdraw all its forces from Hungarian soil. The shocked prime minister summoned Yuri Andropov, then the Soviet ambassador in Budapest, who failed to offer a convincing explanation of the troop movements. Later in the day, Andropov returned to inform Nagy that Soviet forces were taking over all Hungarian airports to "protect the evacuation of Soviet civilians." That was one lie too many. At 4:00 P.M. Nagy convened his cabinet, which after a brief discussion approved his proposal to withdraw from the Warsaw Pact and declare the country neutral. An hour later he summoned Andropov once again, to inform him that the Soviets had left the Hungarians no choice.

Memories of the bloody repression that followed the uprising are still raw in the minds of Hungarians who lived through it. Political discussions tend to take 1956 as their starting point. Janos Kadar, head of the Communist Party for more than thirty-one years after the Russians installed him in power, has come in for a growing share of the blame. According to Maria Ormos, an academician and a member of the Central Committee, documents found in the party

archive directly implicate Kadar in the kidnaping of Imre
Nagy from the Yugoslav embassy, where he had taken refuge as Soviet tanks rolled through the streets of Budapest
firing more or less indiscriminately at apartment houses and
other buildings. Among the documents found, according to
another source, was Nagy's death sentence, signed by Kadar.

Kadar's long rule ended abruptly in May 1988, when a
party conference voted to replace him with Karoly Grosz.
Within a year, Kadar was expelled from the Central Committee and from his last, purely ceremonial post as president
of the party. As the historian Emil Niederhauser reminded
me, even Kadar once conceded that, in view of the Stalinist
excesses that triggered the uprising, calling it a counterrevolution was a misrepresentation. "The greater part of our
historians and the public at large did not accept the official
version," Niederhauser said. "But our schoolchildren still are
being taught not much more about the causes of 1956 than
that it was a 'lamentable event.' I say this with some shame."

Some thirty years afterward, I was impressed by the number
of young Hungarians, children of Communist militants, who
wanted nothing to do with the party. I talked at length with
several of them, all decently educated, some well traveled,
and none enchanted with the theory or practice of Communism. "The party until very recently was still judging
people according to where they stood in 1956 — on one side
of the barricades or the other," said a young manager. "It's
a ridiculous criterion for people of my generation. I was six
years old at the time. Yet I cannot excuse or defend what
happened then, in spite of my father's unyielding belief that
the Soviet intervention was justified."

The son of another unreconstructed Stalinist admitted to
a certain respect for the older man's integrity. "I once asked
him," the son recalled, "whether he would advise me to join

the party, even though I was not a believer, just to get ahead in this society. His answer made me proud. 'No,' he said. 'That would be naked opportunism. If you don't believe, you have no business joining the party.' I liked him better for saying that."

The conflict between fathers and sons, though softened by affection, often produces awkward silences in the family circle. A young social scientist, for example, told me that his father, an elderly physician who joined the party in his student days, had never wavered in his political convictions. "Even after all these years, he can still find reasons to defend the crimes of Stalin and his henchmen," the son said. "So we try to avoid wounding discussions that resolve nothing. I cannot alter his views, and he has given up trying to convince me that the party is eternally right. We shall never agree."

The sons, if not the fathers, take pride in the distance Hungary has traveled from Stalinist dogma. In many respects, present-day Hungary sets the pace of reform within the Soviet bloc. It is a small country busily borrowing ideas from the West (a market-driven economy, substantial freedom of choice and expression) while maintaining a system of government that is not yet markedly different from those of its East bloc neighbors.

The post-Kadar leadership, determined to put the past behind it and to start the country on the road to recovery and reconciliation, promised to hold free multiparty elections. In June 1989, it signed an agreement with the main opposition groups, which were not yet functioning parties, to draw up plans for the transition from one-party rule. "This is a great victory on the road to democracy," said Peter Tolgyessy, a spokesman for the umbrella group of non-Communist associations. "We have waited forty years for this."

The promised restoration of pluralist politics would turn the calendar back to the immediate postwar period — before Matyas Rakosi applied his notorious "salami tactics" and, slice by slice, carved up the opposition parties. That nullified the 1945 election, in which the Smallholders Party rolled up 57 percent of the total vote, against 17 percent for the Communists and the Socialists. Foreign Minister Gyula Horn, a prominent member of the present Central Committee, remarked with apparent regret that the pluralist order then in place had been "liquidated."

Multiparty elections are slated for 1990, and in the new climate more than a dozen new political associations have sprung up like mushrooms after a heavy rain. The Smallholders are back, along with a reborn Social Democratic Party and a scattering of other non-Communist groups that include the Democratic Forum and the Alliance of Free Democrats. The Democratic Forum appears to be the most important of the new associations. It appeals to Hungarian nationalism and has the support of several prominent writers and poets who are known as populists. The Forum is outspoken on the plight of the persecuted Hungarian minority in neighboring Romania. It also has raised a number of social issues, such as Hungary's low birthrate, widespread alcoholism, and a suicide rate that is said to be the highest in the world. It attributes all these evils to the influence of Communist materialism. The Free Democrats, who demand free elections on the Western model and a full range of civil liberties, are known as urbanists because many of them are said to be Budapest residents of Jewish origin. (Hungary's Jewish population of about 100,000 is the largest in Central Europe to have survived the Holocaust. Traditional Hungarian anti-Semitism also has survived.)

The imminent threat of defeat at the polls has thrown the old Communist Party, which preferred to call itself the Hungarian Socialist Workers Party, into disarray and confusion. A party congress in October 1989 adopted a new name, the Hungarian Socialist Party, dropped Karoly Grosz from the leadership, and chose Rezso Nyers, a Social Democrat in his youth, as its new chief. The policy changes adopted at the congress did not go far enough to satisfy the more radical reformist wing, led by Imre Pozsgay, but went too far for Grosz and his orthodox followers, who were expected to quit and form a rump party of their own.

Addressing the congress, Nyers charted a middle-of-the-road course. The renamed party's basic orientation, he said, "cannot be Communist, and it cannot simply be a Social Democratic Party." Nyers added, "We should seek a synthesis, to be created from the coming together of Social Democratic and Communist traditions, values, and practices." He said the Hungarian party would seek to maintain friendly relations with Communist parties that welcome change while also calling for "friendly bonds" with the Socialist International, which includes the democratic Socialist parties of Western Europe.

To many Hungarians the Nyers speech, like the newly adopted Socialist Party program, read like a straddle of conflicting principles. The program, on one hand, promised measures to prevent "exaggerated concentration of power," the rule of law, a government responsible to a parliament elected in "free competition" among political parties — all basic principles of Western democracy. On the other hand, while endorsing the principles of private property in a market economy, the party pledged itself to prevent a restoration of capitalism by "all political means." Small wonder that the patchwork of ideological compromises drew a less than rapturous reception from Hungarians on the right or the left.

"We are feeling our way toward the future," said Pozsgay, the Socialist candidate for president. "We do not know how this experiment will end. We know only that we had to change. Communism had reached the end of its usefulness."

With contested multiparty elections set for the late spring or early summer of 1990, neither the ruling party nor the opposition has projected a clear picture of post-Communist reality for the voters.

It took three months of tough bargaining by Communists and fifteen opposition groups to decide on the shape of the table, the participants, and the agenda for talks about the transition. The opposition demanded two-sided talks with the Communists. It had to accept equal participation for a third side, representing seven Communist transmission-belt organizations, such as the official trade unions and the National Council of Hungarian Women.[1] The outcome was an agreement to hold three-sided talks around a four-sided table. To a considerable extent, Hungary was following the example of Poland, where the ruling party negotiated with Solidarity representatives a sweeping program of reforms that, among other agreements, set the terms for the 1989 election, an unmitigated disaster for the Communists, as it turned out.

The slow pace of economic reform in Hungary, however, remained a source of worry for such party intellectuals as Gabor Fodor, a professor at the party university. "I believe that the hope of pluralism in Hungary is likely to be thwarted not by the Soviet Union, but by our economic situation," he said. "Economic failure could ruin everything, forcing a shift back to the totalitarian methods of the past. This is still a country poor in capital, short of energy, and without a fully qualified labor force.

"We have produced a country without property rights, which means that nobody is responsible for protecting and maintaining state property, and the state owns almost every-

1. Transmission-belt organizations include such mass groups as trade unions, youth and women's associations, peace movements, and other special-interest groups created in the Soviet Union (and copied in other Communist-ruled countries) for the purpose of extending the party's direction and influence over large numbers of people who are not necessarily party members.

thing here. We simply must re-establish capitalism in this country to some degree. It is, after all, an organic development, not something imposed from outside. We must tell the Hungarian people and the world that we are going to make capitalism work for us, of course with social and economic guarantees. We also need to make our currency convertible. Without that step I can't see us getting the wide foreign support we need."

Hungarians speak with remarkable candor about the failures of socialist economics, in part because they measure their quality of life against that of their Western neighbor, Austria. Budapest, after all, is only 150 miles from Vienna and a thousand miles from Moscow. Roughly one Hungarian in ten has traveled abroad in recent years, mostly to the affluent West. The freedom to travel has its effects, as the Communist daily *Nepszabadsag* observed in an editorial: "The yardstick is not the narrow range of goods available to some of our [Eastern] neighbors, but the very full supply seen in Western shop windows. After years of rising living standards, when the principle of 'things getting better year after year' was axiomatic, the current relapse is disquieting to public opinion. This anxiety is one of the characteristic features of the present social climate, and it has a strong impact on our way of life."

The most striking example of disastrous planning can be traced back some forty years to the Stalinist period, when Rakosi, then the party chief, proclaimed a Soviet-style plan to make of Hungary "a land of iron and steel." It was a bizarre blueprint for a country that lacked the essential ingredients of steel making — high-grade iron ore and coal. Rakosi poured billions into white-elephant steel mills that, from the beginning, have required massive subsidies to survive. Hungary's production cost per ton is almost twice that of West European steel companies, which have their own

problems competing with low-cost producers like South Ko-
rea and Brazil. According to the World Bank, Hungary's
1988 budget provided $3.8 billion in subsidies to failing in-
dustries. More efficient companies pay a 50 percent tax on
their earnings to help fund the subsidies to the inefficient.
When other taxes and welfare contributions are added, the
relatively efficient producers, a distinct minority, wind up
paying almost 100 percent of their profits to the government. There are ups and downs, of course, but the latest
estimates suggest that some 40 percent of Hungary's state-
owned companies lose money steadily.

I encountered little disagreement with the proposition that
Hungary's only rational course was to begin shutting down
its worst offenders. Even the departed Kadar, who could
not bring himself to crack down on the deficit producers,
told me in a 1986 interview that Hungary needed to apply
the rules of the market even though that course would be
painful. Efficient use of resources, he said, was no less important in a socialist economy than it was under capitalism.
But he seemed torn between that logic and the guarantee of
full employment contained in Hungary's constitution.

Grosz seemed to be less paralyzed by the idea. At the vast
steel complex on the Danube, once called Stalinvaros, his
regime sanctioned a layoff affecting forty-five hundred of
its fourteen thousand employees. Half of the remaining
workers were expected to lose their jobs over a two-year period. Layoffs started earlier at Ozd, a town of forty-eight
thousand near the Czechoslovak border. Its obsolete steel
works, dating from the nineteenth century, laid off three
thousand workers in 1987. Production dropped by half, although some ten thousand were still on the payroll. According to unofficial estimates, it would have cost the state less to
shut down the whole operation and go on paying the laid-
off workers full wages for the rest of their lives. The steel
workers laid off at Ozd received 75 percent of their normal

wages through the first six months of enforced idleness, dropping to 60 percent for the second half-year. After that, they were on their own.

The optimists in Budapest predict that many new jobs will be created when the private sector expands. The new Law on Corporate Association is intended to stimulate entrepreneurship, free the movement of capital, and allow foreign investors to buy into Hungarian enterprises. It also establishes the right of anyone to form a private company and sell shares to the public. Since the beginning of 1989, private companies have been allowed to hire as many as five hundred employees. The old limit was thirty-five.

About a hundred joint ventures involving Western investors, mostly small businesses till now, are in operation. The new law allows foreign investors to own up to 100 percent of the shares in Hungarian companies. These are radical steps for any East bloc country, far in advance of the economic reforms Gorbachev has introduced in the Soviet Union. They are not, however, risk-free, and many Hungarians remain suspicious of the market. Even those who see no real alternative, if the economy is to resume its stunted growth, betray anxiety about the high cost of failure. Nothing less is at stake, they say, than a relapse into the old, discredited pattern of the command economy.

Hungary was slow to recognize its comparative advantage in fields for which it was better equipped than steel making. Computers, for example. It is hard to think of another country with so long and distinguished a tradition of training creative mathematicians. John von Neumann, a world leader in the design and development of high-speed electronic computers, was a Hungarian schooled in Budapest before he became an American. But the political leadership of the 1960s and 1970s, Kadar included, did not foresee the microelectronic revolution that swept the United States, Japan, and Western Europe. Like Politburo members in other Communist-ruled countries, they thought of heavy industry as the central bulwark of a socialized economy.

Only in recent years has Hungary started to make up for lost time by building a new reputation in the design of computer software. Novotrade, one of several innovative software companies, employs some 150 programmers. All but a handful of them are free-lance designers. They are handsomely paid by Hungarian standards, earning as much as $500 a month, part of it in foreign currency. Novotrade does a thriving business with Western countries, the first Soviet bloc enterprise to crack that highly competitive market. Its most popular exports are computer games. Another Budapest company, Szamalk, sold a data-modeling system to IBM. Hungarian computer scientists at Szki, a third software company, successfully adapted a remarkable programming language known as Prolog, which is widely used in the United States and Japan for research in artificial intelligence.

It is clear that Hungary's best hope of climbing out of its economic difficulties lies with lean go-ahead firms like Szki, Szamalk, Novotrade, and Raba, a company in Gyor that makes farm equipment for export. But the essential resources for new ventures will have to come, at least in part, from sharply reduced losses on the old smokestack industries, a course that makes many *apparatchiki* distinctly nervous.

Agriculture, until recently the bright spot of the Hungarian economy, is no longer booming. Although grain yields have been pushed up three and a half times over the past fifteen to twenty years, Hungary's is high-cost agriculture. The bulk of its farm exports, moreover, go to the Soviet Union and other East bloc countries, which pay in soft currencies, and Hungary has hard-sell problems in the highly protectionist markets of the European Community. Its successes in food production are nevertheless impressive. A visit to the farmers' market off Moskva Ter in Buda on a Saturday morning in late summer offers a feast for the eyes as well as the palate. The display of fruits and vegetables in season, many grown by industrial workers who augment their wages by market gardening, can be spectacular.

These successes were the product of an earlier economic reform, which assigned less onerous delivery quotas to farm families and encouraged rather than compelling them to join cooperatives. Their reward for joining was land that the farmers could work as if they owned it, although they were barred from passing it on to their children. They rented the land and equipment from the state, and they were free to manage their holdings without overt interference from the government. The happy result, a steep rise in farm production and exports, caught the attention of Chinese planners, who sent missions to study the Hungarian experience. Hungary, in effect, became a model for Deng Xiaoping's rural reforms in China, which greatly increased food production there as well by appealing to the farmer's self-interest.

The Russians until recently clung to their system of centrally directed state farms and collectives. They contended that the Hungarian formula might have worked well in a country of 10.5 million people, but it was not the answer for their vastly larger country with problems of a different kind and scale. Moscow did show interest, however, in such Hungarian innovations as the automated chick hatcheries developed by the Raba company. Since 1970, Raba has supplied more than four thousand of these units to the Soviet Union. Demand has grown to the point that the Russians today willingly pay for them in convertible currency.

Another bright moment of my last visit to Budapest was a meeting with Janos Fekete, a relentlessly cheerful man who has since retired as deputy chairman of Hungary's National

Bank. In that position, he was responsible for the tight-money policy Hungary had to impose as a condition for continued support from the International Monetary Fund. Fekete also had the unenviable task of dealing with his country's staggering external debt, some $17 billion in 1988. He took wry comfort in pointing out that prosperous Denmark bore a debt burden that, on a per capita basis, was greater than Hungary's.

His was not the most pleasant of tasks, Fekete said, because it called for saying no to many vested interests, including those deficit-producing industries that kept demanding more credits. "More intelligent countries have managed to shut down some failed plants," he said. "We must, too." If that meant creating temporary unemployment, so be it, Fekete said. His was not, of course, a popular view, but Hungary, unlike most Communist-ruled countries, had anticipated the need to weed out its least efficient enterprises when it passed a bankruptcy law in 1986. "It's true," Fekete added, "that we have guaranteed the right to work in our constitution. In 1945, the party had nothing to promise the people except cheap food and guaranteed jobs. But this can't mean that every Hungarian has a constitutional right to a job *where he lives.* Our people don't like to move, except abroad. Remember that Hungary is a country with a labor shortage, owing to its low birthrate, so the unemployment is likely to be of short duration."

The new course of Hungarian economic policy has meant a number of structural changes of a sort that other Soviet bloc countries have yet to introduce, including the creation of "commercial banks" to handle the day-to-day business of state-owned industries. I visited one of them, the Bank of Budapest, a few steps from the stylish Vaci Utca, for a conversation with Zsigmond Jarai, a knowledgeable young executive in command of fluent English, who had studied economics in Budapest and in West Germany. "We are not real banks today," he said at the outset. "We can't even rate our borrowers." Apparently there is no Hungarian agency that evaluates the creditworthiness of companies seeking loans or underwriters for bond issues. Nor is the bank free to choose its customers. The National Bank of Hungary simply and arbitrarily allocated the "bad companies" on its books to one or another of the new commercial banks. As a result, Jarai's bank wound up with huge loans outstanding to several of the least solvent enterprises in the country.

They included Ganz-Mawag, a company that builds antiquated railroad equipment, and the Tatabanya coal-mining company, another hardship case. "We don't want to force them into bankruptcy," Jarai said. "If that is going to happen it should be the government's responsibility. Rather than stick us with these customers, the government would have done better to finance stronger companies and in this way help to restructure the national economy. If we were free of ideological constraints, we would do the rational thing, but that isn't possible yet."

Jarai, a slender, well-tailored man under forty, is not altogether pessimistic about the long-term outlook if, as he put it, "we have democracy and freedom to innovate." But the state, which holds a 60 percent interest in the new banks, keeps them on a short tether. Some of the banks find themselves with many clients and little money to lend, while others are said to have few clients and more money than they can prudently lend. The Bank of Budapest does a profitable business discounting commercial paper and bills of exchange. But the failing companies it has been assigned as clients have not much future, Jarai conceded, and as long as the government shrinks from forcing them into bankruptcy, they must go on paying interest on their uncollectible loans to stay in business. "The issue is not capitalism versus socialism," Jarai insisted. "It's simply this — if the government is going to allocate all financial resources, then

it doesn't need a capital market." The government appears
to lack the courage of its proclaimed convictions about moving to a market economy.

Wage scales in Hungary are niggardly. Industrial workers
are paid the equivalent of $120 to $130 a month. A family
with two children also receives a government allowance of
some $40 a month. Average *incomes* are higher because so
many Hungarians work at more than one job, that is, in the
so-called Second Economy. Economists estimate, however,
that fully one fifth of the population, some two million citizens at the bottom of the scale, subsist on less than $70 a
month. The numbers are ludicrous, and some Hungarians
are still capable of laughing at their situation.

A Budapest friend announced at lunch one day that sala-
ries were not, after all, very important. "It's just pocket
money," he said, grinning broadly. I didn't see the joke, so
I asked him to explain. "Think about it," he replied. "In this
country, as is well known, the state provides all the essentials
of life — food, housing, health care, education, right? Why
worry about your salary?" Rents are in fact low, and medical
services free in theory. But a wise patient is well advised to
slip his doctor a small envelope filled with forint notes, even
though payment is not required and, in fact, illegal. Everyone understands that a doctor can't possibly live on his state
salary. Another friend set the scene for me. "When I go to
my doctor," he said, "we engage in a little pantomime. I slip
him, say, 3000 forints in an envelope. He protests. I protest.
Then I walk out, leaving the envelope on his desk. We have
understood one another." It's true that 3000 forints does
not amount to much for a visitor from the West, but for
many Hungarians it's the equivalent of two weeks' wages.
For a young physician just starting his career, it more nearly
represents three weeks' salary. In Hungary, honest professionals still earn less than skilled workers.

The depressed economy was on the mind of Elemer Hankiss, a prominent sociologist at the Academy of Sciences, when I called on him. "Until 1981 to 1982," he said, "people had the feeling that Hungary was on the way up. The Polish events, what we knew of developments in East Germany and Czechoslovakia, convinced many people that Hungary was a better place. But in the last six or seven years, the real value of pensions has dropped by no less than 40 percent, and prices keep going higher. We talk endlessly about reform, yet we are terribly slow to act. It's very important that we take fresh steps toward freedom. Much of the opposition comes from party leaders in the counties. I call them the oligarchs. As a group, they are far more conservative than our leaders at the national level. Opposing reform is for them less a matter of ideology than of defending their own powers and privileges."

Some good things have been done, Hankiss said, citing the Second Economy: "That is one of the best things we have done, but we cannot explain it ideologically. It sounds odd, I know, but in many industries people work one shift in the normal way, then earn three to four times as much by working after hours as subcontractors to their regular employer." Other sources pointed out, however, that working two jobs translates into widespread exhaustion and an extraordinary incidence of neurotic disorders.

My wife and I visited a young engineer named Istvan, who exemplifies the two-job trend. His first job as a foreman at the Lenin Steel Works in the city of Miskolc does not pay enough, Istvan said, to ensure his family a comfortable life. "I feel there is too much enforced equality in this system," he added, as he showed us through his tiny though neatly arranged apartment in an ugly high-rise block on the outskirts of the city. "Many common laborers with less education are better off than I am, but that is the value system of the socialist countries." Unlike many other graduate engi-

neers, who prefer to work for themselves driving taxis or
growing vegetables, Istvan said he would never give up the
hope of practicing his profession one day, "even if I have to
feed my family dry bread." His opportunity came when the
enormous deficit-producing metallurgical works, with more
than thirty thousand employees, fell disastrously behind the
planning cycle. His employer then offered Istvan, along with
seven fellow engineers and four draftsmen, a contract to
form an economic planning unit that could make up for lost
time. By putting in twenty to twenty-six additional hours a
week at his part-time professional work, Istvan multiplies
his monthly earnings. But he is not free to seek a better job.
To qualify for his little apartment, he had to sign a written
commitment that he would stay at least ten years longer at
the Lenin Steel Works.

The many hardships Hungarians have endured over the
decades are reflected in official statistics that were kept secret in Kadar's time. They reveal a declining population,
increasing alcoholism, and an alarming rise in neurotic disorders. Hungary is the rare exception in a world of explod-
ing fertility. Deaths exceeded live births by 18,900 in 1986,
a trend that is expected to continue. The number of alco-
holics registered with health authorities rose from thirty-nine
thousand in 1970 to fifty thousand in 1980 to sixty-five
thousand in 1985. *Otlet,* a weekly published by the Communist Youth League, reported the rise in neurotic problems,
attributing it to the sixteen-hour workdays put in by many
Hungarians. The trend is beyond dispute, though some disagreement exists over its cause. A study conducted by the
National Insurance Company did find a correlation between such disorders and the number of hours worked. The
Ministry of Health, in an unrelated survey, found that the
number of Hungarians who use sedatives or similar medi-
cations had increased 3.71 times between 1960 and 1980.
Over the same twenty-year span, the number of young

Hungarians rejected for military service on psychological grounds had jumped from 16.4 percent to 31.9 percent. Normal on-the-job stress is said to be common, complicated by the additional pressure of working a second job after hours.

A psychiatrist quoted in the Youth League weekly said that he knew of workers who, in effect, lease the names of friends in exchange for a share of the extra money they earn by working a second job under a false identity. That is one way of getting around the law that limits work to 160 hours a month. There must be others, and resourceful Hungarians are bound to discover them. *Otlet* condemned the practice, arguing that the humane way of dealing with the problem was to increase wage levels so that workers would not be forced to undermine their health by seeking second jobs or extra shifts.

Hungary's official trade unions, ever obedient to the party, have done little to attack these conditions. Magda Kovacs, an official of the Central Council of Trade Unions, acknowledged that the unions had not stood up to the government in defense of workers' interests in health, education, and housing. "We were not in the habit of criticizing the government," she said. "We have fallen behind in these areas, and housing is the most immediate problem. It takes a lifetime in Hungary to get a flat." She added that the housing shortage was bound to impede government plans to shut down inefficient factories and shift the labor force from one part of the country to another, where jobs might be available. "You can't expect people to spend a second lifetime waiting for a flat in a new location," Miss Kovacs said.

The Trade Union Central Council, whose traditional role had been to prevent strikes or to stop them when they happened, was having to adjust to new conditions after parliament in 1989 legalized the right to strike. "I can't think of a time in the past forty years," Miss Kovacs told me, "when the past and the present have diverged so markedly. It's a time of transition, and the unions also want reform." The official unions, like the Communist Party, have been losing members rapidly, 300,000 in 1988 alone.

Another sign of change was the emergence of new unions, unauthorized and wholly independent of the party. The first of them was the Union of Scientific Workers, soon followed by a Union of Film Industry Workers. To learn more about them, I visited Pal Forgacs, an organizer of the Scientific Workers, in his office on Castle Hill in Budapest. Forgacs, a trade union activist before World War II and in those days a Social Democrat, lost his job after the Communist takeover in the late 1940s. He worked in a factory until 1957, then became secretary of the Oil and Chemical Workers. He also did research on Hungarian conditions for the International Labor Office in Geneva, a specialized agency of the United Nations.

"The idea of starting the first independent trade union in Eastern Europe was raised," he said, "by a group of historians and social scientists at a meeting in December 1987. We decided not to seek the government's permission, invoking a provision of the Hungarian constitution that permits free entry into 'mass organizations.' A couple of friendly lawyers volunteered to do some research. They found that Hungary was bound by the conventions of the ILO, which of course uphold the rights of workers anywhere to form unions." Forgacs recalled that there was trouble in the beginning. The official press published attacks on the union, and one university refused permission for the founders to meet on its premises. But the government did not resort to traditional "administrative methods" and, to the pleasant surprise of the founders, more than five hundred showed up for the union's first conference in May 1988.

Imre Pozsgay, the reformist leader, was the first party figure to accept the new union. By way of explaining the resistance of his Politburo colleagues, he reminded the founders that "it's still a Stalinist party." The union, nevertheless, recruited about ten thousand members in a hundred local branches across the country, mainly at universities, scientific institutes, industrial laboratories, and other institutions.

"The changes that led to our forming the union started with the example of Solidarity in Poland and of Gorbachev in the Soviet Union," Forgacs said. "There was some discussion at the outset of our joining the Public Workers Union, which includes prison guards. But the majority refused, on the ground that we had no business in a union with 'the same ones who will lock us up.' We don't emulate Solidarity in our attitude toward politics. In fact, we have no political line and we are determined not to become one more anti-Communist organization."

Professor Hankiss, the sociologist, is a founding member of the new union. He said the organization was probably too small to make much difference on its own. "But we hope it will serve as a model for other independent unions of non-intellectuals," he told me.

In Hungary's climate of openness, yesterday's harassed dissidents are emerging as respected politicians. One taboo after another has been torn up. Apart from the birth of new independent unions and all the new political groups preparing to contest the 1990 election, the press and even the state television system are enjoying a rebirth of free expression. Something like a hundred new publications have appeared, several offering serious analyses of politics and social trends, and others more frivolous stuff — comic books and magazines that specialize in undraped women. In the department of pure symbolism, Hungarian border guards have turned to tearing down the barbed wire fence along the Austrian frontier, which even with the fence intact had been as open as most in Europe; and the removal of the red star from the national coat of arms, to be replaced by the Crown of St. Stephen, Hungary's patron saint.

Few of these changes would have been possible if the reformers had not captured the high ground in the divided party leadership. Pozsgay and Nyers, both viewed as thinly disguised Social Democrats, also are expected to have their way on the issue of pluralism in politics. Rezso Nyers, a Social Democrat before his party was smothered in the Communist Party's embrace, had been the chief architect of Hungary's 1968 economic reform, the first significant departure from Leninist orthodoxy in the Soviet bloc. In June 1989 he moved up to the chairmanship of the Communist Party's new four-member Presidium.

Nyers summed up his leadership agenda in a single sentence: "We are doing away with Stalinism and the dictatorship of the proletariat and adopting parliamentary democracy based on absolutely free elections." A reporter asked Nyers whether he should be regarded as a Communist or as a closet Social Democrat. "I am a Communist," he replied, "but certainly not in the Stalinist sense. Let's just say that my Communism is deeply rooted in social democratic theory."

But for all the hopeful talk in Hungary about liberalization, a visitor could detect a strong undercurrent of anxiety about the future. Prominent Communist officials worried openly about Mikhail Gorbachev's ability to remain in power if his own domestic reform program failed to produce real results in the next year or two. A senior party official, just returned from a briefing session in Moscow, sounded the most pessimistic note. Gorbachev faced powerful entrenched opposition, he said, and there was little support for *perestroika* among workers and peasants, because they had yet to see any improvement in living standards.

This was the picture he brought back: housing and the infrastructure are in bad shape; food supply is more precarious than in many years past; there is enormous resistance to the cancelation of special privileges that millions of office holders have come to expect as their due; unrest in the Baltic states, Armenia, and other republics has shaken the top leadership; their darkest fear is that if Moscow gives way to these nationalist pressures, the Tatars, Volga Germans, and, above all, the Ukrainians will be emboldened to demand self-determination. "Increasingly," the official said, "Gorbachev's task reminds me of Peter the Great's in trying to impose a revolution from the top down."

He was less explicit, though clearly troubled, about the possibility that if Gorbachev were ousted by Kremlin conservatives, further reform in Eastern Europe might be halted. But he did not minimize the danger of failure at home. "I see no alternative to continued liberalization in Hungary," he said, "in spite of our inflation, industrial inefficiency, and the threat of unemployment. This would mean a further drop in living standards — and that could be dangerous. Ours is not a country of strong democratic traditions. Yet we must go on opening the political process and speeding democratization." The country, meanwhile, continues to fall farther behind the West in providing a decent standard of life for its people, in spite of marginal improvements.

Young people are particularly sensitive to the gap between promise and performance. A recent poll of student opinion at the Technical University in Budapest showed that only 37 percent were optimistic about Hungary's future. The comparable figure was 70 percent in 1983 and 56 percent in 1985. Jozsef Bayer of the Communist Party's Social Science Institute concluded, in a remarkably candid article, that "we would be fooling ourselves if we did not notice that a substantial number of students are beginning to question socialism itself as a sociopolitical order."

The specter of rising unemployment coupled with inflation, officially estimated at 17 percent in mid-1988 but corrected by independent analysts at more like 20 percent, is not the stuff of youthful dreams. Among the middle-aged generation, which made its compromises with "socialist reality" long ago, I encountered a tendency to worry about the correctness of reforms that encourage private enterprise. An official of the Central Committee told me that, in his view, the very existence of the Second Economy proved that the "First Economy" had failed. "We must make it possible," he said, "for a citizen to earn his living by working a single job." Some argued that the party's original decision to legalize the Second Economy had been a grave mistake because it permitted some people to get rich, by Hungarian standards. Ivan T. Berend, a noted economist who also serves as president of the Hungarian Academy of Sciences, dismissed that contention on practical grounds. "There were many hot arguments within the party," he recalled, "over the issue of 'socialist egalitarianism.' But the truth has to be faced that ours is still a shortage economy. We can't afford to stop the Second Economy, because it accounts for something like a third of the national income. We even heard arguments that small private shops should be banned because, when they are few and widely scattered, they can be monopolistic. Others, including myself, took the position that we need more of them. These changes generated a huge debate and a major ideological problem."

One issue that generated no significant tension between the party and the people was the fate of the large Hungarian minority in Transylvania, across the border in Romania. A large anti-Romanian demonstration in the summer of 1988, unofficial but clearly sanctioned by the regime, drew the largest, angriest crowd Budapest had seen in years. Estimates of its size ranged from 40,000 to 100,000, large enough, in any event, to make some government officials distinctly nervous. A Hungarian diplomat I encountered the following day was deeply troubled. "It's all very well," he explained, "to have thousands of people out in the streets shouting anti-Romanian slogans. But what was to prevent their shouting 'Down with socialism'?" What, indeed? I tried and failed to convince him that even if the public was unhappy over the depressed domestic economy, the demonstrators were looking outward, not inward, in a surge of wounded national feeling. Like officials in other Communist-ruled countries, the diplomat had been conditioned to distrust crowds unless they were marshaled and controlled by the party for its own purposes.

In this case there was near unanimity between people and party. Every Hungarian I met was exercised over the scheme of Nicolae Ceausescu, the Romanian chieftain, to tear down between six thousand and eight thousand rural villages, including a great number inhabited by ethnic Hungarians, who number between one and a half and two million. Transylvania, framed by the Hungarian border on the west and the Carpathian Mountains on the east, has been ruled over the centuries by a succession of conquerors — Romans, Mongols, Turks, Germans, Austrians, and Hungarians. With the dissolution of the Austro-Hungarian Empire at the end of the 1914–18 war, the victorious Allies awarded the region to Romania under the terms of the Trianon treaty, and the heavily Hungarian population of Transylvania found itself under foreign rule. Although Hungary briefly reclaimed the northern part of Transylvania as a reward when the authoritarian Budapest government of Admiral Miklos Horthy sided with Nazi Germany in World War II, the region was again awarded to Romania after the Axis defeat. Relations between the two countries, both members of the Soviet bloc, have been less than friendly since then, though they are more embittered today than at any time in the past forty years.

The Soviet Union adopted a hands-off attitude toward the bitter dispute between two Warsaw Pact allies. When Yegor K. Ligachev, Gorbachev's chief rival and critic in the Soviet Politburo, visited Budapest in 1987, he avoided leaning one way or the other. The fact that both countries were in the socialist camp, he said, "gives us the right to hope that contradictions and misunderstandings will be ironed out."

Nothing of the sort happened. Jozsef Benyei, editor of a Debrecen newspaper that serves the northeast corner of Hungary, spoke of psychological warfare in progress. "Yes, there has been a definite upswing of nationalism here," he said. "The Hungarians in Romania are made to feel very uncomfortable there, and that is bound to affect us, too." Csaba Goetz, who manages the Hortobagy state farm near Debrecen, described the trials of families like his own that are divided by the border. Goetz recalled an automobile trip into Transylvania to visit relatives, when his wife and he were detained at the border for eight hours while Romanian customs officers combed through every piece of luggage and confiscated the gifts they were carrying. "We were bringing our relatives a few Hungarian books, magazines, and recordings, chiefly music by Béla Bartók, which are not allowed to circulate in Romania," he said. "They took everything; a most demeaning experience."

Minor harassments of this sort had been going on for years without retaliation by Hungary. But by 1989 the government and party were taking their cue from the aroused Hungarian public. Reports that Hungarian-language schools in Transylvania had been closed, and streets renamed to erase any vestige of Hungarian identity, were no longer soft-pedaled in Budapest. Although Romanian officials kept denying reports of forced assimilation, President Ceausescu's words carried little weight, whether in Hungary, in the rest of the Soviet bloc, or in the West. His plan to demolish the largely Hungarian villages and shift their residents into so-called urban agro-industrial centers made no sense unless his purpose was to subdue or drive out the stubborn Magyar minority, a clear violation of human rights, and to reclaim their land for collective farming.

Ceausescu's response to the mass demonstration in Budapest took the form of a thinly veiled accusation that the Hungarian Communists had revived the minority issue to divert attention from their economic difficulties. A face-to-face meeting between Grosz and Ceausescu in Arad, once a Hungarian town but now incorporated into Romania, did little to improve matters. No progress was reported on the village-razing scheme or on any other issue in dispute. Meanwhile, many thousands of ethnic Hungarians were fleeing Romania with considerable difficulty to seek refuge.

Just as Budapest abandoned its initial caution on the Romanian issue under the pressure of public opinion, it came under pressure from below on an environmental issue. This involved the construction of two dams on the Danube, one at Nagymaros in Hungary and the other 120 miles upstream at Gabcikovo in Czechoslovakia. Work on the Czechoslovak project moved ahead smoothly without a murmur of public protest. But the Hungarian reaction was loud and lively, a measure of the difference at the time between two Communist-ruled neighbors in matters of free expression. In Budapest, unlike Prague, there were demonstrations, critical articles in the official press, protests by prominent scientists, and the formation of new citizens' organizations (one called Danube Blue) to defend the threatened environment.

Opponents of the dam argued that it would scar an area of great natural beauty, known as the Danube Bend, barely a half-hour's drive north of Budapest. Here the famed river forces its way through the mountains in a narrow horseshoe curve toward the Great Hungarian Plain. The protesters, an extraordinary coalition of scientists, environmentalists, members of the parliament, and assorted citizens, argued that the whole project was a colossal mistake, entered into

without public discussion or adequate study of its consequences. They complained that the dam would contribute
to soil depletion, endanger the fresh-water supply of north-
west Hungary, and destroy aquatic life, in addition to dam-
aging the region's beauty. The mystifying aspect of all this
was that no one could list any substantial benefits Hungary
would derive from going ahead with the project.

The few known facts were unpromising. Virtually all the
electricity generated at Nagymaros would go to Austria, which
had guaranteed the financing, for the first twenty years of
operation. Even after the commitment to Austria had been
fulfilled, however, it was estimated that the dam would supply no more than 2 to 3 percent of Hungary's power needs.
There was a passionate debate. The dam opponents turned
out a large crowd for a torchlight demonstration on Margaret Island in the Danube. It carried banners with messages like THE DAM VIOLATES OUR NATIONAL INTER-
ESTS and OUR FUTURE IS AT STAKE. The demonstrators
also demanded a national referendum to decide whether
Nagymaros should be scrapped or allowed to go ahead.

In a newspaper interview, Grosz dismissed the public out-
cry. "There are already thirty hydroelectric power stations
on the Danube," he said. "I don't see why the thirty-first
should make such a significant ecological difference." The
general secretary of the Hungarian party, who inherited the
dam project from Kadar, conceded that if the project had
not been started years earlier, he might have decided to halt
construction, but it had now become a question of national
prestige involving formal agreements with neighboring
countries. Asked whether Hungary would honor its international commitments, he replied, "Yes, certainly."

But the cabinet, in a rebuff to Grosz, disagreed. It voted
to stop work on the Hungarian section of the vast project.
Czechoslovakia protested angrily, serving notice that it would
demand compensation. The Austrians also sounded un-

happy, though they were more polite. While the outcome remained uncertain, Budapest's environmental lobby and the political reformers counted the cabinet decision at least a half victory, which was later confirmed by the parliament. Environmentalists and reformers told one another that Grosz's authority was waning and that the system at last was responding to the voice of the people.

Grosz, whose record suggests a highly ambitious man capable of trimming his principles to the prevailing wind, had been learning to live with setbacks and compromise. A year before the solemn reburial of Nagy and his associates, for example, Grosz warned the "democratic opposition" not to go through with plans for a demonstration marking the thirtieth anniversary of the Nagy execution. He used strong language, threatening "administrative measures" to suppress "enemy and opposition" manifestations. It was an unfortunate choice of words, reminiscent of the Stalin-Rakosi era, when "administrative measures" were synonymous with mass arrests, show trials, and torture. In fact, a small demonstration did take place, and the police used truncheons and tear gas against the participants. Twelve months later the Nagy funeral, arranged by the same opposition forces, drew to the Square of Heroes a huge throng, including Prime Minister Miklos Nemeth, Imre Pozsgay, and other prominent leaders. There was no violence.

Like the cabinet decision to halt the Danube dam project, this was an eloquent measure of Grosz's declining authority and of growing reformist influence. Left to his own devices, Grosz made clear, he would have rigged the 1990 election to make certain that the Communists could not be turned out of office. He preferred a limited exercise of democracy, one that would guarantee his party a majority in parliament. One of his aides conceded that "the first elections will not be real elections." But the reformers in the Communist leadership prevailed. Pozsgay insisted, in an interview with Radio Free Europe, that the election "must be free even if it entails risks for the party. . . . A refusal to accept this risk would amount to setting aside the principle of free elections."

Asked whether he would accept the leadership of a "reform Communist" Party, Pozsgay rejected the term. Any party he led "would not be based on the Communist tradition of clinging to abstract ideals," he said, "but rather on the type of European socialist ideals that characterize the Italian and French Socialist parties, or the Swedish, Austrian, and West German Social Democratic parties." It was a bold statement, filled with risks for Pozsgay and his supporters because it amounted to rejecting the Leninist principles of the party he hopes to lead and turning it toward Western-style democratic socialism.

The pitfalls confronting Hungary's ambitious politicians are so numerous that they will have to be lucky as well as wise in finding the high road to national independence and parliamentary democracy. A great many things must go right for them, and the margin for error is narrow.

The Soviet Union's reaction, of course, would be crucial. Opposition leaders in Hungary, as in Poland, are therefore reluctant to force the pace of change beyond the limits of Soviet tolerance. Miklos Haraszti, an editor of the dissident journal *Beszelo*, which became an aboveground weekly when censorship ended, has written that "we don't have to be warned that post-Communist democracy is best when cooked on a low flame." He added: "Poland and Hungary are engaged in a conspiracy of caution. The democratic movements in both countries have decided to renounce the taking of revenge for earlier failures and to let the Communists retire from power step by step." That will be a delicate exercise.

Hungarians nonetheless behaved as if there was no turning back. On October 23, 1989, the thirty-third anniversary of the 1956 uprising, a vast and jubilant throng filled Kossuth Square in front of the parliament building in Budapest. Matyas Szuros, speaker of the parliament and acting president, proclaimed the new Republic of Hungary from a balcony overlooking the packed square. No longer a "People's Republic," Szuros said, Hungary was now an "independent, democratic and legal state." Five days earlier, the parliament had approved nearly 100 modifications of the 1949 constitution by a vote of 333 to 5, with 8 abstentions. It was a day and evening freighted with symbolism. The green, white, and red Hungarian flag flew all over the city, shorn of the red star imposed by the old Communist regime. That evening, under a huge portrait of the martyred Imre Nagy, a candle-lighted ceremony commemorated the 32,000 Hungarians killed in the uprising and celebrated the beginning of a new era.

Under the revised constitution, the new republic affirmed "the values of both bourgeois democracy and democratic socialism." It abolished the "leading role" of the Communist Party, which had voted to dissolve itself a few days earlier and to campaign in the 1990 election under the Socialist banner. The parliament ordered the dismantling of party organizations in factories and other workplaces, an important element in the party's network for controlling Hungarian society.

The Workers Militia, the Communist Party's private army of 62,000, also was abolished. It had been created following the suppression of the 1956 revolution to protect the party against the people. The militia's continued existence had been a source of anxiety to the new opposition parties, which argued that it was wrong and dangerous for any party to have its own paramilitary force. The Hungarian army lost no time after the vote in parliament, hauling away truckloads of pistols, machine guns, ammunition, and other equipment from

the citadel in the Buda hills that served as the headquarters
of the Workers Militia.

But it was the critical state of Hungary's economy, rather
than the threat of a political backlash, that presented the
most serious hazard to democratization. In the minds of most
citizens, who are neither politicians nor intellectuals, the very
word "reform" has come to stand for harder times ahead.
According to government statistics, food prices in the first
quarter of 1989 were up by 13.8 percent over the same period a year ago; clothing was up by 19.4 percent, and services by 13.9 percent. Economists agree that inflation is not
likely to be contained in the foreseeable future. According
to word-of-mouth reports from Budapest and other cities,
many apartments went dark over the winter of 1988–89 because thousands of families, too poor to pay their utility bills,
had their electricity cut off. The main victims were pension-
ers. Short-term relief of the Hungarian situation cannot come
from the government, which is bound by its agreement with
the International Monetary Fund to go on reducing subsidies to consumers and failing industries. The major creditors, West Germany and Japan, are not expected to over-
look the fact that the billions they loaned to Hungary in the
1970s are still outstanding and that much of the money went
in wasteful subsidies to state industries.

As a result, the public mood is troubled, a source of anxiety to the new political groups preparing to contest the approaching multiparty elections. Handicapped by their in-
ability to match the financial and organizational strengths of
the renamed Communist Party, and deeply divided over
policy questions, the new opposition parties have yet to strike
a spark of real enthusiasm in much of the population. One
reason suggested by Hungarian friends was that the new
parties were created by elites drawn from the ranks of dissident intellectuals and were widely perceived as showing

little concern for the bread-and-butter problems of the masses.

The contrast with Poland is striking. Hungary lacks an engine of change like Solidarity, which after all is a union as well as a popular movement, with its roots in the shipyards, tractor factories, mines, and steel mills. In comparison, the Hungarian opposition seems to resemble a cluster of competing political boutiques whose merchandise, while stylish, interests no more than a fraction of dispirited working-class voters. The essential common touch is hard to find.

# 3

## *Czechoslovakia*

### The Gentle Revolution

T HE PEOPLE of Czechoslovakia, not renowned for im-
petuous action, broke the power of their Communist
rulers in twenty-one late autumn days without a drop of blood
spilled. It was a gloriously gentle revolution.

After many years of underground resistance and systematic persecution, a few hundred intellectual dissidents, joined
by several thousand university students, had overthrown one
of the most doggedly Stalinist regimes in Eastern Europe.
Their leader, Vaclav Havel, an unlikely politician, set the
tone for the vast throngs in Wenceslas Square, instructing
them to remain polite in their moment of triumph, to avoid
violence, and to renounce vengeance against their recent
persecutors. The shy, soft-spoken Czech writer had become
the voice of an aroused nation.

In his 1978 essay "The Power of the Powerless," distributed in *samizdat,* Havel told a story about a greengrocer who
was ordered to post the slogan "Workers of the world, unite!"
in a shop window. He did as he was told. To refuse would
have meant forfeiting the chance of a vacation on the Black
Sea coast or jeopardizing his children's prospects of university admission. People like the greengrocer, Havel wrote,

would have to take down the ridiculous propaganda posters and begin "living in truth" if they wanted to defeat Communism. He argued that the totalitarians were not invincible, that once all the timid citizens learned to say no, the regime's nakedness would be exposed, as in the fairy tale about the unfortunate emperor with no clothes.

Havel was right. But before ordinary citizens dared to say no, they had to overcome their fear of losing something — a job, the hope of promotion, a chance to buy a little Skoda car. The people evidently found their courage in a precipitating incident on November 17, when a group of protesting students in Prague were brutally beaten by the police. They retreated to the university, expecting the police to invade the campus. This time the police did not come after them, for reasons that were never explained. Other citizens quickly sensed that the regime was unable or unwilling to use force again. As they joined the spreading demonstrations, their numbers grew day by day. That was the moment when the people lost their fear, according to Father Vaclav Maly, a dissident Catholic priest whom the fiercely anticlerical government had forbidden to perform his religious rites.

The people had lived with fear, keeping their heads down, since the Warsaw Pact invasion of 1968. Now it was clear to them that the Russians would not intervene. Mikhail Gorbachev had said as much. Besides, Czechs and Slovaks could take hope from the recent experiences of their East bloc neighbors — Solidarity's victory in Poland, Hungary's turn toward parliamentary democracy, and the peaceful October revolution in East Germany. Czechoslovakia was slow to join the procession, but once its people had conquered their fear, they repudiated the old Communist order decisively.

The retreat of the mighty started on November 24, 1989, with the resignation of Milos Jakes, the hard-line party chief, following an outbreak of peaceful street demonstrations.

Within four days, Prime Minister Ladislav Adamec agreed to give up his party's political monopoly. On December 7 Adamec stepped down, and the following Sunday, December 10, Czechoslovakia installed a new cabinet, the first since 1948 with Communists in the minority. President Gustav Husak, a symbol of the disgraced old regime, swore in the new ministers before he also resigned. In the closing days of the year Czechoslovakia made amends in striking fashion for injustices flowing from the Warsaw Pact invasion twenty-one years earlier. Havel, a playwright and essayist, so recently a political prisoner of the old regime, was swept into office as president of the republic on an irrepressible wave of public enthusiasm. At Havel's express request, the parliament also restored Alexander Dubcek to a position of honor as its new presiding officer.

A month before the party's disintegration set in, the police had dragged Havel from his sickbed to a prison ward with the aim of preventing his participation in demonstrations marking the birth of the Czechoslovak Republic in 1918. Yet on November 28, Prime Minister Adamec was negotiating virtual surrender terms with Havel (whom he had dismissed a few weeks earlier as "an absolute zero") and his associates in the newly established Civic Forum. Havel's courage and his powerful moral authority left the Communists little choice.

The surrender terms were remarkably comprehensive. In addition to terminating the Communist Party's forty-one-year political monopoly, the government, with party approval, committed itself to ending compulsory teaching of Marxism-Leninism in the universities, to releasing all political prisoners, and to establishing a commission that would investigate the police beatings of student demonstrators, the event that had precipitated the formation of Civic Forum and ignited the massive protest demonstrations in Prague and other cities. Among other concessions, the government assured the democratic opposition access to the Czechoslo-vak media and the right to publish its own daily newspaper.

Civic Forum was barely nine days old when the regime yielded these concessions. "History has begun to develop very quickly in this country," Havel said. "In a country that has had twenty years of timelessness, now we have this fantastic speed." There would be other demands and other conces-sions in the next several days — for free elections, freedom of speech and religion, and the resignation of President Hu-sak.

The Communist Party was not extinct, but it was fast be-coming invisible. Marian Calfa, the new prime minister, who promised free and democratic elections for parliament, pos-sibly by the end of June 1990, promptly resigned from the party. It would take at least that long for the opposition par-ties to organize, write their programs, nominate candidates, and plan their campaigns.

Czechoslovakia had had no political life outside the Com-munist Party since the putsch of 1948. Both the Socialist and the People's parties had been squeezed and pressured into submission. They were tails, in effect, to the Communist kite. Civic Forum, which did not exist before the November cri-sis, moved into the political vacuum almost overnight. It was a loose coalition of about a dozen mostly illegal groups es-tablished on the spur of the moment in a Prague theater on November 19. Three weeks to the day later, the revived op-position had a majority in the new government: seven min-isters from Civic Forum, two Socialists, and two People's Party men, equally delighted to break free of the Communists, who kept ten cabinet posts.

The first deputy prime minister, Jan Carnogorsky, per-sonified the new politics. Two weeks before he took office, the forty-five-year-old lawyer from Bratislava had been in jail for demanding free elections. He belonged to Public Against Violence, the Slovak counterpart to the Czech republic's Civic Union. The new foreign minister, Jiri Dienstbier, also had served time for dissident activities. In recent years he made his living by stoking a boiler and devoted his free time to the human rights campaigns of Charter 77 alongside his friend Havel. Dienstbier, a prominent journalist and broadcaster until the Warsaw Pact invasion, had to persuade a friend to replace him in the boiler room before he could attend the swearing-in ceremony of the new cabinet.

The other first deputy prime minister, Valtr Komarek, had been head of the economic forecasting institute in the Academy of Sciences and in his new position will doubtless have major responsibility for restructuring the Czechoslovak economy. Vaclav Klaus, the new finance minister, and Vladimir Dlouhy, head of the planning commission, also came from the forecasting institute. Although both Komarek and Dlouhy were Communist Party members, both had the endorsement of Civic Forum. In my talks with them more than a year before the old regime's disintegration, both Komarek and Dlouhy impressed me as incisive critics of the existing economic order in spite of their party membership. They should now have the clout to put their ideas into practice.

Perhaps the most unusual member of the new cabinet was Petr Miller, an electrician like Lech Walesa in Poland and now the minister of labor and social affairs. Unlike the intellectuals in most of the leadership positions, Miller was a worker, a foreman actually, at the big C.K.D. electrical works on the outskirts of Prague. Real members of the working class were rare among the founders of Civic Forum. Recalling his first encounter with the dissidents, Miller told John Tagliabue of the *New York Times:* "They were looking for representatives of different groups. Someone said, 'We need a Catholic,' and one was found. Then someone said, 'We need a worker,' and they said, 'Take Miller.' "

He turned out to be an invaluable ally of the dissident

intellectuals, artists, and students who took part in the creation of Civic Forum. Miller startled them by delivering on
his promise to bring ten thousand workers into the center
of Prague to join their demonstration. Delivering a speech
for the first time in his life, he rallied the C.K.D. work force
and found that it shared the general indignation over the
brutal police beatings. That example galvanized hundreds
of thousands of workers in other parts of the country to join
the two-hour general strike a few days later to demand free
elections and the end of Communist rule.

Prague, a melancholy city long burdened by the people's
sense of loss over what might have been, had by all accounts
been transformed. Where so much had been forbidden,
suddenly everything was possible. People who used to go
about their business wearing dour expressions now turned
a smiling face to their neighbors as they assembled in the
city center surrounding Wenceslas Square. No longer silent,
they chanted democratic slogans, sang patriotic songs, and
made a joyful noise tinkling tiny bells and jingling their key
chains, which symbolized the unlocking of doors. Many wore
Havel for President buttons. This Prague was not the city I
had seen in late summer of 1988.

I had been impressed then by the capital's enduring beauty.
The church domes and spires were freshly gilded. In the
magnificent Old Town, medieval squares, palaces, and
monuments had been lovingly restored at enormous cost.
Unlike Warsaw, the city bore no scars of war. Unlike downtown Belgrade or the back streets of East Berlin, Prague was
neither drab nor scruffy. Compared with the capitals of other
Communist-ruled states, Moscow included, this was a city of
abundance. Shop windows were loaded with consumer goods,
expensive but available. Food stores displayed arresting as-
sortments of meats, sausages, bread and rolls and pastry,
cheeses, wines and liquors. The streets of the central city,

other than Wenceslas Square (now reserved for pedestrian traffic and taxis), were filled with automobiles. Yet in conversations with a foreign visitor, many citizens sounded defensive, apologetic, less than proud of their material progress. A young economist, born after the Communist Party captured power in 1948, spoke in mocking tones of "our sausage socialism." He said the consumer comforts had been bought at the cost of investment in the country's future. It keeps the people quiet, he said. Don't be misled by the shop windows; they are a poor substitute for the political and economic reforms the country needs. You can't have one without the other. But the hard-line leadership of the party and state endured, stubbornly resisting real change, refusing to face the truth about the crisis of socialism in Eastern and Central Europe.

In the age of Mikhail Gorbachev and *perestroika,* Czechs found it difficult to blame Moscow for their manifest lack of movement toward a freer, more open society. It was not at all clear that Gorbachev's Politburo would raise objections to reforms far bolder than any the Prague leadership had dared to contemplate — reforms of the kind that Alexander Dubcek began to introduce during the brief Prague Spring of 1968 only to be overthrown in a massive invasion by Russian, East German, Polish, Hungarian, and Bulgarian troops.

Dubcek remained a nonperson in his own country, living in obscurity in Bratislava although still widely admired in Western Europe. When the twentieth anniversary of the Warsaw Pact invasion was being observed elsewhere, Dubcek found himself under friendly siege by foreign newspapermen and television teams. His quiet message to the outside world was an endorsement of the reforms Gorbachev had been introducing in the Soviet Union. With typical modesty, he traced a certain parallel between his own New Course reform program of 1968 and Gorbachev's *perestroika,* without claiming prior authorship. "It is indispensable," Dubcek said of Gorbachev's reform campaign. "I salute it and I support it, because I find in it a profound connection with what presented itself to us twenty years before. Had there been a political leadership in the USSR at that time similar to the one today, the military intervention . . . would have been unthinkable." In an interview with West German television, Dubcek spoke of Czechoslovakia's having lost twenty years owing to the Soviet intervention, a lost opportunity for "our country and for socialism."

Jiri Pelikan, who worked closely with Dubcek during the short-lived effort to establish "socialism with a human face" in Czechoslovakia, was less guarded in an interview with Radio Free Europe. "The Prague Spring," he said, "could have served as a reformist laboratory for the entire Soviet bloc. Conditions for economic reform and for political democratization were, in fact, more favorable in Czechoslovakia at that time than they are in the USSR today, with the crucial exception that Gorbachev need have no fear of tanks from the neighboring countries. Instead, he has to face resistance from the party and state bureaucracy, an explosive nationality issue, and a very bad economic situation, particularly with regard to food and the supply of consumer goods to the public. Czechoslovakia, in contrast, is a relatively small country with just two nations, economically developed, with democratic traditions. In 1968 it had a great deal of confidence in the Communist Party as an institution capable of reform and ready for dialogue."

Pelikan, who emigrated to Italy after the Soviet invasion, made the central point that at least in one country, for a few precious months, a Communist Party had found a way to reconcile individual freedoms with socialism: "The party was democratizing itself; censorship was abolished; institutional guarantees were given to secure freedom of expression, of assembly, and of religion; foundations were laid for . . . a lawful state; and travel was made virtually free for all citizens." It was past time, he added, for the Soviet leadership under Gorbachev to declare that the crushing of the Prague Spring was a blunder, Brezhnev's blunder, and to guarantee that what happened in 1968 would never happen again.

A year later Gorbachev did just that. But the Prague regime felt no powerful pressure from below to "fill in the white spaces" about who in the Czechoslovak leadership had invited the Warsaw Pact invasion. I found no counterpart in Czechoslovakia to the broadly supported and insistent demands of its Polish neighbors that Moscow fully and formally acknowledge Soviet responsibility for the murder of more than four thousand Polish officers whose mass grave in the Katyn Forest was discovered in 1941 by advancing German troops. That's what Poles mean when they speak of "filling in the white spaces."

The only Czechoslovak voice openly raised in demand of the truth was that of Charter 77, the human rights organization, which appealed to Moscow for a "factual assessment" of the events that led to the invasion. Havel, a leading spirit of the Charter group, insisted that "nothing can change in our country without reopening the theme of 1968." Two questions continued to be posed in conversation by Czechoslovaks in and out of Charter's ranks: Did the Brezhnev regime in Moscow make the decision on its own to crush the Prague Spring, or, as the Soviets later claimed, did it start the tanks rolling at the invitation of certain unnamed Czechoslovak Communists? And what evidence existed to support the justification that the invasion was necessary because the country was threatened by "counterrevolution"?

But the crew of party bosses installed by the Russians after the invasion was still more or less intact. Gustav Husak, Moscow's chosen successor to Dubcek, had the main responsibility for dismantling the achievements of the Prague Spring. He retired to the ceremonial post of Czechoslovakia's president in December 1987, and Milos Jakes took over the party leadership. His main contribution to the process of "normalization," a term suggestive of George Orwell's "newspeak," had been to cleanse the party's ranks. As the purger in chief, Jakes supervised the expulsion of 500,000 party members who were found to be unreliable, that is, unduly sympathetic to Dubcek's liberal reform program.

The purged party showed little interest in, or commitment to, reforms of the sort that Mikhail Gorbachev was launching in the Soviet Union. Lubomir Strougal, the only member of the Prague leadership openly to advocate economic reform, lost his job as prime minister and his seat on the Politburo in 1988. Gorbachev's message to the leadership when he visited Prague was that the "frank admission of oversights and blunders, and the resolve to repair them, [can] only strengthen the prestige of socialism . . . Minor repairs will not be enough. An overhaul is in order." Nothing of the sort happened in Prague, almost as if Leonid Brezhnev were still in charge.

According to Rudolf Slansky, Jr., a member of Charter 77, the Jakes regime had little to fear from the people. "Daily life is without problems," he said. "The shops are filled, even if the quality is low and the prices are high. But the general economic situation is very bad. We are consuming at the cost of our future development. Our industry needs modernization, yet investment has been cut back sharply. The terms of trade have been deteriorating. If you take 1970 as a hundred, then we are at about sixty-six today."

Czechoslovakia, unlike Poland, Hungary, and Yugoslavia, is not weighed down by large external debts. Her conservative Communist leaders prudently shunned the loan windows when the big foreign banks were under pressure after the Arab oil embargo to recycle billions of petrodollars in the 1970s. The "internal debt," on the other hand, is enormous and steadily growing. Sophisticated Prague economists define internal debt as the sum total of investments deferred in recent years: housing not built or renovated, run-down railroads that can't afford the new rolling stock they desperately need, factories still operating machinery and equipment that was installed in the 1920s and 1930s. The country's industrial base, originally built to serve the needs of the Austro-Hungarian Empire, has been described as the "museum of the Industrial Revolution."

With the disintegration of the empire at the end of World War I, the newly created Czechoslovak Republic was left with two thirds of all its manufacturing facilities, a physical plant that once served a market of sixty million people: Austrians, Poles, Ruthenians, Slovenes, Italians, Magyars, Slovaks, Romanians, Croats, and, of course, Czechs. The boom years of the 1920s saw that industrial base expand. By 1939, Czechoslovakia ranked just behind France and ahead of Italy in per capita domestic product. Following World War II and the Communist takeover in 1948, the Soviet Union pressed Czechoslovakia to expand its large, undamaged heavy industry in order to export machinery to the entire Eastern bloc in exchange for raw materials. That is the pattern to this day. The Russians supply oil, natural gas, and iron ore in exchange for heavy machinery from Czechoslovakia, a curious reversal of the traditional pattern, in which the colonies send raw materials to the metropolitan power in exchange for finished goods.

As long as 80 percent of Czechoslovak exports go to the Soviet bloc, quality is not of paramount concern. In fact, the quality of Czech export products, a matter of national pride during the First Republic of Thomas Masaryk and Eduard Benes, has been slipping over the past forty years. Valtr Komarek, now deputy prime minister, acknowledged that much of the country's huge output of steel, machinery, and shoes did not meet Western standards and was therefore of little interest to markets outside the bloc. Like the Soviet Union, Czechoslovakia looks to the West and to Japan for the more advanced technology it would need to upgrade its production. But that kind of technology would have to be paid for in dollars or deutschemarks or yen, and Czechoslovakia's hard-currency earnings were too sparse. In short, a Catch 22 situation. For Dr. Komarek, who argued that in view of its skilled labor force and strong industrial tradition, his country should be doing as well as Austria or Belgium, the solution lay in "market socialism and democratization." He did not conceal his conviction that the "social costs" of real restructuring would be heavy and unpopular.

Komarek and his staff produced a massive blueprint for radical reform that was designed to put Czechoslovakia on a new track by the year 2010. His plan called for a series of wrenching changes over time. It meant, among other hardships, cutting back steel production to half the present level of fifteen million tons a year, with comparable reductions in brown coal output. It probably also meant abolishing some 500,000 industrial jobs, not all at once, admittedly, and creating new jobs in the weak services sector to take up the slack. "This will be painful," he said, "but we must do it. We have a paradox here. Everybody is for reform, but few are willing to close a factory or make people move. There is fear of social conflict." His plan also called for less wrenching changes in, for example, the shoe industry. Czechoslovakia, Europe's biggest producer of cheap shoes, earns some $135 million a year from exports. "We get $4.00 to $5.00 a pair today," he said. "If we made shoes of higher quality, like the Italians, we could be left with $15 to $20 a pair."

One of the great mysteries of life in Czechoslovakia has been how people managed to live so well and work so little. Along with the East Germans, Czechoslovaks have enjoyed the highest living standard in the Communist bloc. An astonishing number of families own cottages in the countryside, which for the most part they built themselves. By midafternoon on a Friday, the exodus from Prague would begin, the streets, coffee houses, theaters, and concert halls abandoned to tourists — mainly Germans and Austrians — and to off-duty soldiers. Close students of this phenomenon have observed that the cottage owners worked much harder on weekends for themselves — building, repairing, painting, cutting grass, digging in their little gardens — than they did on weekdays working for the state. The weekly retreat to the countryside has been described as part of an "internal emigration" from the prevailing dreariness of life under Communism. Many people fell into the habit of doing as little as necessary in their workaday lives and saving their creative energies for private pursuits — sports, weekends in the country, or gardening. There was a popular saying, roughly translated, that "socialism beats working." Cynics spoke of a social compact between the party and the people: social peace in exchange for consumer comforts.

The spirit of free enterprise was not dead in Prague in 1988. Virtually every Czech we met earned more, in legitimate or semilegitimate ways, than official statistics would suggest. A lawyer wise in the ways of the underground economy estimated that Prague alone had more than fifty thousand millionaires — not dollar millionaires, of course, but people whose net worth in crowns could be measured in seven digits. At the top, according to this source, were Czechoslovaks employed outside the country — diplomats, engineers and technicians, members of trade missions, employees of United Nations agencies. Their hard-currency savings were convertible into crowns at no less than five times the official rate. Next in line were the professional athletes (hockey and tennis stars, for example), whose skills commanded high dollar incomes. In much the same category were musicians, writers, and other artists who performed or were published abroad. A more surprising category of the new rich included members of agricultural cooperatives.

Their modest wages were multiplied by their participation in the profits, particularly when several family members worked together and pooled their earnings. Members of construction cooperatives also have done well. Many built solid, thoroughly modern houses for themselves on the outskirts of Prague and rented out rooms or apartments to foreign visitors.

The one clearly illegal category involved so-called parasites — black market operators, moneychangers, owners of private taxis, prostitutes and their protectors. This may have been the largest category, to judge by the frequency of solicitations addressed to foreign tourists. It would be difficult to conceive of a product or personal service that was not for sale in Prague, a far cry from the Prague I remembered from the mid-1950s. Then my wife and I were guests at the Alcron, an art nouveau hotel building a hundred yards off Wenceslas Square. Although our room was moderately comfortable, reading was out of the question by night or day. The room was dark and the lighting dim, a characteristic of many European hotels of the period. We marched off the next morning to buy larger light bulbs. At one shop after another we met the standard response: "Sorry, we have run out." We kept walking until we discovered an electrical shop where the initial response sounded faintly encouraging. "I'd be happy to sell you a light bulb," said the man behind the counter (pause), "if you will also buy a radio." No deal; we had a radio. Apparently the five-year plan had produced an oversupply of radios and a scarcity of light bulbs.

On the same visit to Prague, I ran out of razor blades one morning. Simple: I bought a packet of Czechoslovak blades, known generically in Prague as *zhiletki*. This struck me as touching evidence of brand-name loyalty in a country where the genuine article had not been seen for many years. The first blade I tried seemed to lack a cutting edge, so I tried a second. Again it glided over my soapy face, leaving the whiskers more or less intact. It was faintly comforting to come across a newspaper cartoon some days afterward in which St. Nicholas was asking a mature Czech gentleman what he would like for Christmas. "What I want," he replied, "is *zhiletki* that cut."

Thirty years have passed since that encounter with the artificial scarcities of crude economic planning driven by ideological compulsions. But the comparative abundance of the 1980s masked deep structural problems, low worker morale, and rigid, overcentralized planning. Dr. Komarek's institute calculated, for example, that compared with the average for a group of advanced capitalist countries, Czechoslovakia used 63 percent more energy, two and a half times as much raw steel, and almost twice as much cement to manufacture $1000 worth of finished product. Planning in Czechoslovakia was based on the number of physical units to be produced, not on their money value. The only incentive the system offered was fulfillment of the plan. When an enterprise fell short of the numerical goal, the government usually came to its rescue by increasing the input of materials or manpower. Knowledgeable economists called this the "soft budget constraint." Prices and wages were fixed by the central authorities, not by management. There was little incentive for industrial managers to invest in modernization of their facilities. The unpredictable flow of materials has been another problem. As one economist expressed it, "The needed resources are never, or hardly ever, in the right place at the right time in the required quantities. This circumstance leads managers to hoard materials and creates a permanent state of industrial crisis."

A major obstacle to further reform, encountered also in Poland and Hungary, is described as the "social cost" of shutting or scaling down factories and mills that run chronic deficits. The year-to-year losses of many enterprises are variously ascribed to poor management, obsolete equipment, the rigidity of planning processes, and the seductive appeal of the guaranteed Soviet bloc market for low-quality goods, which undermines efforts to compete in hard-currency markets by raising quality. But the overriding principle under Communist rule was that restructuring must not be carried out "at the expense of the justified social security of workers." That was the argument against rationalization of the economy raised by local and regional party chiefs. Many weeks before Dr. Komarek's reform plan was submitted to the Politburo for consideration, party officials of the Ostrava coal-mining region made known their intention to fight any curtailment of production. As long as the party had the last word on economic decisions, real reform was stultified. The outlook is brighter now that the Communists' supremacy has been effectively canceled. But a great many economic distortions remain to be corrected.

Public unhappiness with the conditions of life was reflected in bitter jokes. One, widely repeated, went like this: "Citizens who earn 5000 crowns a month or less are the *builders* of socialism. Those who earn more than 5000 crowns are the *beneficiaries* of socialism. Those who earn more than 10000 crowns are the *proprietors* of socialism." Like its Soviet bloc neighbors, Czechoslovakia is more generous to miners and industrial workers than to professionals. Doctors are notoriously underpaid, a circumstance that breeds corruption in medical practice. The salary of a skilled surgeon, 6000 crowns a month, is identical with a plumber's. A university graduate trained in computer science starts at 2000 crowns, while the starting wage for a subway motorman is 3400 crowns. Disparities of this kind disheartened the student generation and its parents. Unlike the students of 1968, who rallied behind the Prague Spring leadership, the generation of the eighties tended to shun politics until the tide of change in Hungary, Poland, and the Soviet Union lifted hopes that Czechoslovakia could not forever go on resisting the inevitable. A West German correspondent who talked his way into a political lecture on *perestroika* at Prague University reported that the students appeared to be laughing at the lecturer much of the time. Toward the end, a student brought down the house by standing up and comparing the idea of restructuring in Czechoslovakia to the opening of a new whorehouse staffed by the same old whores.

It was with surprise and pleasure that middle-aged to elderly members of the Charter 77 movement noted the enthusiastic participation of some ten thousand young people in a demonstration and march on August 21, 1988, to commemorate the twentieth anniversary of the Warsaw Pact invasion. They cheered the name of Dubcek, called for the Russian army to go home, chanted *Svoboda* (Freedom), and raised homemade banners bearing the name of Thomas Masaryk. It was an isolated and apparently spontaneous happening. The Charter movement had no part in organizing it.

Milan Kundera, the distinguished Czech writer who chose exile in Paris when the Soviet tanks rolled into Prague in 1968, has thought a great deal about what he calls "the misfortune of nations." In a published interview, Kundera said: "In a fascist, dictatorial state everyone knows that it will end one day. Everyone looks to the end of the tunnel. In the Empire to the East, the tunnel is without end . . . Yes, the tortures, the sufferings are the same. But the tunnels are of very different lengths. And this changes everything."

Jaroslav Seifert did not live to see light at the end of Kundera's tunnel. The poet, a Nobel laureate, stayed at home in Prague until his death at the age of eighty-four. A friend of his recalled that in 1956, when Stalinist repression was at its height in Czechoslovakia, Seifert had said: "If an ordinary person is silent about the truth it may be a tactical maneuver. If a writer is silent he is lying." Truth seeking and truth telling, in fact, became the ruling passion among Czechoslovak writers, politicians, journalists, lawyers, economists, and engineers during the heady Prague Spring. Seifert joined them with a long poem titled *Prague Castle,* which he completed in July of that year. Imagining himself part of a noisy crowd in the castle courtyard, the poet wrote:

> But how I wished amid that din to
> yell out several faltering words,
> a prayer that some hand should wipe away
> the fear residing in those waiting eyes,
> for I so want to believe the time has come at last
> to call murder by its proper name of
> Murder!
>
> Knavery, albeit crowned with laurels
> would be knavery once more,
> lies once more lies as in days of yore.
> And brandished pistols would no more open
> innocent doors.
>
> But I wanted too much
> in this century and in this land
> where the illusory tree in bloom
> so quickly turns to sand.[1]

As so often in the dismal past, the censor had the last word. He struck out those final, bitter lines when the poem was reprinted in the 1970 edition of Seifert's collected works. Like Alexander Dubcek, who promised his countrymen "socialism with a human face," the poet wanted too much for his time and place.

The Communist Party of Czechoslovakia lagged far be-

1. Quoted in Jan Ladislav, "Encounters with History or Une Education Sentimentale 1938–1968," in *The Prague Spring: A Mixed Legacy,* Jiri Pehe, ed. (New York: Freedom House, 1988), p. 12. Poem translated by A. G. Brain.

hind its Polish, Hungarian, and Soviet counterparts in coming to terms with the truth about 1968. Not until the December day in 1989 when Mikhail Gorbachev described the Prague Spring reforms as "right at that time and . . . right now" did the disintegrating Czechoslovak party swallow hard and reluctantly agree. Vasil Mohorita, a youthful member of the Politburo, said, "We are of the opinion that the entry onto our territory of five armies of the Warsaw Pact was not justified, and the decision to do so was wrong."

With the collapse of the neo-Stalinist regime, Czechoslovakia at last closed a dark chapter in its postwar history. For twenty-one years human rights had been routinely violated. The riot police, under party orders, had perfected a repressive technique of crowd control, using attack dogs, water cannon, tear gas, and truncheons against peaceable demonstrators. In January 1989, when a group of human rights activists led by Vaclav Havel attempted to lay flowers on the spot where a student named Jan Palach had committed suicide by fire twenty years earlier in despairing protest against the Warsaw Pact invasion, the police made several hundred arrests. Havel, who had served more than four years in prison for earlier offenses, was sentenced to an additional nine-month term that was later reduced to four months.

On October 28, 1988, police had used the same tactics to disperse a crowd of some five thousand, assembled in defiance of a government ban on unofficial observances of the Czechoslovak republic's seventieth birthday. Many were beaten and kicked and had their arms twisted as the police dragged them off into waiting vans.

Freedom of assembly, a basic human right enshrined in the Helsinki Accords of 1975, was strictly limited to occasions blessed by the party. Measured by other Helsinki standards — freedom of thought, expression, religion, and travel — Czechoslovakia under the iron rule of Gustav Husak and Milos Jakes had a dismal record. It was a wretched distinction for a nation that, unlike its Warsaw Pact allies, had been a liberal democracy from 1918 to 1938.

Havel, whose writings were banned for twenty-one years in his homeland, had become one of the moving spirits in Charter 77, a group of human rights advocates formed in 1977 to monitor and expose the regime's violations of decency. Like other celebrated Czech and Slovak writers, Havel lived and worked under more or less constant police surveillance even when he was out of jail. "You live in fear for your manuscript," he recalled. "Until such time as the text which means so much to you is safely stowed somewhere, or distributed in several copies among other people, you live in a state of constant suspense and uncertainty — and, as the years go by, surprisingly enough, this does not get easier but, on the contrary, the fear tends to grow into pathological obsession."[2]

The playwright's total dedication to the long struggle for truth and civil liberties led some of his admiring friends to suggest that his true vocation was political leadership, precisely the role in which he found himself when the Communist apparatus collapsed. "I sometimes feel that Havel became a playwright by mistake, that he really should have been a politician," the Czech writer Ivan Klima told me. "His essays are better than his plays."

Charter 77 never pretended to be a mass movement. It started with a membership of 241 dissenters from various walks of life — liberals, democrats, Christians, Communist reformers, even some who considered themselves revolutionary Marxists. By its own description, Charter was "a loose, informal, and open association of people of various shades of opinion, faith, and profession united by the will to strive individually and collectively for the respect of civil and human rights." It had no platform or political program. Havel

2. Quoted in *Index on Censorship*, October 1986.

once described the movement as "an icebreaker with a kamikaze crew." Its essential purpose was active defense of human rights, which a Charter document defined as "assets of civilization" that all governments were obligated to honor.

In addition to defending human rights through the power of the word, Charter spread its interests to encompass threats to the environment, religious and ethnic rights, social and economic problems, music and literature. At its peak, Charter had fewer than two thousand members. All had signed its founding document, an act of courage because the consequences could be harsh: official harassment, loss of jobs, house searches, endless interrogations by the secret police, crude pressures against close relatives. Charter nonetheless kept pressing for an honest reassessment of the Prague Spring and the Soviet-led invasion that throttled it, with due credit to Alexander Dubcek's short-lived regime as the true precursor of Gorbachev's "new thinking" in the Kremlin. The difference between Prague 1968 and Moscow 1988 had after all been summed up by a Kremlin spokesman in two words: "Twenty years."

The old regime appeared to be of two minds about how to handle the increasing popular support of Charter and newer protest organizations. Having crushed the independence celebration through brute force in October 1988, it tried a permissive track in December when Charter and four other independent organizations sought — and received — permission to celebrate the fortieth anniversary of the Universal Declaration of Human Rights. Thousands turned out for that event, the first officially authorized independent rally in twenty years. There were no arrests this time.

By an overwhelming show of hands, the demonstrators adopted a resolution calling on the Communist leadership to honor its international commitments by releasing political prisoners, restoring full freedom of religion, and assuring all citizens of their rights of free association, freedom to travel,

and freedom of information. Father Vaclav Maly, a former
Charter 77 spokesman, found the regime's unexpected show
of tolerance puzzling. "I was surprised not to be in jail," he
said. "Our rulers take a step backward, and then a step forward."

Czechoslovakia may be the only modern state that for thirty-
five years did not allow its citizens to celebrate the anniversary of their national independence. But in spite of the
Communist campaign of calumny, President Masaryk and
the First Republic, established in 1918 out of the wreckage
of the Habsburg empire, were not erased from folk memory. Masaryk was, after all, the founding father of the independent Czechoslovak state, revered long after the state
had been dismembered by Nazi Germany. In 1987, on the
fiftieth anniversary of Masaryk's death, the Communist daily
*Rude Pravo* published a commemorative article, the first in
almost two decades. Even more surprising was *Rude Pravo*'s
publication of excerpts from the memoirs of Eduard Benes,
Czechoslovakia's second president, who succeeded Masaryk
in 1935 and died soon after the Communist takeover in 1948.
In keeping with these signs of change, the party leadership
announced in 1988 that October 28, the birth date of the
First Republic, would again be celebrated as a national holi-
day.

It was a strange celebration. Milos Jakes, President Husak, and Prime Minister Ladislav Adamec led the official observance at Prague Castle and then presided over a public
rally in Wenceslas Square. Husak announced a limited am-
nesty, one that excluded repeat offenders, citizens involved
in corruption, and those who had tried to leave the country
illegally "and still maintained a hostile attitude toward the
socialist system." It was not, however, the only celebration in
Prague. Charter 77 and four other independent groups held

their own rally in the square the next day to demand political change and wider freedoms. Hundreds of police, some with dogs on leashes, turned on the demonstrators, who shouted "Shame" and "Gestapo" at the officers of the law. Western journalists saw the police beating demonstrators and scattering them with water cannon and tear gas. The disorderly scene unfolded under a large official poster reading ALL POWER IN THE CZECHOSLOVAK SOCIALIST REPUBLIC BELONGS TO THE WORKING PEOPLE.

The steps toward restoring Masaryk's good name and reinstating the independence day observance impressed many citizens as part of a design by the Communist leadership to overcome public apathy by reawakening national feelings. Czechoslovkia, however, is a country of two separate and distinctive peoples, Czechs and Slovaks, who for the most part show few signs of brotherly feelings toward one another. The Slovak minority (roughly one third of the total population) speaks its own language, as it did when Slovakia belonged to Hungary. Czechs live in Bohemia and Moravia and speak their Slavic language. Many of them believe that the Slovaks alone gained something from the suppression of the Prague Spring, which happened to be led by Dubcek, a Slovak. It was Dubcek who saw to it that Slovakia received political autonomy in 1968, the only reform of the Prague Spring that was not revoked the following year by Husak. A disgruntled Czech intellectual told me: "These are two wholly different nations. The Slovaks had no independent history until 1848. Our history goes back a thousand years. We Czechs save our money and dislike showing it. Slovaks throw their money around. They are mostly Roman Catholics. We have large Protestant church groups as well. The Slovaks have a national inferiority complex. They have tried successfully to take what they could from the common treasury on the ground that they are poorer than we. When we meet a person for the first time, it's more important to know whether he is a Slovak or a Czech than whether he is a Communist or a non-Communist."

He also complained that Slovaks got more than their fair share of positions in the federal ministries after 1968, a reward, he suggested, for their quick conformity with the new Soviet-blessed order. The outburst might have shocked me at another time, but this was 1988, the year of inflamed nationalist protests within the Soviet Union and in several other Eastern countries. Clearly, the Marxist belief that nationalism as an expression of "bourgeois class interests" would disappear with the advent of socialism was looking rather shaky. As for Marx's dictum that religion was the opium of the people, the demand for a fix appeared to be growing in socialist Czechoslovakia. A Prague friend, himself an atheist, came away in a state of shock during my visit when he accompanied another foreign visitor to a Catholic church. "This was an ordinary Tuesday," he recalled, shaking his head in disbelief. "Yet the church was filled — more women than men, it's true, and many of them elderly — but an astonishing number of young people as well."

The Czechoslovak government, among the most overtly anticlerical in Europe, was slowly shifting toward increased tolerance of religion. After six months of negotiations with the Vatican, it agreed, in June 1988, to the consecration of three new Catholic bishops. But the Catholic Church, in particular, has a great deal of lost ground to make up. After 1968 the number of functioning priests dropped by 65 percent. For generations past, long before the Communists took power in 1948, the church had been losing adherents, owing to its close identification with Austrian oppression under the Habsburg monarchy. The losses continued through the Industrial Revolution as millions of villagers moved into the cities, many leaving their faith behind. But religion appears to be on the crest of a powerful revival today. Few of the

the Czechs or Slovaks I met disputed the impression that the Catholic Church had been strengthened by withstanding decades of official harassment. Although hard facts are scarce, it's estimated that Czechoslovak Catholics number about six million, roughly a third of the population. The venerable primate and archbishop of Prague, Cardinal Frantisek Tomasek, took the government to task time and again. "Catholics are aware of their rights," he wrote in a letter to the prime minister. "They will continue to demand them and are determined to make sacrifices . . . In the name of Catholics, I declare that we demand a change in the attitude of the state toward the church." The primate gave his full support to a thirty-one-point petition, signed by some 500,000 of the faithful. It demanded, among other things, strict separation of church and state, an end to restrictions on religious instruction, and the abolition of laws that prohibit any criticism of Marxism-Leninism in sermons. "The voice of the believers is being heard loudly now," he said in a magazine interview. "It is something new, and the authorities must listen."

It cannot have escaped the notice of the Communist authorities that, year by year, many more Catholic pilgrims made their way to a fifteenth-century shrine of the Virgin Mary above the walled medieval town of Levoca, in Slovakia, where they sang hymns, celebrated mass at two-hour intervals, and lined up to make open-air confessions through the summer night. In July 1988, the pilgrims numbered 280,000, an increase of 50,000 over the previous year. Unlike years past, there were no reports of police harassment or interference in 1988. The government appeared to draw a line between the faithful, who were too numerous to be punished, and militants such as Ivan Polansky from the town of Dubnica, who was sentenced to four years in prison for publishing illegal religious literature. Another religious activist, Augustin Navratil, was convicted on charges of disturbing the

peace and slandering a public organization for his leading
role in the thirty-one-point petition campaign. He was committed to a psychiatric institution for the fourth time in ten
years. Cardinal Tomasek found it remarkable that in a country like Czechoslovakia, where loyalty to faith demanded
sacrifice, large numbers of young people were joining the
religious revival. Their motives were not political, according to Father Vaclav Maly, the priest who lost his license
to preach or to wear clerical garb because he was meeting
young people in private apartments to discuss human rights.
He believed that many young people were drawn to religion
because they wished to be accepted into a community, rather
than live alone in what he called an atomized society.

Prague's ancient Jewish quarter, on the other hand, marks
the near extinction of another religious community that,
however small in numbers, made a great contribution to science, philosophy, and letters in the Czech lands over a span
of almost a thousand years. Most of the 375,000 Jews who
lived in Czechoslovakia before Hitler annexed and dismembered the country did not survive the Holocaust. Their
number in Prague is fewer than two thousand today, and
seven of their nine synagogues have been turned into state
museums or storehouses. They contain thousands of religious objects — rare books, hangings, vestments, silver rit-
ual objects — confiscated by the Nazis and apparently intended for a postwar museum that was to be dedicated to
the species they were busily exterminating.

Now the Prague Ghetto, among the oldest and probably
the best preserved in Europe, has been turned into a museum of another kind: a memorial to the vanished past and
a tourist attraction that appears to draw non-Jews and Jews
alike. There is the Jewish Town Hall, with its unique clock
in which Hebrew letters take the place of numbers, and the
Altneu (Old/New) Synagogue, seldom used for worship these

days, which dates from 1270. The synagogue is a small, dark space below street level with low-hanging arches in the Gothic style. Its most prominent feature is a dusty red banner, or a replica, presented to the Jews of Prague by Charles IV, Holy Roman Emperor and king of Bohemia in the fourteenth century.

It was here that Yehuda Loew ben Bezalel, a legendary rabbi, cabalist, and philosopher, prayed and studied the Talmud. He is better known as the creator of the Golem of Prague, a manservant made of clay whom the legendary rabbi endowed with life and then was forced to destroy because the Golem ran amok. The tomb of Rabbi Loew dominates the Old Jewish Cemetery, where the Jews of Bohemia buried their dead for four hundred years. The rabbi died in 1609. On a narrow ledge of the tombstone, tourists like to deposit little slips of paper, each held in place by a pebble, on which they inscribe their thoughts, hopes, or requests to the Almighty. On the day of my visit, there were fluttering messages written in Spanish, Hungarian, Italian, German, Czech, Yiddish, and Russian. One message read:

> Viva il Communismo
> Viva la Democrazia

Another, in German, read:

> Freedom is as precious as air.
> May real peace and freedom come
> Where it is needed most,
> The DDR [German Democratic Republic]

Rabbi Loew's tomb, grander than the rest, is also better preserved. The others, literally thousands upon thousands of weathered, crumbling headstones, tilt and lean crazily, as if the Golem had flung them about randomly, without rhyme, reason, or design. Tourists wind along the twisting paths through the ghostly burial place, scanning the weather-worn inscriptions on the tumbled markers in search of meaning, then turn away to seek more cheerful surroundings. Only occasionally does someone ask after the grave of Franz Kafka, who spent much of his short life in the Prague Ghetto. But Kafka lies in a new Jewish cemetery out in the suburbs. Our guide said, "You can find his grave easily, but you can't buy his books here in his native city, even though an edition was promised long ago." Because Kafka, like many Prague intellectuals of his time, spoke and wrote in German, certain of today's literati do not consider him a Czech writer.

The official guidebook to Prague contains no mention of Kafka, although a bronze bust and plaque mark his birthplace, an ancient apartment house near the Old Town Square in the center of the medieval city. It was a group of foreign writers, not Czechoslovaks, who installed the bust in 1964, forty years after Kafka's death. When his famous novel *The Trial* was published in Czech for the first time, in 1937, it was said to have sold three copies. Its ominous opening sentence ("Someone must have been telling lies about Joseph K., for without having done anything wrong he was arrested one fine morning") proved a remarkably chilling forecast of the torments many of Kafka's countrymen were soon to undergo at the hands of their Nazi conquerors and later at the hands of the Communist power structure. All his writings were banned, of course, during the German occupation. When at long last *The Trial* was republished in 1958, it produced a shock of recognition among young readers who had some knowledge of the murderous show trials of the early 1950s. But the trend toward more lenient censorship did not last. With the Soviet invasion of 1968, Kafka's writings disappeared once again.

Soon after the political upheaval that started in November 1989, Prague welcomed the return of artists and intellectuals who had left the country after the 1968 invasion. Ota

Sik, the economist chiefly responsible for the economic reforms that were quashed after Soviet tanks rumbled into Prague, was met with cheers in Smetana Hall at a concert played by the Czech Philharmonic in tribute to Civic Forum. Sik is now a citizen of Switzerland. The orchestra's conductor, Vaclav Neumann, wore a large Civic Forum badge on his lapel as he led the musicians through Beethoven's Ninth Symphony. Vaclav Havel then introduced the Forum members of the new cabinet, including foreign minister Jiri Dienstbier, who sat in the box of honor. The jubilant crowd joined the orchestra, chorus, and soloists in rapturous applause for the revolution against Communism.

A few days earlier, Czechoslovakia lifted the ban on some of its most talented writers, including Milan Kundera, who lives in Paris, and Havel. Joseph Skvorecky writes, teaches, and publishes Czechoslovak literature in Toronto. Pavel Kohout has lived in Vienna since 1978, when he was refused permission to re-enter Czechoslovakia at the end of a visit to Austria. He was at work on a new play for the Burgtheater when we talked in his favorite Viennese coffee house.

Ivan Klima, who returned to Prague voluntarily from a teaching position in the United States after the Warsaw Pact invasion, kept writing, although his stories remained unpublished in Czechoslovakia for more than twenty years. To support his family, Klima worked at odd jobs as a land surveyor's assistant and as a male nurse. Several of his books — *A Summer of Love, My Merry Mornings,* and *My First Loves* — have been published in other countries. Klima is not a joiner. He did not even sign the founding document of Charter 77, which campaigned for the restoration of human rights over a dozen years. "I never sign anything I haven't written myself," he told me, "except appeals for the release of political prisoners."

In 1988, when I visited his apartment on the rural edge of Prague, Klima said that he kept in touch with the outside world by listening to foreign broadcasts because there was so little honest information in the Czech newspapers. "We are informed," he said, when the talk turned to events in neighboring Poland. "We listen to Radio Free Europe, the Voice of America, and the BBC." He had also recently subscribed to *Moscow News* for information about the progress of Mikhail Gorbachev's reforms in the Soviet Union. Its coverage, he explained, was more enlightening than anything the Prague press was allowed to print.

There is also the case of Jiri Ruml, deputy editor of a weekly news magazine, *Reporter,* which blossomed briefly in the Prague Spring and was then suppressed. Two decades older, and wise in the ways of dealing with bureaucracy, Ruml began negotiating with the government in 1988 for permission to publish an independent newspaper. The paper, *Lidowe Nowiny (People's News),* took its name from a Prague newspaper that was banned in 1952. Several monthly issues had been distributed in *samizdat* format when Ruml decided to apply for registration of *Lidowe Nowiny* as a legitimate aboveground publication. It would then be entitled to adequate newsprint and the right to use state-owned presses. Ruml hoped to move step by step from monthly to daily publication of a newspaper that did not submit its material to official censorship. In his conversations with the Federal Office for Printing and Information, Ruml cited the precedent of widening press freedom in the Soviet Union: If *glasnost* was permitted, even encouraged in Moscow, why not in Prague? The government countered with a legal objection: Only organizations belonging to the National Front, the Communist Party transmission-belt organization, could publish newspapers. Ruml and his editorial board were prepared for that objection. They pointed out that Pacem in Terris, an association of Catholic priests friendly to the government, did not belong to the National Front. Why not form a Society of Friends of *Lidowe Nowiny*? Although the paper continued to appear "as an experiment," Ruml and Rudolf Zeman, a fellow editor, were arrested in October 1989 on charges of subversion. The opposition paper's license to publish legally has now been granted and its editors released from jail, thanks to the gentle revolution.

Even the party press, not widely admired for its investigative zeal, for unexplained reasons recently discovered such life-and-death issues as the people's health. *Prace,* the daily newspaper of the Communist trade unions, reported that Czechoslovakia ranked twenty-fifth among twenty-eight European countries in life expectancy. Between 1960 and 1985, *Prace* found, life expectancy rose by one tenth of a year even as West Germany over the same period gained 5.3 years. Czechoslovak men now have a life expectancy of 67.3 years; women, 73.9. The figures suggest that Czechoslovaks die between four and seven years earlier than the citizens of other developed countries. They also rank first among the citizens of 150 United Nations member states in mortality rates for cancer, coronary diseases, and strokes. About 20 percent of the population suffers from diseases directly linked to environmental pollution.

Not so many years ago, East European officials tended to dismiss concerns about pollution. They said it was a problem unique to capitalist societies, and its main cause was the profit motive. As socialist industries were not under pressure to turn a profit, private ownership having been abolished, the problem could easily be handled by enforcing uniform standards. That comforting though false assumption has now been exploded, and Czechoslovakia has done little to make up for lost time. The country's pollution problems, Valtr Komarek has said, "show the bankruptcy of the traditional socialist model of industrialization."

The four most heavily polluted countries of the region — Czechoslovakia, East Germany, Poland, and Hungary — all burn high-sulfur brown coal as their primary energy source. The sky above their power plants is black with combustion products, including sulfur dioxide, which has destroyed large forest areas and seriously damaged historic buildings and monuments. Their automobiles still burn leaded gas and do it inefficiently, adding to the murk that hangs over many cities. I noticed in Prague that some drivers had developed the habit of switching off their engines while they waited for a green light at busy intersections. When I asked one driver whether he was trying to save gasoline, he laughed. "No," he said, "I'm just doing my bit to cut down on pollution. Our government, as you know, does nothing at all."

The rivers of Czechoslovakia, even the fabled Moldau, whose natural beauty inspired Bedrich Smetana's tone poem, are choked with sewage. In an average year, 1.2 billion cubic meters of waste are dumped into the rivers. Less than one third of that staggering quantity passes through a water-treatment plant before being released into the rivers. Much of the problem is attributed to the system of industrial management that is common to the Soviet bloc countries. Managers are appointed by the party and judged on their performance in meeting centrally assigned production goals, not on their efficient use of resources or their success in dealing with pollution. When an enterprise is fined for polluting the air or water, it is not the manager who pays. Since the state owns all property, it winds up paying the fine. It can be argued that many American managers are equally negligent. But the huge land mass of the United States, Czech ecologists say, can absorb far more pollution than their own small country, so cramped for space that action to control pollution is, or should be, an absolute imperative.

Most, a town in Northern Bohemia, is cited as a worst-case example of what can happen when production is worshiped without concern for people. Some twenty-five years ago, Most was found to be sitting on a rich coal deposit. The district authorities shrewdly decided to tear down the town so that they could get at the coal. The displaced residents were eventually moved into new apartment buildings nearby, a process that took years. The strip mining of brown coal began more promptly, releasing clouds of sulfur water into the air. The stench was overpowering, but, as a member of the Most district committee acknowledged, "we were so busy building the new town that we didn't pay much attention to the environment. When the snow in town started turning black, we knew we had to do something." Black snow was not the worst of it. The strip mining left a manmade canyon several kilometers long beside the row of new apartment houses, and the air was so foul that mothers feared to walk their babies outdoors. Today, Most has started doing something to make life more tolerable. It plans to install desulfurization equipment and filters in the municipal heating plants. There is talk of converting the town's residential heating from coal to natural gas from Russia. But it has taken a quarter-century to move a very short distance.

The government in Prague has not been altogether idle. It issues occasional directives and resolutions on the worsening environment, but the practical results have been meager till now. A study by Charter 77 found that Czechoslovakia ranked number two in the whole of Europe when it came to sulfur dioxide pollution. In Prague itself, according to the Charter report, the amount of sulfur dioxide in the air exceeds the officially permitted limit by more than 20 percent. Concentrations of nitrous oxide, the product of automobile exhausts, were estimated at 200 to 300 percent above the permissible level. The government was anything but grateful for well-meaning interventions of this kind by independent groups. When a study group calling itself the Ecology Club of Bratislava produced a sixty-page report listing the environmental hazards the region was facing, the government at first ignored it, then confiscated two thousand copies of the document, and finally denounced it in *Pravda,* the Slovak Communist paper. A *Pravda* editor said the facts in the report were "80 percent correct," but what troubled him most was that the study had been used by Western media "as a criticism of the socialist system." The technology for controlling air, water, and soil pollution is as costly in the East bloc as in the West, and a major clean-up will demand far higher budget priority than it has received in Czechoslovakia.

Czechoslovak intellectuals I met did not dwell exclusively on such problems as the state of the physical environment or the stagnant economy. They kept alive the hope that one day "socialism with a human face" might become a reality, not through the destruction of the existing political system but through gradual change. They had enough of drama, they said, in 1938 and 1948 and again in 1968. Solidarity's long struggle to transform the structure of the Polish regime gave them courage. Above all, they put their faith in what they call "parallel activities," such as Charter, and the ferment of ideas being published in *samizdat* publications, which, for lack of access to a printing press, circulated from hand to hand in typewritten form. A Slovak writer, Milan Simecka, who had served time in prison for his opinions, stated the case for gradualism in an interview with the novelist Eva Kanturkova, published in an underground magazine. "Have we made any mark on the character of the regime?" he asked. "I'm afraid not. But we have made a mark on the way people think in this country, on the national culture. We've also done something to polarize [thinking about] morality here. That all amounts to quite a bit. It will be more obvious in a few years' time.

"We are fully aware that the pluralism of ideas here is possible only thanks to the wider context of European intellectual pluralism, and because isolation is now unthinkable with the existence of modern mass media . . . Thirty or even twenty years ago, such parallel activities as ours would have been nipped in the bud, and nobody would have been the wiser, as indeed happened in the past."

Modest hopes, but life in Czechoslovakia imposed certain sober limits on the aspirations of even its most talented and courageous citizens. Like other residents of Bratislava, Simecka watches Austrian television every day, and he is not enchanted by the squabbles of Austrian politicians he sees on TV. "I much prefer looking at the pluralism of life there, the plurality of opinions, the plurality of the press, radio, and television, the plurality of language, ideas, and beliefs, the plurality of trades and shops, not to mention the plurality of travel agencies, restaurants, and publishing houses . . . All that provides the basis for a truly European lifestyle. We'd need only a few crumbs from that table to feel better, freer, and more cheerful . . . It is the only concrete and tangible thing that it makes any sense to work for, practically speaking."

The gentle revolution should offer brave souls like Milan Simecka more than a few crumbs of comfort.

# 4

## *Poland*

### The Second Coming of Solidarity

IN THE MIRACULOUS SUMMER of 1989, Catholic Poland installed a new prime minister, a tall, taciturn man named Tadeusz Mazowiecki, whose beliefs were rooted in the gospel of Christ, not of Marx and Lenin. Even nonbelievers called it a miracle that Solidarity was asked to form a government that, for the first time in more than forty years, would not be dominated by Communists. A Soviet newspaperman who asked the little-known prime minister whether he considered himself a socialist or perhaps a social democrat received this calm and doubtless astonishing response: "Simply put, I'm a Christian, a Catholic who follows the social teachings of the Catholic Church, which emanate from the instructions of John Paul II." Soviet tanks did not roll into Warsaw, as they had rolled into Budapest and Prague when Communist dogma and Soviet hegemony were challenged.

For anyone who remembered Hungary in 1956 and Czechoslovakia in 1968, the change was breathtaking. The Kremlin sent Mazowiecki a congratulatory message that, while hardly effusive in tone, assured the Poles that "friendship and all-around cooperation" would continue even if the

Communist Party was no longer in command. Mikhail Gorbachev telephoned the new Warsaw party chief, Mieczyslaw Rakowski, urging the Communists to accept a back seat in the coalition government led by Solidarity. The Communists, who had been threatening to make life difficult for Mazowiecki, promptly announced that they were prepared for "partnerlike cooperation." Even the KGB signed on to the new policy. Its chief, Vladimir Kryuchkov, hurried to Warsaw, met the prime minister, and endorsed him as "a solid man."

Poland was passing through a political transformation that would have seemed utterly inconceivable a year earlier. It started in the winter of 1989, when General Wojciech Jaruzelski, who had imposed martial law and had outlawed Solidarity in December 1981, decided that drastic remedial action was called for. The economy was in shambles, two successive Communist "reforms" had failed to arrest the decline, and much of Polish industry was paralyzed by strikes. The time had come, Jaruzelski was persuaded, to legalize and negotiate with Solidarity.

A series of so-called round-table negotiations followed; they set the stage for national elections in early June. Suddenly the trade union called Solidarity found itself in the business of politics — nominating candidates, creating constituency organizations, printing posters, pamphlets, and newspapers, raising money. Its negotiators had agreed that the Communists, after more than forty years in power, should be guaranteed a majority in the Sejm, the lower house of Poland's legislature, by limiting the number of seats Solidarity would contest. The voters, however, were in no mood to respect the rules of the game. Almost as if it were a free election, they buried the Communist Party's tattered claim to legitimacy, electing ninety-nine out of a hundred Solidarity candidates to the newly created Senate and sweeping every one of the lower-house seats that Solidarity was allowed to contest. The outcome could only be read as a humiliating, all-but-total rejection of Communism.

Even the party potentates who ran unopposed on the Communists' "national list" felt the wrath of the voters, who rejected all but one of the thirty-six leadership figures on the list by scratching out their names on the ballot. The victims included Rakowski, then Poland's prime minister, Interior Minister Czeslaw Kiszczak, Defense Minister Florian Siwicki, and Wladyslaw Baka, the party secretary in charge of economic policy. The tremors were felt throughout the Soviet bloc.

By allowing the people to register their opposition to Communism, the Polish party shocked the hard-line leaders of East Germany and Czechoslovakia. Nothing of the sort had been permitted in Eastern Europe since the 1940s. It was certainly not the kind of blunder that Todor Zhivkov would have made in Bulgaria, or Nicolae Ceausescu in Romania. Almost nothing had changed in those Balkan countries since Gorbachev launched his reform programs in the Soviet Union. Hungary's reform politicians, on the other hand, were encouraged and delighted by the Polish outcome as they geared up for their own exercise in pluralist politics. Gorbachev and the men around him said little, strenuously avoiding even the appearance of intervention in their external empire.

Their minds presumably were on more immediate problems within the boundaries of the Soviet Union — economic failures, enormous budget deficits, inflation, coal strikes, and surging nationalism in much of the internal empire: the Baltic states, Armenia, Georgia, Moldavia, and Central Asia.

The historic April accords and the June election in Poland marked the high tide of political change in the Soviet bloc. But it was clear in retrospect that the grand compromise between the Polish party and Solidarity, which legalized the union, laid down the election arrangements, and provided for the uncontested election of General Jaruzelski to the new post of president, involved miscalculations on both sides. The Communists erred in assuming that the short, seven-week run-up to election day would work in favor of their candidates, although none of them had ever run in a contested election. Their built-in advantages — incumbency, money, organization, media access — did not appear to count for much. Solidarity, by contrast, clearly underestimated the depth and intensity of anti-Communist sentiment among the voters, which worked in favor of its own inexperienced candidates. Unprepared for a victory of near-landslide proportions, the Solidarity deputies suddenly found themselves in the parliament without having agreed on a common strategy for applying their newfound political muscle.

Zbigniew Bujak, Solidarity's district leader in Warsaw, neatly framed the bewildering dilemma that confronted his legislative colleagues. "An enormous responsibility has fallen on Solidarity," he wrote a few days after the votes were counted. "How should an opposition behave when it has the majority?" Anywhere but in Poland that would have been an absurd question. In traditional parliamentary democracies, of course, victorious majorities govern, and defeated minorities go into opposition. But in this and other respects, Poland was a special case. Many weeks would pass before Solidarity overcame its disinclination to govern.

Lech Walesa's political instincts told him that, although Solidarity was now the dominant force in Polish politics, the prudent thing was to remain in opposition and refuse to join a governing coalition with the Communists. He preferred to wait for the next election, in 1993, which would be completely free, as agreed in the round-table negotiations. Besides, the economy was a hopeless mess created by the Communists, and the clean-up should be left to them. "The safe road is the evolutionary road," Walesa told Henry Kamm of the *New York Times.* "Everything has to be calculated very well on the computer. We want to stay on the reform course and not provide arguments [that can be used] against us by those who are just waiting for them." He had in mind the still-potent conservative faction in the Communist leadership, which had opposed the union's restoration to legal standing even after Jaruzelski, Kiszczak, and Rakowski had advocated it. Another cautionary element seems to have been Walesa's concern that Poland's East bloc allies would not hold still for Solidarity's accession to power.

Solidarity's challenge to the existing order had already produced momentous changes, and some of its new members of parliament were nervous about forcing the pace. Krzysztof Sliwinski, managing editor of Solidarity's new and legal newspaper, *Gazeta Wiborcza,* enumerated the gains achieved: "We have won trade union pluralism. There is increased freedom of expression and movement. More than 80 percent of Polish farmers own . . . their land. A strong, independent Roman Catholic Church protects the deepest moral values of the land. And the opposition has freely elected members in parliament. So, although Poland cannot be called a free and democratic state, it already does not fit into any totalitarian Communist straitjacket. It is no longer a satellite country of a great imperial power."

But there was no sign of euphoria sweeping the country. Poles had grown weary of political games and unfulfilled promises. Few of them dared to hope that the Communists, though defeated at the polls and ruling by consent of Solidarity, would yield power if push came to shove.

It soon became brutally clear, however, that the Communists lacked the votes to go it alone, their apparent majority in the Sejm notwithstanding. Two smaller parties, the United Peasants Alliance, with seventy-six seats, and the Democratic Party, with twenty-seven, which had been puppets on a Communist string for the better part of forty years, were showing signs of unwonted independence. Denied their endorsement and the support of Solidarity, General Kiszczak resigned after barely two weeks as prime minister. Even General Jaruzelski, though assured of the presidency by the terms of the April accord, squeaked in by the margin of a single vote, but only with the connivance of a group of Solidarity deputies who deliberately spoiled their ballots or stayed away in order to reduce the number of affirmative votes he needed to survive. Apparently the Solidarity mavericks wanted to make sure of Jaruzelski's election without having to vote for him. Solidarity's virtually total control of the Senate, moreover, meant that even if the Communists managed to patch together a government, they would be unable to pass major legislation without the union's assent. It looked like a recipe for certain deadlock.

Politicians on all sides were painfully aware that the government, whatever its ultimate composition, could not long postpone action to restructure and revive the ruined economy. Letting things drift could lead to collapse. The Finance Ministry had warned that, with inflation running out of control in 1989, and industrial output flagging, such collapse was imminent. There was not much disagreement among economically literate Poles about the bitter medicine to be administered — further increases in consumer prices, reduced investment, and the shutdown of many money-losing state companies. That necessarily meant spreading unemployment.

At this point, Lech Walesa took charge. Abandoning his preference for the oppositionist role, he met secretly with the Peasant Party leader, Roman Malinowski, and found him willing to support a Solidarity prime minister. Together, Walesa and Malinowski called on President Jaruzelski, whose alternatives were limited. Unless he accepted a prime minister from Solidarity's ranks, Jaruzelski would be forced to call new elections and risk a second humiliating defeat. The general prudently agreed to appoint a Solidarity man. Walesa chose Mazowiecki.

The new prime minister, a hawk-faced Catholic layman, editor, and lawyer, exemplifies the extraordinary alliance between industrial workers and intellectuals that has distinguished Solidarity from trade unions in other countries. The alliance was forged in August 1980, when Mazowiecki initiated an appeal signed by sixty-four scholars, scientists, and assorted cultural figures in support of the Gdansk shipyard workers, who were then striking for the right to form an independent union, along with higher wages and civil liberties. The document read, in part: "In this struggle, the place of the entire progressive intelligentsia is on their side. That is the Polish tradition, and that is the imperative of the hour." On behalf of the signers, Mazowiecki and Bronislaw Geremek, the bearded, pipe-smoking medieval historian at present Solidarity's leader in parliament, delivered the document to Walesa, who thanked them warmly. "But what we need are not petitions," he said. "What we need are experts, people like you, to talk to the government on our behalf. Please give us your help." The two intellectuals agreed to stay on in Gdansk as advisers to Solidarity, and after the union was outlawed they helped to guide its underground activities. Neither man was schooled in economics or administration. But with the second coming of Solidarity, as it has been irreverently described, they found themselves saddled with the task of somehow putting Poland on the road to economic recovery.

On his triumphal return to Gdansk nine years later as the head of a yet-to-be-formed government, Mazowiecki readily conceded that, in view of the enormous tasks ahead, Poland needed bread more than it needed a prime minister. "Today, when we open this historic chapter," he said, "we must reject a feeling of hopelessness. It must be rejected because no one can do anything without believing that it can be done."

His inspirational tone was tinged with melancholy when he spoke of the dark outlook that had driven thousands of young Poles to emigrate. "We must believe that this nation . . . can reach the stage where life will be better in Poland," he said, "so that no one lacks anything in Poland, so that no one leaves it."

The urge to emigrate is most powerful among members of the eighteen-to-forty generation, born and schooled within the Communist system. They have developed a rugged immunity to pie-in-the sky promises of a bright socialist future. Jobs are hard to find. Upward mobility has vanished, and living standards continue to decline. Living without hope year after year has started a flood tide of emigration. More than 500,000 Poles, mostly young and many of them educated, left the country for good between 1980 and 1987, and the exodus has continued. When I visited Warsaw in 1988, young Poles were lining up as early as 5:00 A.M. outside the West German, Australian, British, and American embassies to apply for visas. "I don't want to leave forever," a sturdy, tow-headed mechanic told me as he waited in line. "This is my home. All I want is to work in the West for a couple of years. Then I can save some money, real money, I mean, not zlotys, then come back, and perhaps build a house for myself. Otherwise there is no hope, none at all."

The Communist regime used to describe these emigrants as "mean-spirited" people, driven by materialism. Church spokesmen talked more compassionately of the "emigration of despair." In a reflection of the darkening mood, large numbers of young Poles saw no useful purpose in higher education. The official press has conceded that "an education is no longer a factor that ensures an adequate standard of living." In fact, the Communist reward system has long been rigged against careers that require a university degree; physicians and academics stand at or near the bottom of the wage scale, well below factory workers. One serious result has been a dramatic decline in university enrollments. The proportion of Polish youth attending universities dropped from seventeen per thousand inhabitants in 1975 to thirteen per thousand in 1983. That left Poland behind Bolivia, Costa Rica, Panama, and Peru.

Even among young people attending universities, hope has been in short supply. A 1987 survey of student opinion found only 2 percent in agreement with the proposition that the Polish government was pursuing the right policies and achieving good results. A survey of Lodz University students the same year found the majority opposed to any "further construction of socialism"; some 45 percent said they favored the restoration of capitalism. A prominent sociologist interpreted these findings as part of a wider process of "alienation from all state institutions" that was most pronounced among the young.

Poland's student generation is not, however, alone in its disenchantment with things as they are. If the 1989 election proved nothing else, it unquestionably exposed the failure of the Communist Party to win and hold the support of the people it has ruled for more than forty years. The outcome was less a triumph for Solidarity than a near-total rejection of Communism. The party, nevertheless, still commands the permanent instruments of state power — the army, the security police, and the vast bureaucracy, which can be expected to resist or sabotage truly radical reforms. The raw numbers are instructive.

Until its repudiation at the polls, the Polish Communist Party claimed 2.3 million members. According to Solidarity estimates, 700,000 were retired bureaucrats and former managers of state industries. An additional 900,000 were state employees in one category or another. In short, 1.6 million party members, or 70 percent of the total membership, could be said to have a vested interest in resisting change, if only to preserve their jobs and privileges. But with the party's dissolution in January 1990, its diminishing ranks split. The advantages that went with party membership were no longer sufficient to hold the old structures in place.

There is, of course, no warrant for assuming that all card-carrying members are necessarily wedded to the party until death do them part. It's worth recalling that within two years of Solidarity's founding in 1980, the Polish party lost one fourth of its total membership. Whether Solidarity, now re-born as a governing party as well as a trade union, will be able to exert comparable magnetism into the 1990s remains to be seen. It has suddenly inherited all the accumulated problems the Communists failed to solve over four decades in their fidelity to the teachings of Marx, Lenin, and Stalin. Prime Minister Mazowiecki looks elsewhere for guidance. "I am a believer," he said, "and I believe that Providence cares for us."

Poland's Communist Party, meanwhile, was going through a crisis of faith. "We need a wholly new definition of the word 'socialism,'" Mieczyslaw Rakowski told me in 1988, a few months before he took office. "It may take ten years, perhaps longer, to give the concept fresh meaning, but it must be done. I can assure you that nobody in Poland today is ready to go to the barricades in defense of the 'dictator-ship of the proletariat.'" Rakowski, editor of the Warsaw weekly *Polityka* before he entered the upper reaches of the party hierarchy, once was reputed to be a Communist of liberal stripe. That reputation took some hard knocks when Rakowski served as the government negotiator in the 1981 negotiations with Solidarity, which led to martial law.

His stubborn refusal to discuss or consider the legaliza-tion of Solidarity put Rakowski at odds with many reform-minded Poles, who saw that as the first step toward national reconciliation and the ultimate revival of Poland's moribund economy. When I raised the question of reopening talks with

Solidarity, Rakowski cut me short. "Poland does not need an antisocialist party," he snapped. There was nothing more to be said — not then, at any rate.

The Communist retreat from that extreme position started in August 1988. Neither the government nor Solidarity had a credible program for dealing with the problems of an exhausted, virtually bankrupt nation. Solidarity's membership had dwindled. It was no longer a mass movement. The union's diminished ranks were torn by disagreements, and a wave of angry strikes, mostly unauthorized, was creating havoc in the economy. What finally brought the two sides together was a dawning realization that each needed the other to share the responsibility — and the blame — for a long-delayed effort to turn the economy around that would demand heavy sacrifices from the people. Walesa, whose appeals for talks with the government had been rejected till then, played his cards shrewdly. Most Poles, he said, did not "care a fig about Walesa or Solidarity," but they would support the union movement as long as the government persisted in making people's lives miserable. The regime's pollster, Colonel Stanislaw Kwiatkowski, was of much the same mind. He wrote in a Warsaw newspaper article that the government's own bumbling was responsible for the worrying round of August strikes, the second in four months. Something had to be done.

It started with a quiet meeting in a Warsaw suburb between Walesa and General Kiszczak, the officer who seven years earlier had signed the martial-law order that led to Walesa's eleven-month internment. Kiszczak, then minister of the interior, had an astonishing proposal: if Walesa could persuade the strikers to go back to work, the regime would consider restoring Solidarity's legal status as an independent union. The stakes were high. If Walesa succeeded in ending the strikes, the government would have to negotiate at last with the union it had outlawed and somehow failed to crush. If he failed, Walesa and Solidarity would lose a great deal. It was an offer Walesa could not refuse.

Within three days, he had halted the strikes — and promptly found himself accused of capitulation by many embittered younger workers. But Walesa, whose courage and instinctive political skills had seen him through more difficult moments, defended his leadership at a post-strike rally in Gdansk with a self-confidence bordering on arrogance. "I have not been a traitor and I will not be a traitor," he said. "You wanted more [than I could deliver], especially my adversaries. But I am not going to toy with Poland. I extinguished the strikes and I will extinguish any others that happen." Walesa had long believed, and Kiszczak now agreed, that only with Solidarity's full participation was there a chance of turning around Poland's ruined economy. Other party potentates took longer to convince.

As late as November, with the strikes ended, Rakowski's government was still refusing to negotiate and Solidarity was still technically an outlaw organization. In January 1989, the regime at last agreed to negotiate. In April, though only after a tearing clash within the Central Committee of the party, the regime legalized Solidarity and invited the union's participation in Poland's half-free election, the first since Communist rule was established after World War II. The Central Committee meeting was a close call for General Jaruzelski and his supporters. But the disastrous state of the Polish economy left them no more promising alternative. When hard-line party leaders attempted to derail the agreement with Solidarity, Jaruzelski threatened to resign, a threat in which he was joined by Kiszczak, Rakowski, and General Florian Siwicki, the defense minister.

"Coming to terms with Solidarity must have looked like the only way out for Jaruzelski," a foreign diplomat told me. "The plain fact, which the general refused to acknowledge for so many months, was that Solidarity had a far stronger claim to legitimacy — in the eyes of the people — than the Communist Party."

The regime, in short, needed to borrow against Solidarity's line of credit if it was to impress foreign lenders and the long-suffering Polish people with its determination to bring order out of economic chaos. The risk to Solidarity was considerable. The union's leaders knew that they would have a hard time persuading the people to accept new hardships as the only way to correct mistaken policies by Communist regimes that had repeatedly betrayed their promises in years past.

Poland's predicament, as expressed time and again by politicians, diplomats, journalists, bankers, and academics with whom I talked, came down to this: unless drastic steps were taken without delay, Poland would sink to the level of a Third World country. Its growth rate was among the lowest in Eastern Europe. The average citizen's standard of living was, next to a Romanian's, the lowest in the Soviet bloc. The American dollar had become the standard measure of market value; the wretched Polish zloty counted for almost nothing. Where, other than in Poland, would a Communist newspaper *(Gazeta Krakowska)* make a point of publishing the black market dollar-exchange rate several times a week?

Warsaw taxi drivers, a tough and skeptical lot, I discovered, prefer to ignore their fare meters because they are marked in zlotys and, in any case, lag far behind the inflation rate. During my last visit, I noticed a small notice pasted to each meter; it read 3X. This meant the passenger had to multiply the fare reading by three. More recently, I was told, the taxi meters read 7X and, in the spring of 1989, attained the dizzying height of 12X. That was enough to put taxis out of reach for any Pole without access to black market profits. No great loss, as it happens, because the cabbies prefer to pick up foreign passengers and negotiate the fare in dollars or deutsche marks.

A Warsaw department store on Marszalkowska Boulevard has taken a leaf from the cabbies' book. It sells brand-name imports in several stylish boutiques, but only for twenty-odd foreign currencies. The zloty is taboo. All prices are listed in dollars, although deutschemarks, Swiss and French francs, Austrian schillings, pounds sterling, and Italian lire are gratefully accepted. This necessarily limits the clientele to Poles with generous relatives in the West, or those with a hoard of hard currency earned outside the country. The boutiques, nevertheless, have done a land-office business in Italian designer jeans, Dutch chocolates, Austrian ski boots, and other pricey imports.

But for the majority of Poles, who lack access to foreign money, shopping tends to be a frustrating exercise. They spend long hours queuing up not for luxuries but for scarce necessities — soap, cheese, acceptable cuts of meat, fresh vegetables, and, scarcest of all, toilet paper. Most of these shortages defy rational explanation. They became the stuff of mocking commentaries in the city of Wroclaw by a troupe called Orange Alternative, which brings the theater of the absurd into the streets. It has drawn large crowds with tongue-in-cheek announcements like this one: "Socialism, with its extravagant distribution of goods, as well as its eccentric social posture, has put toilet paper in the forefront of people's dreams . . . At 4:00 P.M. in Swidnicka Street, let us take our toilet paper and distribute it to the people bit by bit. Let us share it justly. Let justice begin with toilet paper."

This was another message by Orange Alternative: "Recent events indicate that we will have to live lean today so as to get fatter later." Living lean is not, of course, a matter of choice in Poland, unlike the calorie-counting, cholesterol-avoiding Western countries. There is no great demand for oat bran. In the late summer and early autumn, Poles were looking to the West, chiefly the European Economic Community, to put meat on their dinner tables. In one of its final acts, the Rakowski government lifted all controls on food prices in a single stroke that doubled the price of cheese, quadrupled the cost of milk, and sent most other prices through the roof.

Rakowski's dramatic lurch in the direction of free-market economics might have made sense if it had been done less abruptly, in stages. But with typical bureaucratic bull-headedness, it ignored the inevitable time lag between the desired effect of stimulating increased food production in the uncertain future and the immediate impact of wildly surging prices on a nation in poverty. "Poland's future will be decided in the shop queues and not in parliament," the Solidarity newspaper *Gazeta Wiborcza* commented in a front-page article by its editor, Adam Michnik. "The new prices have created a sense of shock, and empty shop shelves provoke bitterness. It is clear to all that we must react. Urgently."

Food shortages and price rises have often triggered social and political upheavals in Poland. They set off the strikes that gave rise to Solidarity in 1980 and were suppressed only by the imposition of martial law. Prices and shortages also figured in the strikes that finally drove the Jaruzelski regime to negotiate with Solidarity, which in turn led to the union's rebirth and its eventual victory at the polls in June 1989. They do not, however, exhaust the Polish catalogue of pressing human problems.

Public health officials acknowledge, for example, that much of the country's milk, which in some districts tends to be bluish in color, is not fit for human consumption unless it has been brought to a boil. A report by the Polish Academy of Sciences concluded that 40 percent of the milk supply contained unacceptable amounts of microbiological contaminants. Medical services are primitive in many parts of the

country. Even in Warsaw, it took a full week of tireless lob-
bying and string pulling before a friend of mine, suffering
from a serious heart ailment, was admitted to the intensive
care unit of a major hospital. The courteous staff sent him
home the following day. "They apologized for the unfortunate inconvenience," my friend recalled, "but the electricity
had failed and the water supply had broken down. So they
unhooked all of us from the life support equipment and
closed the place down for the weekend."

Doctors and nurses are grossly underpaid and over-
worked. A staff physician at a Lodz clinic earns roughly half
the wage of an average industrial worker. Life expectancy
in Poland has been declining over the past quarter-century.
Official statistics show that in 1965 a thirty-year-old man could
look forward to 41.7 additional years of life. By 1988 his
predictable lifespan had dropped to 39.7 additional years.

Poland is an acknowledged environmental disaster zone —
particularly in the vicinity of such industrial cities as Krakow, Katowice, Wroclaw, and Lodz — which adds to the
health risks. The Vistula River, flowing through Krakow and
Warsaw on its northward course to the Baltic Sea at Gdansk,
is an open sewer poisoned by industrial waste. The skies over
Krakow and Katowice are dark with smoke and acrid fumes
from nearby iron and steel works. Government officials concede that nothing is being done because the country can't
afford scrubber technology. The ancient stonework of medieval Krakow is rapidly eroding under attack from air-
borne pollutants. As for the dying forests, a tourist guide
dismisses that concern with an outworn joke. "An environ-
mentalist," he says, "is someone who, seeing a man fall out
of a tree, rushes up to the tree and asks, 'Are you all right?' "

Throughout its modern history, Poland has been dogged by
misfortune at the hands of more powerful neighbors. Tsarist Russia, Prussia, and Austria erased it from the map of

Europe in 1795 in a three-way partition. More than 120 years would pass before Poland was reconstituted a sovereign state, at the end of World War I. That brief interlude of independence ended on September 1, 1939, when Hitler's armies invaded from the west, followed in a matter of days by Stalin's armies invading from the east, as arranged in the secret protocols to the so-called nonaggression treaty signed on August 23, 1939, by Foreign Minister Vyacheslav M. Molotov for the Soviet Union and his Nazi counterpart, Joachim von Ribbentrop. That pact, more accurately described as a treaty of joint aggression, ultimately robbed Poland and the Baltic states of their independence.

The fiftieth anniversary of the Stalin-Hitler pact that divided Europe, and Poland itself, into German and Soviet spheres of influence could not pass unnoticed in the astonishing summer of 1989. In the lower house of Poland's reborn parliament, Communists joined Solidarity deputies in a unanimous vote condemning the secret deal as a cynical "example of imperialist thinking and secret diplomacy" at the expense of weaker nations. A day earlier, even the Polish party Politburo denounced the secret protocols as violations of international law. The Kremlin, which for decades past had heatedly denied the existence of the secret protocols, lamely conceded that the Soviet Union and Hitler's Germany had "without a doubt" concluded such agreements.

Stalin had locked in his land grab at the end of World War II. He annexed 100,000 square miles of Eastern Poland for the Soviet Union and, by way of compensation, agreed with the Western allies that some 50,000 square miles of German territory should be placed under Polish rule. This led to one of the largest and most disruptive population movements Europe had seen as Poland's frontiers were, in effect, shifted 150 miles to the west. As many as ten million Poles and Germans were transported from their homesteads and farms — Poles to the newly acquired former German territories in the west and displaced Germans into what remained of Hitler's shattered Third Reich.

Poles have long memories, particularly for grievances against Russians and Germans. They have not forgotten or forgiven Stalin's brutalities: the massacre of thousands of Polish officers whose remains were later found in mass graves in the Katyn Forest, near Smolensk; the fact that units of Marshal Konstantin Rokossovsky's First White Russian Front sat on the east bank of the Vistula and did nothing to help while overwhelming German forces crushed the Warsaw Uprising in 1944; and his refusal to honor the Yalta agreement on free elections for Poland.

Stalin's supreme postwar insult may well have been his secret decision to impose Soviet commanders on Poland's armed forces. With the late John Scott of *Time,* I had stumbled on evidence pointing to the clandestine Russification of the Polish army in June 1946. That was three years before the Poles announced that the same Marshal Rokossovsky, who on Stalin's orders had not lifted a finger while the Germans killed 200,000 Poles in the streets of Warsaw, had been appointed Poland's defense minister.

Scott and I, driving to Warsaw from Berlin, had been arrested at a road barrier and ordered back to the city of Poznan for interrogation. The young officer who studied our passports and visas was pleasant enough but was unable to explain what had gone wrong. "I have my orders," he said. To make certain that we would get to Poznan, he assigned us a teenage guide armed with a submachine gun. We had traveled perhaps ten miles, enveloped in gloom, when I spotted a rare and splendid sight ahead — a shiny 1946 Ford V-8 with a miniature Stars and Stripes fluttering from its radio antenna, headed in the opposite direction. Uncertain how the armed soldier in the rear seat would react, I flagged the oncoming car rather timidly and pulled up. So did the driver of the gleaming American car, who turned out to be an American embassy courier named Jake Vermeulen. We slipped him a scribbled message for Arthur Bliss Lane, the American ambassador in Warsaw, with instructions that he lose no time delivering it personally. Slightly less disconsolate now, we pushed on to Poznan, rattling across an ancient drawbridge into a castle courtyard.

Here we were delivered into the hands of two officers in Polish uniforms, both wearing Soviet war medals. They spoke Russian, as did Scott, who had worked in the Soviet Union during the Great Depression and married a Russian woman. Our interrogators took a passionate interest in John's American passport, holding its pages up to the light, one by one, and muttering in Russian about "crude forgeries." Before long, however, they decided that John must have been a Red Army deserter, because his passport clearly showed that he had left the Soviet Union in 1941, the year of Hitler's invasion.

A couple of anxious hours followed. The gloomy old castle was beginning to feel like a prison. While John fenced with his interrogators in fluent Russian, I had plenty of time for dark thoughts. When, for example, would I see my young bride again? And how would she receive the news, when it reached her in Washington, that John and I were missing behind the Iron Curtain? The term was on everyone's lips at the time, owing to Winston Churchill's recent speech at Fulton, Missouri, warning the West that the Soviet Union was bent on a course of postwar expansion. A shrill telephone interrupted my reverie. The caller was Poland's minister of public security, Stanislaw Radkiewicz, who, as we later learned, scolded our interrogators for stupidity and ordered our immediate release. Thanks to Jake Vermeulen's heavy foot on the gas pedal, our message had been delivered, and Ambassador Lane had lodged an immediate protest with Radkiewicz. In an extraordinary reversal, our interrogators were now offering apologies. It was nothing more serious, they said, than a case of mistaken identity; there were "counterrevolutionary bandits" in the area, and that made people nervous. Giddy with relief now, we invited our captors to join us for dinner that evening in a Poznan hotel.

In the course of that long, boozy dinner we interrogated our interrogators. They insisted, of course, that they were honest-to-God Poles in spite of their Stalingrad medals and their fluent Russian. We pressed them to concede that they were, in fact, Russians masquerading as Poles. No, no, they kept saying. They were true Poles who happened to have fought with the Red Army at Stalingrad and they had now been repatriated. The elder of the two, a Colonel Morozov, smiled crookedly when I remarked that Morozov did not sound like a Polish name. I suggested that if he were going to remain in Poland he would do well to change it. This time the colonel burst into loud laughter. We read it as confirming our suspicions.

Stalin, who did not much care for Poles, once said that Communism fitted Poland about as neatly as a saddle fitted a cow. That may explain why he liked the idea of surreptitiously planting Soviet officers in key positions throughout the Polish armed forces to make certain of their reliability. The Rokossovsky appointment, once announced, came as a clear affront to Polish pride. But it was not until 1956, with Stalin long dead, that Nikita Khrushchev agreed to recall Rokossovsky at the urgent request of Poland's new Communist leader, Wladyslaw Gomulka. The last of the lower-level Soviet officers like Colonel Morozov stayed on in Poland for years after.

Communism had not always been so widely detested in Poland. In his classic study *The Captive Mind,* the great Polish poet and Nobel laureate Czeslaw Milos vividly recalled the influences and illusions that radicalized his own prewar generation of intellectuals:

> The Eastern world, which we knew only from books, seemed to us like a world of progress when we compared it with conditions we could observe at first hand. Weighing the matter rationally, we were convinced that the future lay with the East. Our country was in a state of paralysis. The masses had no say in the government. The social filter was so contrived that peasants' and workers' youth had no access to the secondary schools and universities . . . Infinitely complicated national minority problems (and our country had a high percentage of minorities) were resolved in the most chauvinist spirit . . . Can one wonder that we looked to Russia as the country where a solution had been found to all the problems that beset us, as the country which alone could save us from the misfortunes which we could so easily visualize as we listened to Hitler's speeches on the radio?[1]

A radically different Poland emerged from the crucible of war. Stalin and Hitler between them had liquidated prewar Poland's minority problems. The greater part of the Jewish population, three and a half million strong in 1939, did not survive the Holocaust. Today there are fewer than five thousand Jews in Poland. The White Russian and Ukrainian minorities became unwilling Soviet citizens when Stalin annexed Eastern Poland.

Stalin's surgery had turned Poland into an ethnically homogeneous state in permanent allegiance to Moscow under the eternal guidance of the Communist Party — or so it seemed until 1980. The breakthrough came in two installments. First, the rise of Solidarity, described by the philosopher Leszek Kolakowski as the single event that, more nearly than the Russian or Chinese Revolution, resembled the authentic working-class revolution long predicted in Marxist theory. It was a fourteen-month struggle of industrial work-

1. New York: Vintage Books, 1981, pp. 146–147.

ers against the owners of the means of production, in this case the Polish state embodied in the Communist Party. The party prevailed by declaring a state of war against the workers in December 1981, filling the jails with Solidarity militants and their allies in the intelligentsia. Then, in the second stage, a movement that refused to disintegrate or die under the hammer blows of the police and army came back to triumph at the polls. Offered a real choice for the first time in 1989, the voters cleanly canceled the Communists' political monopoly and turned the country in a new direction.

Poland today is embarked on a difficult, perhaps impossible, course. Never before in a Communist-ruled country has a broad social movement attempted to win power and replace the discredited system through peaceful parliamentary means. Poland's powerful drive toward self-determination has raised alarms among hard-line Communists in spite of Lech Walesa's promise that the new Solidarity-led government will continue to honor its Warsaw Pact commitments and leave Communist ministers in charge of the army and security forces. There are powerful men in the Kremlin who doubtless consider the Polish developments dangerous on strategic as well as political grounds. If Gorbachev should stumble, they may yet be tempted to deal harshly with the unruly Poles.

As the largest of the subject nations, the land bridge between Soviet territory and East Germany, Poland remains a keystone of the alliance system. Its standing army of thirteen divisions accounts for close to a third of the combined Warsaw Pact forces, excluding, of course, the massive Soviet contingent. But ever since the Polish army played its part in the suppression of Solidarity in 1981, its value as a military asset of the Soviet high command has been discounted by strategists within the bloc. There is fragmentary evidence that the Soviets, concerned about protecting their lines of supply and communication with Red Army units facing

NATO forces in Germany, have tried to reduce their dependence on Polish territory by developing alternative routes, including increased reliance on seaborne shipments through Baltic waters.

Purely military considerations of this nature, if not altogether obsolete as the fear of war recedes, are less salient in the 1990s than they appeared to be at the height of the Cold War. Gorbachev's careful record of nonintervention in Hungary, Poland, East Germany, Czechoslovakia, Bulgaria, and, of course, Romania, suggests that the old limits on deviation have been stretched to a degree that would have been unthinkable even six months before Solidarity's second coming. Consider the dramatic contrast between the Kremlin's reaction to the Prague Spring in 1968 and the Warsaw summer of 1989.

In Czechoslovakia there was not the slightest sign that the Communist Party, led by Alexander Dubcek, was losing control of events or was threatened with overthrow. In fact, by making itself the principal agent of liberalizing reform, it earned a degree of enthusiastic citizen support never matched till then in Eastern Europe. Dubcek's regime abolished censorship, moved to democratize the political system and restructure the economy, drafted sweeping guarantees of human rights and civil liberties, and was overhauling the corrupted legal system. The Kremlin's brutal response — tanks roaring into the streets of Prague — crushed for twenty-one years the hope that peaceful reform was possible under Communist rule.

Many of the same reforms have been promised in Poland. Here the locomotive of change was an indomitably anti-Communist trade union, and the Communist regime has grudgingly yielded a portion of its power at the will of the voters. Soviet tanks did not roll, and a telephone call from Gorbachev cleared the way for Mazowiecki to form his new coalition government. It's early to draw the conclusion that

Solidarity is in power to stay. Much can still go wrong. A resurgence of strikes and bread-and-meat riots could open the door for an eventual return of the Communists. But Poland has a fighting chance of becoming the first country to refute the Leninist dogma that Communism is irreversible, that once a Communist Party is in power, there can be no turning back.

The country's postwar history dictates low-key expectations. Three times since World War II — in 1956, 1970, and again in 1976 — Polish workers have confronted security forces in the streets of Polish cities to protest food shortages and generally wretched conditions, leading in each case to the downfall of a Communist regime. That could also be the fate of Prime Minister Mazowiecki's new Solidarity-led government if, like his Communist predecessors, he should fail to seize the moment and begin to rebuild the crippled economy. The inescapable link between Polish misery and Polish political turbulence remains a threat to stability.

Forty years of Communist misrule and economic mismanagement have created an unholy mess that is bound to take years to overcome, together with a great deal of luck and more than token assistance from the West. The economic and social infrastructure is on the verge of collapse: hospitals and clinics suffering a lack of medical supplies; butcher shops displaying what Warsaw housewives call "naked hooks" in the absence of meat; state industries running enormous deficits that can be funded only out of the people's standard of living, which has been declining for at least a decade. A deaf person must wait six years for a hearing aid, and newly married couples are told they can expect to move into their own small apartment in thirty years.

Finding a way to put more bread and meat on Polish dinner tables is Solidarity's first intimidating task, though not the only one. It must inspire Western creditors to provide more generous assistance and, at the same time, convince the population that belt tightening now will be rewarded by a better life in the future. The Communists, meanwhile, retain control of the army, the police, and the *nomenklatura*, a secret list of some 900,000 positions that till now have been filled exclusively by party-approved candidates. These are the men who run every significant enterprise and institution in the country — state industries, financial institutions, the official bureaucracy, even hospitals, schools, and universities. An attempt to reduce their numbers and their powers may be the first tough test of the new government's authority.

Jan Winiecki, a respected Polish economist, has suggested that the best way to get rid of the *nomenklatura* would be to pension it off. He has calculated, not altogether in jest, that the gain in economic efficiency would more than offset the cost of all those pensions. Mieczyslaw Rakowski had another idea. Before losing his parliamentary seat and the prime ministry, Rakowski pushed through a National Consolidation Scheme that authorizes "experiments" in the transfer of state property to private entrepreneurs. Rather than rely solely on their pensions, certain members of the *nomenklatura* alertly took advantage of the new legislation to prepare soft landings for themselves in the small but growing private sector. This scheme, which soon became known as the "enfranchisement of the *nomenklatura*," permits knowledgeable managers to steer business toward new companies in which they had the foresight to acquire shares, and to lease them factory space and equipment owned by the state.

One member of the *nomenklatura* who seized his opportunity early on was Marek Ogrodzki, chairman of a state-owned company that manufactures electronic components. In 1986 he asked the minister of industry to lease him the enterprise. When the government hesitated, Ogrodzki agreed to let the employees vote on the proposed transfer, and 70 percent approved. Although the state claimed 50 percent of the company's income instead of the usual 40 percent, the entrepreneur took over. He fired 280 of the 1,000 workers, taking advantage of the looser law on private companies, and output increased even as the costs of production dropped. A happy outcome from the government point of view. But other attempts at privatization by insiders have been more controversial. Some have been accused of cheating the state by placing too low a value on company assets and acquiring them at fire-sale prices. Ryszard Bugaj, an indignant Solidarity deputy, calls that "nothing less than the plundering of our national wealth." The counterargument heard in Warsaw is that, while some degree of corruption is probably unavoidable, any step toward privatization should be encouraged.

The catalogue of Polish problems goes on and on. But the hope persists that under new leadership the country can begin to move with clarity and purpose to emancipate itself, step by careful step, from a system of misrule that dates back to Stalin's time. Certain obstacles are already visible: obstruction by the *nomenklatura* and disruptive maneuvers by Polish party diehards who cannot be expected to go into oblivion without a struggle.

A more immediate danger confronts Solidarity and the millions of Poles who gave it their votes. Painful austerity measures can be expected to generate social unrest on a scale that would undermine Solidarity's chances of survival. Easing the pain of those unavoidable measures ought, I believe, to be a matter of high priority for the United States, its prosperous European allies, and Japan. The response till now of President Bush and other Western leaders varies from halfhearted to niggardly. The President has said that he hopes the Poles will get along without "an airlift of money." That seems a wholly inadequate reaction to the challenge that Poland represents today as it struggles with an external debt of $39 billion and a crippled economy.

It is undeniably and sadly true that Poland's Communist rulers squandered many of those borrowed billions in the 1970s and failed to rebuild the economy. But that truth should not be held against the new leadership in Warsaw, which came to office through the ballot box and is determined to break with the totalitarian past. If the West insists on a policy of cheese paring, it will forfeit a historic opportunity to help the Poles move toward independence, parliamentary democracy, and the rule of law, precisely the course that successive Washington administrations have been urging on them for many years. It is an opportunity that, once missed, may not soon return.

# 5

## *The Other Germany*

E AST GERMANY, or, formally, the German Democratic Republic, has never been a state like any other. From its birth in 1949, with the Soviet Union in the role of midwife, the GDR was a rump state cut off from the larger nation, with precious little democracy. The moment its formidable apparatus of coercion fell to pieces in October 1989, the GDR's separate existence came into question. Egon Krenz, the party chief and head of state for all of forty-six days, argued that "without the Communist Party there is no German Democratic Republic." The people, busy demonstrating for the freedom long denied them, were shedding no tears over the prospect that the party might disappear. They were out in the streets shouting "Resign" and "Germany, one fatherland."

On December 3, Krenz did resign, along with the party's entire Central Committee and the Politburo. The long-silent people of the GDR were carrying out their own October revolution with lighted candles in their hands. They marched for basic liberties with extraordinary self-discipline and good-humored determination not to quit until real change was assured. It was a form of citizen protest not seen in the GDR since the 1953 workers' uprising was put down by

Soviet tanks, the first nonviolent revolution in German history.

At least two turning points can be identified. The first occurred on March 19, 1989, when Hungary became the first East bloc state to sign the 1951 United Nations Convention Relating to the Status of Refugees and its 1967 protocol. That action was little noticed at the time. The convention's operative principle, which Hungary embraced, was that no refugees should be returned against their will to a country where their life or liberty would be threatened. The Hungarians had their own reason for signing the document. They were not about to return more than 10,000 ethnic Hungarians who had fled Romania's campaign of forced assimilation in 1988. But the principle, once accepted, applied equally to East Germans.

It took several months before word of Hungary's action reached many citizens of the GDR. In May, when Hungary dismantled its barbed wire barriers along the Austrian border, East Germans began arriving and formally requesting asylum. Their numbers grew, and on September 10 the Hungarian government announced that all East Germans were free to leave the country legally and resettle in West Germany. The GDR regime protested bitterly, but the Hungarians stood firm on the principle of *non-refoulement,* a French term taken from the text of the UN convention, meaning that no refugee should be forced to return under threat of persecution. Tens of thousands of East Germans took advantage of the opportunity to leave their country, most of them young workers and professionals the GDR could ill afford to lose. Krenz called the late summer exodus "a great loss of blood."

Thousands more crossed into Czechoslovakia and Poland, camping out in the West German embassy compounds while they waited for permission to emigrate westward. Day by day their numbers climbed. In early October bloody police violence broke out in Dresden when local residents tried to clamber aboard a train carrying the refugees across GDR territory to asylum in the Federal Republic. The police beat them off, and the entire country was now on edge.

In Leipzig, where the weekly Monday peace service at the Nikolai Church was expected to draw a large crowd of protesters on October 9, tensions ran high. Then came the second turning point (*wende* in German). Large numbers of police, soldiers, and secret service agents had been assembled in a show of force and, under orders from on high, issued live ammunition with orders to shoot if necessary. According to Markus Wolf, the GDR's retired spy chief, who later emerged as a reform advocate, "There was a written order from [Erich] Honecker for a Chinese solution. It could have been worse than Beijing."

As the critical moment approached, prominent Leipzig citizens and party officials met to discuss ways of preventing a deadly confrontation between the unarmed peace demonstrators and the formidable security forces. Meeting at the home of Kurt Masur, the internationally celebrated conductor of the Gewandhaus orchestra, they managed to head off a slaughter of the innocents. Krenz, then the Politburo member in charge of security, rushed to Leipzig and, by his own account, helped see to it "that these things were solved politically" rather than by force. When tens of thousands of demonstrators took to the streets that evening, the police did not intervene.

It had been a close call, closer than most people knew. Christof Hein, an East German novelist and playwright, talked with young members of the security force shaken by the experience of being ordered to shoot their countrymen. "They were pale and agitated as they spoke," Hein recorded in his crisis diary.[1] " 'We're just regular draftees,' they said.

1. The *New York Times Magazine* published excerpts from Hein's crisis diary on December 17, 1989.

'We had our orders.' They sense the contempt of the populace and feel that they themselves are victims. Even these
young soldiers have been violated." Hein added, "We have
been living in a country we are just now getting to know."

There was no resisting the revolutionary tide, which soon
undermined the existing Stalinist order, established under
Walter Ulbricht's regime and ruled since 1971 by Erich Honecker, who was ousted by the Politburo on October 18 in
favor of his "crown prince," Egon Krenz. A hard-fisted Honecker disciple, Krenz made himself instantly visible, plead-
ing for public acceptance as a reformer in factory meetings
and street crowds. "The situation in the GDR is loaded with
tension and highly contradictory," he said. "There is a mood
of awakening that has never been known until now."

Addressing a large, less than friendly crowd outside the
headquarters of the Socialist Unity (Communist) Party, Krenz
offered his vision of the future. "We want a socialism," he
said, "that is economically effective, politically democratic,
morally clean and, most of all, has its face turned to the
people." In short, a socialism that had never existed in the
Soviet bloc. The people were not persuaded.

Concession followed concession. Krenz legalized the freedom of travel to the West. He ordered holes punched through
the Berlin Wall, which suddenly became an ugly irrelevancy.
East Germans by the tens of thousands poured into West
Berlin through the new openings for a glimpse and taste of
its long-forbidden attractions. Although each day some 2,000
to 3,000 stayed on in the West, the majority returned to their
homes and jobs in the East.

Under Krenz's brief leadership, the Communist Central
Committee promptly drew up a reform program that promised, among other things, "free, democratic and secret elections." They are expected to be held in May 1990. The document included pledges by the party to guarantee freedom
of assembly and to bring the dreaded state security appa-

ratus, which Krenz so recently headed, under control of the Volkskammer, the GDR's pathetic imitation of an elected parliament. The language of official discourse also changed. Krenz avoided repeating Honecker's boastful claim that the GDR, in contrast to the Federal Republic, had become "a society in which the exploitation of man by man has been abolished." There would be no more talk of an East German utopia behind the wall.

Krenz blamed the old leadership under Honecker for allowing problems to pile up unsolved while millions of what he called "honest Communists" could do no more than drop an occasional hint that something was amiss. Krenz understood the need of the hour. To survive in a revolutionary period he would have to live down his thuggish reputation. That ruled out any show of concern or gratitude toward Honecker, his seventy-seven-year-old mentor. Like the coachman in the Russian tale who threw his passengers to the wolves, one by one, to save himself, Krenz decimated the party's senior ranks. Some were allowed to resign under pressure. Others were expelled from the party. A handful, including Honecker, also were placed under house arrest.

The purge failed, however, to establish public confidence in the party or its new leader. Between September and the end of 1989, the Socialist Unity Party lost more than a half million members. The sudden disintegration of Communist authority was not easily explained. Too much could be made of the GDR's proximity to the West and the seductive television shots from the far side of the wall portraying life in a freer and far richer Federal Republic. That was hardly a novel experience for most East Germans. For many years they had spent their evenings in front of their TV sets, most of them tuned to West German channels. There were other influences at work for which the Federal Republic was in no sense responsible.

Among the most important of these was the Soviet Union's

welcoming attitude toward reform and its obvious willingness to see the old dogmatists toppled. Mikhail Gorbachev
was not a favorite of the East German party elite. But rank-
and-file citizens of the GDR spoke of him as "Gorby," a term
of affection as well as respect. Not a single East German I
met inside or outside the official circle seemed to feel that
way about Honecker. Gorbachev lifted their hopes and expectations for eventual change.

The Protestant churches in the GDR played an indispensable role by offering shelter, a degree of protection, and
moral support to home-grown dissident groups, much as
the Catholic Church had done in Poland during Solidarity's
darkest days. The Federation of Evangelical Churches even
helped the dissidents collect and expose evidence of vote
fraud by the Communists in recent local elections. In one
East Berlin district, church-based poll watchers interviewed
voters and counted five times the 1,600 negative ballots recorded in the official tally. The federation dared to demand
a government investigation of its fraud charges, not an
everyday occurrence in the GDR. Bishop Gottfried Fork acknowledged that some of the dissident groups "oppose the
government in a non-Christian way," but the church, he
added, had a duty to protect the oppressed. It was no acci-
dent that the Gethsemane and Zion churches in East Berlin,
like the Thomas and Nikolai churches in Leipzig, became
rallying points for the democratic opposition.

The people, moreover, were not as gullible as the party
chiefs imagined. Honecker and others in the leadership never
tired of assuring them that all was well in "the first peasants'
and workers' state on German soil." If the system fell short of
perfection, they said, that would be taken care of in good time
under the party's wise leadership. But the people, well aware
of the system's shortcomings, saw the clear contradiction between the official lies and the gritty Orwellian reality of their

condition. "The ordinary human being became a tiny cog degraded to an object of the . . . political system," according to Professor Michael Schumann of the Law Academy in East Berlin, addressing a party congress after both Honecker and Krenz had fallen from power.

The most powerful force for change may well have been the mass exodus of East Germans in the late summer and early autumn of 1989, helped immeasurably by the Hungarian government's decision to open its border for emigrants to the West. The exodus demonstrated that intelligent, resourceful people could take their lives into their own hands, outflanking the wall and making nonsense of their repressive government's design to run the country as if it were a prison. That message was not lost on their fellow East Germans.

In the first flush of victory, unification with West Germany began to look like a natural outcome of the revolution in the East. The cry of many, though not all, the demonstrators was one nation, one state, no borders, and as soon as possible. But toward the end of 1989, second thoughts were being expressed in both Germanys. Richard von Weizsacker, president of the Federal Republic, cautioned in his first interview with East German television that "what belongs together will grow together, but it must grow together — there should be no effort to push it."

The West German chancellor, Helmut Kohl, who had been one of those pushing for early confederation, backed off to appease his worried European neighbors, the United States, and the Soviet Union. The common thread linking their expressions of concern was that hasty steps toward all-German unity would upset the stability of Europe. "The goal of our policy," Kohl said, "never has been and never will be to establish an over-powerful Germany in the middle of Europe, as many in the Council of Europe, in London, Rome,

and Paris fear — just look at the newspapers." He added,
however, that eventual unification "remains our political
goal."

East Germany's new prime minister, Hans Modrow, proposed a web of treaties to develop cooperation between the
two Germanies, with the GDR remaining intact as a separate
and sovereign state. Gregor Gysi, the new head of the crumbling Communist Party, was sufficiently concerned about the
rising demands for unity to appeal to the United States for
help. "I feel that Germans in this century have lost the right
to create the risk of instability and war," Gysi said in an interview with Craig Whitney of the *New York Times.* "If the
continued independence of the German Democratic Republic is in the interests of stability in Europe," he added,
"then you [Americans] should think about whether you want
to leave help for the GDR up to a single neighbor country,
and thereby create dependency, or whether it wouldn't be
better to share the responsibility, to prevent the emergence
of Greater Germany."

Mikhail Gorbachev, who talked on the telephone with Gysi
soon after the forty-one-year-old lawyer took office in East
Berlin, told him that the Soviet Union would reject any attempt to infringe on East German sovereignty. Gorbachev
is reported to have said that "on the stability of the German
Democratic Republic depends, in no small degree, the stability of the European continent."

Although the Soviet leader has openly encouraged the recent political changes in Eastern Europe, the GDR presents
a far more knotty strategic problem for the Kremlin. Some
380,000 Red Army troops are stationed on East German
territory, confronting NATO's front-line forces in West
Germany. A substantial thinning of the forces on both sides,
the goal to which Gorbachev and President Bush recommit-
ted themselves at the Malta summit conference, could be the
first step toward untying that knot. But long-term stability

in the heart of Europe also will require a final peace treaty confirming Germany's present borders on the East. A rush toward unification, driven by resurgent nationalism, could lead to demands for the recovery of western Poland, the Sudeten region of Czechoslovakia, and other territories taken from Hitler's Germany at the end of World War II. Unification of the Germanys, in short, is a far more complicated proposition than simply erasing the line that separates two states.

The two German states that emerged from the ruins of Hitler's Third Reich in 1949 are in every respect unequal. The Federal Republic in Bonn has more than three times the population of East Germany and more than twice the land area. It is also far richer and more self-confident, a major economic power by any standard, and a pillar of the North Atlantic alliance. East Germany, the western anchor of the Soviet empire and the Warsaw Pact, lags far behind in most respects. It is poorer, grayer, and cuts a less conspicuous figure on the world stage. Honecker in recent years was reduced to pressing the claim that his rump state was more authentically *German* than the Federal Republic.

Honecker's appeal to German nationalism took the form of an exercise in historical revisionism. A team of historians at the Academy of Sciences was put to work reassessing three indisputably large figures in all-German history: Martin Luther, Frederick the Great, and Otto von Bismarck. They decided that all three had not been reactionary figures, after all, but revolutionaries in their fashion. Bismarck was reclaimed for the state of workers and peasants in a best-selling biography, *Bismarck: Archetypical Prussian and Founder of the Reich.* The author, a long-time Communist historian named Ernst Engelberg, said he had written the book to counter what he called the "disgraceful anti-Prussianism" that prevailed in West Germany following the Nazi defeat in World War II. Kaiser Frederick II of Prussia in historic bronze was restored to his pedestal, facing east on Unter den Linden, after languishing for decades in a Potsdam warehouse. He, too, was the subject of an admiring biography, by Professor Ingrid Mittenzwei, which earned Honecker's praise. As for Luther, who had been glorified by the Nazis as an uncompromising German nationalist, the Marxist historians discovered that in the context of the sixteenth century he was actually a precursor of revolution.

I asked one of the academicians, Professor Conrad Grau, to explain these startling revisions. "Since the end of the 1960s," he replied, "we have learned that it is simply impossible for us to escape German history. All those kings and nobles, even the Third Reich, are part of the history we share with the Federal Republic. We have simply learned to accept the legacy of our common history, the negative along with the positive." It was perfectly natural, he said, for a Marxist like himself to place a high value on revolutionary activity and, looked at from that perspective, even Bismarck qualified, although his had been a revolution imposed from the top. "We don't glorify Bismarck," Grau said. "He will never be a hero to us. But we draw a more realistic picture today of the man in his time. It should be remembered that he said we must have a revolution in Germany. He also said that we Germans must come to terms with Russia."

In rehabilitating Frederick II, Professor Grau acknowledged, the historians had to overcome a powerful modern prejudice. They remembered that in the Hitler years Frederick had been held up as a model for all good Nazis and that his "daily sayings" were broadcast throughout the country on the orders of Paul Joseph Goebbels, Hitler's propaganda minister. "At first our Marxist historians took the wrong position," he said. "They reacted to the symbol, not the man. Today we see Frederick's genius as well as his limitations."

The case for Martin Luther turned out to be more complicated. His break with the Church of Rome and his espousal of German nationalism, of course, had caught the public imagination. In political matters, however, Luther was a conservative, and the early Lutheran churches were subject to the power of local princes, hardly a sterling recommendation for contemporary Marxist historians. They felt more comfortable with Thomas Munzer, a Luther contemporary who preached the radical doctrine that God had willed the overthrow of the existing order. The Peasants' War, an uprising of peasants and workmen that broke out in 1524, found Luther and Munzer on opposite sides. While Luther condemned the revolt, Munzer became its leader in Thuringia and paid with his head when the uprising was suppressed. As both a peasant leader and a theologian who had attempted to set up a communal theocracy, in the town of Muhlhausen, Munzer seemed a more appropriate hero for East German Marxists. But Luther was too large a figure to pass over. So in 1983, as the five hundredth anniversary of his birth approached and with an international commemoration planned, the historians decided to credit him with having helped to instigate what they called the "early bourgeois revolution." It required far less ingenuity for the revisionists to re-evaluate Munzer as a leader of the "far left wing" of the same "early bourgeois revolution" when his five hundredth anniversary was observed in 1989.

In a narrow geographical sense, the East German state is entitled to claim its improbable revolutionary heroes. Both Frederick the Great and Bismarck were quintessential Prussians, and Prussia represents a considerable swath of the GDR's territory. Luther, moreover, was born in Eisleben, Saxony, and it was at Muhlhausen that Munzer was beheaded for his part in the Peasants' War. Both towns lie within the boundaries of the GDR. Munzer apart, however, the others can scarcely be regarded as ideological allies of the men who ruled East Germany until recently. For Honecker and his Politburo colleagues, the appeal of such as Luther, Bismarck, and Frederick the Great rested on their symbolic importance for all Germans, West and East. Honecker's historical takeover bid may seem bizarre, but its clear purpose was to advance the GDR's claim to international respect and recognition as an authentic German state.

That respect increased in recent years, owing in large part to the GDR's economic performance rather than to the ingenuity of its historians. So long as its western borders were blocked by the wall, East Germany was not widely regarded as a normal state. But there could be no dispute over the proposition that GDR citizens worked harder and more skillfully than any of their eastern neighbors, including the Soviet Union. The outer edges of Berlin, Leipzig, and other metropolitan areas were marked by row on row of tall new apartment buildings. These were more modern and better designed, though less spacious on the interior, than the pompous Soviet-style blocks dating from the 1950s and 1960s along what used to be called Stalinallee in Berlin. According to government estimates, fully half the population of seventeen million was rehoused by 1990, a considerable achievement, although it took forty years. But a great many GDR citizens still have to make do with dilapidated prewar housing. Within one mile of the swarming Alexanderplatz in the center of East Berlin, street after street of ancient apartment houses still bear the marks of war. They look as if they have not been painted or plastered in fifty years.

The countryside between Rostock on the Baltic coast and Berlin looks moderately prosperous: tidy village streets, many of them cobblestoned, an impressive number of new brick-over-cinder-block farmhouses with tiny Trabant automobiles out front and towering television antennas on the roofs, all pointed westward. It seemed apparent, as we were told in the summer of 1988, that most farmers were no longer fighting the collectives. Not everyone was doing equally well, in spite of the regime's claim to egalitarianism. When I was at lunch in a Rostock restaurant with a West German friend, our waitress responded with an extraordinary show of gratitude to a tip of 2 marks, $1.15 at the official rate of exchange. The meal had been a disappointment, but her broad smile made up for that. *"Jetzt kommt Freude auf,"* she said, a turn of phrase unfamiliar to me; roughly translated, it means "Now for the moment of joy." One had to conclude that tips seldom came her way.

On closer examination, we discovered large disparities between occupations. Baltic fishermen, for example, earned 2200 marks a month, twice the average wage of 1100 marks ($628 at the official unrealistic exchange rate). A factory director's wage was four times that of an average worker, but an old age pensioner had to get by on 350 marks a month, roughly $200. Rents, bread, and trolley car rides were ridiculously cheap, but household appliances seemed exorbitant when measured against monthly incomes. A miniature refrigerator, perhaps one fourth the size of a standard American model, cost almost $900, and the price of a small washing machine was more than $1000.

In addition to high prices for most durable goods and clothing, East Germans had to put up with long delays before getting their hands on products they could afford. "It's not the lack of money that bothers me," said a forty-year-old professional. "My wife and I have put aside money for a new car, but thirteen years have passed and we are still waiting." More commonly, couples waited four months for a color television set. Some GDR citizens, comparing their situation with those of other Soviet bloc countries, took pride in what had been achieved under the existing system. Others, probably a larger number, argued that it made little sense to compare the GDR with less developed countries to the east. They preferred to look westward, where fellow Germans operating in a free society had greatly surpassed the GDR's standard of living. Hard numbers were difficult to come by, but no one I talked with denied that West German television had a larger, more enthusiastic audience than the domestic network. Millions of East Germans spent their days working in the East and their evenings living vicariously in the West, thanks to television. Measured against the prosperity they saw reflected on the tube, their own situation looked rather sad, and they knew it. Yet the leadership under Honecker discounted the need for change. Its attitude toward Mikhail Gorbachev's reforms in the Soviet Union was ambiguous at best.

"Ours is a cautious reaction," said one official who cautiously asked to remain anonymous. "We don't question Gorbachev's international initiatives. We welcomed, for example, the removal of intermediate range missiles on both sides. But with regard to our own domestic policies, we have reservations. Most of the changes Gorbachev is introducing in the USSR we, in fact, carried out ten years earlier. Of course, we can't afford complacency; we are too close to the West to be complacent. But we don't need institutional reforms on the Soviet pattern. What we must do is extend and deepen the social and political changes we carried out earlier."

A more colloquial expression of this enduring skepticism toward Soviet *perestroika* was put in the form of a question by Kurt Hager, an elderly member of the East German Politburo: "If your neighbor put up new wallpaper in his home would you feel obliged to put up new wallpaper in your own?"

The wide, and constantly widening, disparity between consumer prices and production costs started more than thirty years ago, when the leadership under Walter Ulbricht decided to freeze prices of meat, butter, sausage, milk, bread, and other basic foodstuffs as well as apartment rents, heating, electricity, and transport services. A trolley ride, for example, cost 20 pfennigs, or the equivalent of a dime, in 1988, as it did in 1958. Economists estimated, however, that the cost to the state of providing that service was five to ten times the passenger's fare. As costs rose over the years, the state kept prices more or less level through a system of subsidies. As a result, according to a government publication, the state in 1985 paid out an additional 78 marks for every purchase of food worth 100 marks.

Professor Walter Becker at the Hochschule fuer Oekonomie in Berlin confirmed that the rents East Germans paid were purely symbolic, making no provision for obsolescence, repairs, and maintenance. The rent for his own large apartment was 110 marks, or some $60 a month. Dr. Becker noted that although the Soviet Union and Poland had raised many consumer prices to adjust for cost increases, nothing of the sort was being done by the GDR. It was an article of faith on the part of the GDR's early leadership, he said, to keep prices of basic foods and rents absolutely stable. That kind of rigidity was no longer admired by economists and planners in the Soviet sphere.

The GDR, while retaining the most rigid of central planning systems, somehow managed to avoid the worst blunders of other East bloc countries. It is a country poor in resources — no hard coal, no sheet steel of the kind that is used to build automobiles, and its historic source of industrial equipment has been the Ruhr in West Germany. The main advantage it possesses is human, a skilled and disciplined work force. Germanic thoroughness, job training, and effective exhortation made the difference. Western diplomats who have studied the numbers tend to agree that the population of East Germany lives better today than at any time in the past fifty years, far better than citizens of other Communist-ruled countries. The consumer subsidies certainly helped, though at a stiff price. Subsidies took a huge slice of the national budget, roughly one fifth of the 260

billion mark total. Dr. Becker put his finger on another unsolved problem. "With us," he said, "energy and steel are
always in short supply. We've had to try to use them more
sparingly and we still have some distance to go compared
with the West." He pointed out that, for lack of sheet steel,
Trabant automobile bodies were being made of plastic materials. The Trabant is a remarkably ugly little car, under-
powered and a heavy polluter of the air. Its two-stroke engine burns a mixture of oil and gasoline.

After 1971, when the East Germans started to modify the
old Stalinist model of economic planning, they experi-
mented with vertical and horizontal systems in search of
increased flexibility and less delay in applying new technologies. They tried to make some companies less dependent
on government ministries, and found, according to Dr.
Becker, that "when you leave them alone they behave like
monopolists." The trouble with too much centralization, on
the other hand, was that it tended to inhibit innovation. They
settled on a system of industrial combines (*kombinate* in German), 129 of them, and each supposedly directed by a super-
manager. Each *kombinat,* in effect, was granted monopolistic
powers over a whole industry. Some were small, employing
no more than ten thousand workers. One had eighty thousand employees. The idea was that the managers would take
responsibility for the whole production process, including
research and development as well as foreign trade. They
also had more flexibility in allocating funds than the earlier
system allowed. Dr. Becker made no extravagant claims for
the *kombinat* system, but over the past five years, he said,
there had been an encouraging increase in the application
of new technology. Skeptics argued that the system still
amounted to centralized planning — with one layer of bureaucracy removed. The results were far from spectacular.

I found it revealing that not one of the East German officials, economists, or journalists I met mentioned the gener-

ous assistance their country has received from West Germany since 1971. It has taken several forms: payments amounting to more than $2 billion a year, never reported in the GDR media, for upkeep of the autobahns between West Germany and Berlin that run through East German territory, and fees paid for transit rights; the use of subway tunnels; waste disposal; ransom payments for East Germans who wanted to go west; and the border-crossing fees West Germans had to pay to visit the GDR. A second substantial category of assistance took the form of credits from commercial banks in the West that were guaranteed by Bonn. This assured year-by-year flow of billions of deutschemarks has been a source of considerable envy in other Communist-ruled countries, like Poland and Hungary, with their heavy burden of external debts and scarce hard-currency reserves. Another significant advantage not shared by other bloc countries was the GDR's access to the vast European Common Market for its export products, an unintended privilege it owed to the late Chancellor Adenauer. It was Adenauer who, at the time the Treaty of Rome was being negotiated, stipulated that there was only one legitimate German state. The consequence was that GDR products entered the Common Market freely as products of a hypothetical undivided Germany.

In short, the two Germanys had come a long way toward the goal set by Chancellor Willy Brandt in 1969 of "two states in one Germany." Brandt's design for a new *Ostpolitik* (Eastern policy) made possible the limited cooperation between Bonn and East Berlin, although talk of eventual unification was discouraged in the GDR. Not until Walter Ulbricht was replaced by Honecker in 1971 did East Germany show interest in East-West détente. At the end of the following year, the two Germanys signed their *Grundvertrag* (basic agreement), in which Bonn recognized the GDR's separate existence as a legitimate state. Before long a number of Western governments, including the United States and Canada, established diplomatic relations with East Germany.

That agreement produced the first tentative signs that on matters of foreign policy, German-German policies above all, Honecker had his own ideas. He was prepared to strengthen and defend his ties with the Federal Republic even when the Soviet Union objected. Open differences between East Berlin and Moscow became apparent in the early 1980s, when the Soviet Union, having failed to block the stationing of Pershing II intermediate range missiles in West Germany, signaled a policy turn toward "socialist self-sufficiency." The obvious intent was to rally the countries under its imperial domination against the United States and West Germany. The GDR, Hungary, and Romania refused. Honecker, determined to protect his improving relations with West Germany and the flow of economic assistance from Bonn, stressed the need to "limit the damage." Far from cutting ties with the West, he eased the procedures for emigration to the Federal Republic and soon received a large additional loan. The Kremlin reacted with a warning through *Pravda* that behind the show of West German generosity lurked a design to subvert the "socialist order." In September 1984, Honecker postponed his long-planned trip to the Federal Republic, obviously at Moscow's insistence.

Compared with its East bloc neighbors, Honecker's GDR was doing rather well. But for most East Germans that cramped perspective had become irrelevant in the late 1970s and early 1980s. Denied the freedom to travel as they wished, they were seeing the world vicariously, thanks to West German television, and making comparisons, mostly unfavorable, with conditions at home. East Germany's first stab at economic reforms had been timid, and change came slowly. The leadership, stodgy and self-satisfied, would not be rushed.

The Politburo, substantially unchanged since the Brezhnev era, remained a gerontocracy that was plainly antagonistic to the reform ideas initiated by Mikhail Gorbachev. Several of its members had their first taste of power in the Stalin era. All spent the greater part of their lives in the service of the Communist Party. Stephan Hermlin, a prominent East German writer, remarked, "We are ruled by a pope and a college of cardinals. This party of ours is generally unwilling to listen to the people." He traced this leadership attitude back to 1945, when Berlin was in ruins and the Communists were a tiny minority even in what was then the Soviet sector. Once in power, however, they came to think of themselves as members of an elite. "They say, 'We are the enlightened ones,' " he continued, "and their discussions are limited to the elect."

The reformist urge ran strongest among East German writers, and there is evidence that it started long before the Gorbachev era. One piece of evidence that recently came to light was an essay written in the 1950s (but not published until long after his death) by Johannes Becher, once the GDR's minister of culture and among its most honored citizens. Becher minced no words, describing Stalinism as "the tragedy of the century." He castigated himself for his silence in the 1930s and 1940s, when Stalin and his henchmen were murdering old Communists and intellectuals. Becher could not excuse his own silence, he wrote, by accepting the party's justification that the brutal policies of the period were necessary because "socialism came to power in a backward country."

A second recent article wakened ominous echoes that rang even louder. It was written by Nadja Stulz-Herrnstadt, daughter of a candidate member of the East German Politburo who was expelled from the party for protesting the brutal suppression of the 1953 workers' uprising in the GDR. Rudolf Herrnstadt had appealed in vain for the leadership to follow a more humane policy. His daughter called for the posthumous rehabilitation of her father, who fell victim to a party purge directed by Honecker after Soviet tanks had crushed the uprising. Both Becher and Herrnstadt were regarded as German patriots of the left who fought Hitlerism at the risk of their lives. Publication of these articles in the intellectual periodicals *Horizont* and *Sinn und Form* could not have endeared their editors to the leadership, least of all to Honecker, although no action is known to have been taken against them.

Other voices were raised from time to time, demanding an end to literary censorship and protesting the expulsion of important authors and poets from the Writers' Union. At a conference of the union in 1987 Christa Wolf, one of East Germany's most admired writers, pressed her colleagues to "rethink old positions" and to analyze the consequences of what she said was the unwarranted expulsion of several writers who had protested the deportation of Wolf Biermann, a popular and gifted lyricist-troubadour, in 1976. Since then, she said, a number of important East German writers had left the country "because they found that [in the union] there was no chance to discuss their problems openly." Christa Wolf's international reputation won her a degree of immunity from the crude pressures less renowned writers had to face in dealing with the copyright office, which decided what could and could not be published in the GDR.

Guenter de Bruyn, another prominent writer who spoke at the 1987 conference, denounced the continued literary censorship, what he called the mandatory "authorization to print." The system in place, he said, damaged the self-confidence of writers, especially younger writers, and caused some of them to leave the country so that they could write and publish freely. De Bruyn taxed the regime with an irrational fear of the printed word, pointing out that electronic media transcend national boundaries every day. He added that enforced silence about environmental issues, a topic that several East German writers nevertheless did tackle, served no rational purpose but did get in the way of correcting old mistakes. *Neues Deutschland,* the party newspaper, reported only that de Bruyn had "pleaded for change in the current practice in publishing books." Stephan Hermlin, who, like Christa Wolf and Stefan Heym, had signed the petition protesting Wolf Biermann's expulsion from the GDR, said it was plain silly for the government to ban Friedrich Nietzsche's nineteenth-century writings. He also called for more civil treatment of East German writers who had emigrated to the West.

I visited Hermlin at his home and met his Russian wife, the most enthusiastic cheerleader for *glasnost* and *perestroika* I encountered in the GDR. Hermlin did not lag far behind. "This is the second time in history," he said with great animation, "that the USSR has been in the vanguard of socialism. The first time was from 1917 to 1932." That left a gap of more than fifty years between Stalin and Gorbachev, including the period of the Moscow trials, World War II, and its aftermath, when Stalin carved out his empire in Central and Eastern Europe. Hermlin conceded that, like millions of Communists around the world, he had been a true believer throughout Stalin's most murderous years. "I know it's hard to understand how powerful was the impact of the USSR, even in the Stalin years. I admit that I was very enthusiastic about Stalin in my youth. I joined the party at sixteen and went to Spain in the civil war at twenty-three. I remember all the great writers who expressed solidarity with Stalin's judges, not with their murdered victims. We all knew, of course, that in any revolution innocent people would be killed. Such was life. So we said yes to the Moscow trials."

Hermlin, the son of a German father and an English mother, spent the war years in France and Britain, then moved to Frankfurt in the American zone, where he worked with the Hessische Rundfunk. A Soviet official sought him out there and persuaded him to come to East Berlin, promising that the city would be rebuilt as a major cultural center.

"I was extremely eager to be part of this rebuilding," Hermlin recalled. He did not dwell on the difficult moments he must have gone through over the years but sounded firmly convinced that real change was inevitable. "It's exciting to see what is happening in the Soviet Union after so many years of oppression," he said. "I'm certain we in the GDR will do the same. After all, we are only at the beginning of socialism in this country. It took bourgeois society five hundred years to reach the present level of freedom and productivity. I'm confident we will get there, too."

Hermlin, a founder of the Writers' Union (he holds membership card number two), used a personal gauge to measure the degree of change that had occurred. Recalling the protest against Biermann's expulsion, Hermlin said, "We were treated as outcasts in the Writers' Union. I estimate that 90 percent of our colleagues were against us. If a similar thing were to happen today, I'm confident that we would have the support of more than 50 percent of the writers." He attributed the gradual change in attitude to several elements, including "more profound study of Marx's and Lenin's writings" and, of course, developments inside the Soviet Union since Gorbachev came to power. Hermlin insisted, however, that pressures for greater openness had been under way in East Germany for a considerable time before Gorbachev. "Writers were struggling against censorship in the Soviet Union, also in the GDR," he said. In one respect, he added, the GDR was ahead of the Soviet Union and other countries of the East bloc. Only in East Germany, he said proudly, had six volumes of Sigmund Freud's psychoanalytic writings been published.

The political leadership, however, did not share the intellectuals' excitement over the "new thinking" in Moscow. It was therefore with astonishment that readers of *Neues Deutschland* on July 1, 1988, found two whole pages devoted to the Soviet party conference then in progress, and to the particular session in which an unknown delegate named Melnikov, prompted by Gorbachev himself, demanded the ouster of such party worthies as President Andrei Gromyko and the editor in chief of *Pravda*. This was strong meat for East Germans, and, doubtless under party instructions, *Neues Deutschland* treated the story at arm's length. It was placed on pages 11 and 12, not on the front page; the summary of the Moscow meeting had been supplied by Tass, the Soviet news agency, not by the paper's own Moscow correspondent or the East German news agency; and the front of the paper, six pages' worth, was monopolized by a tedious budget discussion in the Volkskammer, the GDR's legislature.

The winds of change blowing from the East forced the leadership to tread a narrow line in these delicate matters. On one hand, loyalty to the Soviet Union demanded that they not wholly ignore what was happening in Moscow; on the other, they were reluctant to risk infecting the citizenry with ideas about democratization, Gorbachev style. But thanks to the reach of West German television, the public was relatively well informed about matters the GDR did not allow to be disseminated.

Until recently, dissidents who were prepared to openly demonstrate their disaffection faced the hard choice between arrest and exile. Thirty were arrested, and more than a hundred others later taken from their homes, for participation in a January 1988 demonstration for human rights. In fact, it was a counterdemonstration that threatened to disrupt an official commemoration of Karl Liebknecht and Rosa Luxemburg, leaders of the German revolutionary left who were killed in 1919. The human rights activists apparently did nothing more than unfold a large banner on which they had inscribed the famous words of Rosa Luxemburg: "Freedom can only be real if it is freedom for those who think differently." Most of the demonstrators caught up in the police sweep were released, but for Stephan Krawczyk, a popular folk singer, and his wife, Freya Klier, a stage director, the consequences were more serious. Charged with treasonable activities, and faced with jail sentences of two to twelve years or immediate emigration, they left for the Federal Republic.

Dissenting groups in East Germany tended to cluster around a handful of causes. Some focused on environmental issues, some on civil liberties, and others on so-called peace issues. Their survival and their ability to function owed a great deal to the support and protection they had been receiving over the past decade from the churches.

The East German Protestant Church, separated from its counterpart in the Federal Republic since 1969, is the only major institution that since 1978 has enjoyed officially sanctioned autonomy. It brings together Lutheran and Calvinist churches under the Federation of Evangelical Churches, in a wary and tense relationship with the state and party. I visited its headquarters in a run-down building on a shabby street that had so far failed to qualify for restoration. My host, Herr Gunther, a lay spokesman for the evangelical group, filled me in on its development. "We said from the beginning that the state may choose atheism, but it won't get rid of God in this country, and that it is possible to have the church in socialism. Some of the politicians may have believed that they could put us in a ghetto. There was the symbolic fact that no new churches were to be built. But the position of the church remains that we are neither against nor in favor of socialism. We want to be free to *do* as well as to preach."

What this meant, he said, was that the church considered the issues of ecology, peace, human rights, and the administration of justice to be legitimate concerns of the people. And, as one of the only open institutions allowed to operate in the GDR, the church could legitimately allow activities of this kind to be pursued under its roof. "We will have reached the limit only when people in the church want to reject socialism," he said. "We have no quarrel with the state over the issue of peace. There are differences, however, over human rights, freedom of information, and the right to travel. We have said to the state that people should be freer to travel outside the country. Fear not, we said; they will return. But we also have taken the position that pastors of the church must not leave."

Gunther's comments fit with a statement by Manfred Stolpe, deputy chairman of the Federation of Evangelical Churches, that the church should be "neither the Trojan Horse of counterrevolution" nor a "transmission belt of the Socialist Unity Party." In other words, according to Stolpe, the church was not and should not become a social movement but must go on providing succor for those who sought its help.

The church's understanding of its live-and-let-live accord with the state was not invariably shared by the other side. In March 1988, the state started censoring church newspapers. "By law, no censorship exists," Herr Gunther said. "We have five church papers, sold only by subscription, with a total circulation of under 200,000. Their main concern is to have open discussion of church matters, including information about synods that take up human rights issues. But we have been forced to reprint sections of these papers when the censor objected. Now we are told that certain topics are forbidden. An Easter issue of one paper appeared with white spaces where the censor had deleted statements by a bishop. We need to persuade the Communists to acknowledge our difficulties, not alone our successes. We shall need more courage."

More recently, the authorities prohibited publication of a passage from a prayer that was to be read during an ecumenical congress in the city of Magdeburg. The censored passage called for "a process of change and renewal in our society." Concerned over the deterioration of church-state relations, Manfred Stolpe said the situation had become "absolutely intolerable." This turn of events was marked by the detention of eighty people who were among some two hundred activists attempting to hold a silent march in protest against the censoring of church publications.

Demands for the right to emigrate sharpened the church-state disagreements. In 1984 the GDR allowed some 25,000 to emigrate, to that time the peak figure. After 1984, the numbers declined, and in 1987 only 11,500 emigration visas were issued. Many would-be emigrants spent years waiting for an answer from the authorities. When an application was rejected, the reason was seldom given. Those who applied frequently lost their jobs and lived in isolation while they waited. The trickle of emigrants turned into a flood in the summer and autumn of 1989.

The Honecker government was not alone in seeking to block or discourage emigration. Long before the exodus through Hungary, the emigration issue had divided the peace and human rights movements in East Germany. There were endless discussions and debates between those who were determined to leave as soon as possible and others who argued that the right thing for any dissident was to stay and keep pressing for change from within. There was division also within the church. When the general superintendent of the Protestant church in East Berlin announced the setting up of a spiritual advisory center for would-be emigrants, his office was soon crowded by hundreds of people. This prompted another church official to complain bitterly. The church, he argued, was not a travel agency, and its business was to provide spiritual comfort, not practical assistance.

Another point of church-state friction dated from the introduction of compulsory military training in the schools for all ninth- and tenth-grade pupils. The church sharply criticized this step and then became a rallying point for conscientious objectors in advocating nonmilitary forms of national service. The response of state officials was to urge that the church stick to its spiritual business and restrict membership to genuine believers. "It's wrong for people to use the church for political purposes," one party member told me. "These developments may go beyond the limits agreed to between the church and the state." His plain implication was that the business of churches was to worship God and stay out of politics. But the Protestant churches appeared driven to stand up to the Communist regime, in part, as some Berliners suggested to me, to regain the respect they forfeited in the 1930s and 1940s when they failed to oppose the deformations of German society wrought by the Nazis.

Walking one afternoon in the Marx-Engels Forum, a vast grassy space in the center of East Berlin — dominated by a statue of Karl Marx, seated with his hands on his knees, and Friedrich Engels standing beside him — I wandered over to the Marienkirche, where a poster caught my eye. It read DER GELBE STERN (The Yellow Star), the badge of shame that Jews were forced to wear during the Nazi era. Inside, in a low-ceilinged room, I half stumbled into an exhibit of photographs documenting the life of Berlin's vanished Jewish community. It was the first indication I had seen that anyone remembered the Jews of Berlin. Here they were, captured on film as they had lived in this city, not as they died in the gas chambers: the bearded elders, the mature businessmen and professionals, the children at school and in summer camps. Every once in a while a recognizable face appeared and under it the grim notation: "Murdered in Auschwitz" — or another death camp.

Here were the Jews of Berlin, smiling, gossiping, playing volleyball, or reading like perfectly normal people, except, of course, that the state was about to order their extermination. Three or four Germans stumbled in off the street, as I had, and wiped their eyes in leaving. The exhibit, clearly, was not a raging success. Yet it had been mounted with care, conceivably with love, by East German Christians associated with the antiwar movement of the Federation of Evangelical Churches. I picked up the *Berliner Zeitung* the following day and read on page 2 an account of how five young thugs, described in the German text as "rowdies," were going to be tried for defacing and toppling gravestones in a Jewish cemetery. On page 3, as if there were no connection with the story on the facing page, was the surprising headline JEW-ISH CULTURE IS PART OF OUR ROOTS. The topic once again was a Jewish cemetery, this one in the Schoenhauser Allee, and the second story was upbeat. The paper reported that because there were so few Jews left alive in East Berlin, a group of volunteers had spent their free time in the cemetery, cutting back fifty years of overgrowth, carting away the trash, and replacing toppled headstones. It was a job that members of East Berlin's Jewish community, mostly old and feeble, and numbering fewer than two hundred, could not do for themselves. The first grave at the Schoenhauser Allee was dug in 1827, and by 1942 there were twenty-four thousand of them. Among the contributors to German culture buried there, according to the newspaper, were the painter Max Lieberman, the composer Giacomo Meyerbeer, and the museum director James Simon.

I mentioned the newspaper accounts to my historian friend at the Academy of Sciences, Professor Grau. "It is a fact," he replied, "that German history without Jews is not comprehensible. Their role in German life through the centuries was major and significant. It is regrettably true that we still have a small number of anti-Semites in this country, and we prosecute them when they commit criminal acts. But forty years have not been long enough to get rid of all vestiges of the past." Grau acknowledged that certain age-old prejudices were still part of common speech. He cited the expression "noisy as a *Judenschule*" (Jewish school) and its counterpart, "*Polnische wirtschaft*" (Polish economy), used ironically to describe a poorly managed enterprise, as symbols of a discredited German past.

The official fiction that the GDR bore no responsibility for the crimes of the Nazi era because it was, by its own declaration, an antifascist state had obviously worn thin, too thin to warrant repetition. Besides, at the time of my visit Honecker had set his sights on an official visit to Washington and, like the Nazis before him, believed that American Jews were enormously influential. This calculation, that Jews held the key to an invitation, probably explained his promise to rebuild the ruined synagogue on Oranienburger Strasse, the largest in undivided prewar Berlin. Honecker also offered to provide $100 million in aid to Jewish victims of Nazi persecution. He specified that the money be shared among needy Jews from Germany who were now American citizens, leaving no room for doubt that this gesture as well was designed for its supposed impact in the United States. Once again, though on a far less generous scale, the GDR was belatedly imitating the Federal Republic, whose restitution payments to Holocaust survivors exceed $40 *billion*. Neither the United States government nor the government in Bonn was greatly impressed by these symbolic — and tardy — steps. A more important obstacle, certainly, than Jewish displeasure was the Berlin Wall. An American diplomat put it bluntly: "As long as the wall stands," he said, "I find it inconceivable that any administration in Washington would roll out the red carpet for Erich Honecker." None did.

Large international issues were of little moment to ordinary citizens of the GDR, as I discovered in traveling to Dresden and Leipzig by second-class railway wagon. People talked freely, I found, if addressed in German. A retired metal worker, for example, said that he was content, even pleased with his conditions, but that he disapproved of the younger generation's greed for material possessions. "My late wife and I spent half our lifetime scrimping for our children's benefit," he said. But the young people of today, including his two grown daughters and four grandchildren, seemed to him insatiable. "They expect everything," he continued. "Not only a nice apartment but color television, an electric refrigerator, and a washing machine right from the start. They refuse to wait and save until they can afford these things. Now they demand bananas. I ask you, doesn't everyone know that Germany is not somewhere in the tropics? We don't grow bananas here, and when we import them they are shockingly expensive. What nonsense, bananas!" The important things, he said, were cheap food, low rents, and free medical care — and all these the young took for granted.

The train to Dresden was old, shabby, and overcrowded. With the approach of noon, many of the vacation-bound travelers carefully unwrapped sandwiches or hunks of sausage. The rest of us started shuffling toward the Mitropa food wagon in search of a snack. I fell into the slow-moving line behind an elderly gentleman, who chattered interminably about the weather (sunny) and the state of the crops in the fields (stunted, for the most part). The old man voiced no complaints, but whenever the line stopped moving he would turn to me with a sly smile and say, *"Vorwaerts, immer vorwaerts,"* in what I took to be an ironic comment on the regime's eternal urging to move the country forward by harder work. To my surprise, only a few of us bought food on reaching the counter. An astonishing number had shuffled through the line for at least forty minutes to buy cigarettes and warm beer. I was spreading mustard on my sausage when a woman beside me lighted up, then paused in embarrassment. "I should have offered you a cigarette," she said, "but I have read that Americans want to live forever." The GDR apparently had yet to mount a public campaign against smoking.

Dresden itself, described in prewar travel guides as a jewel box of a city, was demolished and incinerated on February 13 and 14, 1945, barely three months before the end of World War II, by American and British bombers. Its past grandeur is hard to grasp as one walks the streets today. To one side of the Old Town the planners re-created a sprawl of flat, thoroughly undistinguished buildings more reminiscent of Moscow than of Saxony. The street names recall dead German Communists and Russian heroes: Ernst Thaelmann Strasse, Juri Gagarin Strasse, Lenin Platz, Leningrader Strasse, Karl Liebknecht Strasse, August Bebel Strasse, and Karl Marx everything. For a glimpse of the city's ancient glories a traveler is better advised to visit the Albertinum, whose art collection includes five Canaletto paintings of Dresden in the eighteenth century, together with Albrecht Duerer's *Dresden Altar Triptych,* Vermeer's stunning *Girl Reading a Letter at an Open Window,* and other masterpieces. The Zwinger gallery, the Semper opera house, and the old Catholic cathedral were all rebuilt at enormous cost to the state, but the old Royal Palace and the Frauenkirche are still in ruins.

Germany's royal past and proletarian present confront one another throughout Dresden. The German-Soviet House of

Friendship stands on one side of a broad street that runs parallel with the right bank of the Elbe River, facing on the far side of the street a gilded equestrian statue of Frederick Augustus II, the elector of Saxony who became king of Poland in 1697. The old Augustus bridge nearby, destroyed in the war, was rebuilt and renamed for Georgi Dimitrov, the Bulgarian Communist leader who served Stalin faithfully as secretary general of the Comintern (the Communist International) from 1934 until its dissolution in 1943. This juxtaposition of past and present is equally characteristic of East Berlin. Unter den Linden remains the main axis of power today as it was in the time of the Hohenzollern kaisers, of Bismarck's Reich, and of Hitler's, too. It is here and along the narrower intersecting streets that one finds the government ministries, monuments, and museums clustered together within the space of, say, six Manhattan blocks. This quarter of the half city still resembles the imperial capital it once was. West Berlin, a livelier place, does not possess that look or feel of empire.

Most of the official buildings were in sorry shape when the fighting ended in 1945, but many have now been restored. The main exception is the ugly concrete bunker where Hitler cowered underground while the Red Army conquered the surrounding streets. In 1988 a giant crane hovered over the site as construction workers prepared to build an apartment block on top of the wreckage. "I don't think it's a bad idea to build housing there," an East German historian said. "That will be better than leaving an empty space — and it was empty. Nothing usable was left after the fighting."

I visited one of the usable buildings on Leipziger Strasse to talk with Dr. Joachim Herrmann, director of the Central Institute for Ancient History and Archaeology. As I was leaving, Dr. Herrmann remarked, "This used to be Bismarck's office." Indeed, the large building, somewhat the worse for wear, had once housed the Prussian prime minister's office and the offices of his subordinates. My host might have mentioned that a more recent prime minister of Prussia also worked there, in the 1930s. His name was Hermann Goering. Unlike Bismarck, he had not been rehabilitated.

# 6

## *Decline and Fall in the Balkans*

NEITHER BULGARIA nor Romania looked like a candidate for revolution when the Soviet bloc started splintering in 1989. Nicolae Ceausescu, Europe's last Stalinist dictator, had ruled Romania for a quarter-century. Next door, in Bulgaria, Todor Zhivkov had been in power for thirty-five years. With Erich Honecker in East Germany and Milos Jakes in Czechoslovakia, Zhivkov and Ceausescu made up the so-called Red Rejection Front in opposition to the reforms urged upon them by Mikhail Gorbachev. Zhivkov paid lip service to reform and Ceausescu rejected it outright, even after Honecker's downfall on October 18 sent the unmistakable message that change could no longer be postponed.

On November 10, Bulgarian television brought the nation an unforgettable scene: a stunned Zhivkov hearing his own "resignation" announced at a Central Committee plenum. There is no reason to suppose that the resignation was voluntary. Zhivkov had lost his power in a coup engineered by Petar Mladenov, his eventual successor, with the decisive support of Dobri Dzhurov, the defense minister, and the blessing of the Kremlin.

On December 22, Ceausescu also reached the end of the road. He fled Bucharest by helicopter following a bloody massacre in the city of Timisoara, where Ceausescu's security police had shot down more than four thousand demonstrators. The dictator and his wife, Elena, were captured the following day. His last speech as president, in front of the former royal palace on December 21, had been interrupted for almost three minutes by shouts of "Down with Ceausescu," "Free elections," and "The army is with us."

Although the long-suffering people of Romania have no tradition of rising up against their oppressors, the Timisoara massacre sealed Ceausescu's doom. On Christmas Day, he and his wife Elena were summarily executed after a swift trial by a military court. The case against him had been made nine months earlier in an open letter, never published in Romania but widely reproduced outside it, which amounted to a criminal indictment. The letter was signed by six apparently unregenerate Communists with unbroken records of party loyalty. "At a time when the very idea of socialism, for which we fought, is discredited by your policy, and when our country is being isolated from Europe, we have decided to speak up," they wrote. "We are perfectly aware that by doing so we are risking our liberty and even our lives; but we feel duty-bound to appeal to you to reverse the present course before it is too late."

The signers included two former members of the Romanian Politburo, Gheorghe Apostol and Alexandru Birladeanu; Corneliu Manescu, once foreign minister and president of the United Nations General Assembly; Constantin Pirvulescu, ninety-four years old, a founder of the Romanian party; Grigore Raceanu, a veteran Communist; and Silviu Brucan, former ambassador to the United States and once acting editor of the party newspaper, *Scinteia*. Their indictment centered on these points:

- The Ceausescu plan to tear down thousands of rural villages and force the removal of their inhabitants to three-story apartment blocks runs counter to Article 36 of the Romanian constitution.

- A decree forbidding all contacts between Romanian citizens and foreigners, illegal because it was never approved by the legislature or published, is being used to threaten people with harassment, arrest, and loss of jobs.
- Ceausescu's pet project, which involves the destruction and rebuilding of central Bucharest, is under way in violation of existing laws. Its cost has tripled, owing to changes that Ceausescu orders "every month."
- Securitate, the State Security Service, directs its efforts "against workers demanding their rights, against old members of the party, and against honest intellectuals exercising their rights to petition . . . and freedom of speech . . . guaranteed by the constitution."
- Factories and public institutions are under orders to force their employees to work on Sundays, violating both the constitution and the labor code.
- The privacy of mail and telephone services is systematically violated. "To sum up, the constitution has been virtually suspended and there is no legal system in force. You must admit, Mr. President, that a society cannot function if the authorities, starting from the top, show disrespect for the law."
- Economic planning no longer works in Romania. A growing number of factories lack raw materials, energy, or markets. Collective agriculture is in disarray. Peasants working their private plots, which account for only 12 percent of the arable land, produce 40 percent of the vegetables, 60 percent of the milk, and 44 percent of the meat.
- Harking back to the plan for "systemization of villages," the signers addressed Ceausescu directly: "Why urbanize villages when you cannot ensure decent conditions of urban life in the cities, namely adequate heating, lighting, transportation, not to mention food? A government that

for five winters in a row has been unable to solve such vital problems . . . proves itself incompetent and incapable of governing. Therefore, we are not pressing on you any demand in this respect."

· The mass emigration of ethnic Germans, Hungarians, and Jews is the result of a policy of "forced assimilation" that should be renounced.

· Romania under Ceausescu is increasingly isolated. Several European countries have closed their Bucharest embassies. Romania has lost its most-favored-nation status for trade with the United States, and the European Economic Community is unwilling to extend its trade agreement with Romania.

Again addressing Ceausescu directly, the authors mentioned his frequent stress on summit meetings as decisive in improving relations between states: "But how are you going to improve Romania's external relations when all the leaders of the non-Communist nations of Europe refuse to meet with you? Romania is and remains a European country and as such must advance along with the Helsinki process and not turn against it. You started changing the geography of the countryside, but you cannot remove Romania to Africa."

Finally, the signers called on Ceausescu to cancel the village-urbanization plan, restore the constitutional guarantees on the rights of citizens, and put an end to the export of foodstuffs, which threatens "the biological existence of our nation." They did not ask for the end of Communist rule, only for a constructive dialogue that might save the system.

Ceausescu did not acknowledge the letter, but a few days after copies reached the West, the office of the prosecutor general in Bucharest announced that the secret police had uncovered a "grave action of betrayal" by an official of the Romanian Foreign Ministry, Mircea Raceanu, whose adoptive father was one of the signers of the letter.

The younger Raceanu's arrest and swift indictment looked like a transparent effort by the regime to discredit the letter's authors, at least by association, and to prepare for a Stalin-style show trial. Raceanu, who had been in charge of Romania's relations with Central and South America, stood accused of having spied for an unidentified foreign power since 1974. Following the denunciatory letter to Ceausescu, all six of the signers were arrested and sent into a kind of internal exile, forbidden contact with anyone other than their police guards and, according to some accounts, also denied medical attention. Manescu and Brucan, both seventy-three years old and in failing health, nevertheless surfaced as members of a newly formed National Salvation Front, an improvised political alliance of anti-Ceausescu army officers, dissident Communists, and student leaders. They moved quickly to establish a provisional government, with Manescu briefly at its head.

The Ceausescu dictatorship earned for Romania a uniquely unsavory reputation even among most of its East bloc allies. Some called it an insult to socialism. With the possible exception of Albania, Romania had the most depressed living standard in Europe. Basic foods had been rationed since 1981. Bread, milk, cheese, meat, and fish were all in short supply. Bucharest housewives wasted hours standing in line for necessities that tended to vanish from the shelves before their turn came. In winter, electricity was rationed and apartments were chilly as a matter of state policy. Inside temperatures could not exceed 45 degrees Fahrenheit, a limit imposed by law.

Ceausescu's harsh austerity program appeared to serve several conflicting purposes:

1. To wipe out Romania's external debt (some $12 billion at its peak) by 1990, using resources squeezed out of the wretched living standard of a long-suffering nation. Virtually everything that could be exported, food as well as manufactured goods, was shipped out of the country. Ceausescu justified his draconian measures on the ground that eating less was good for the people's health. In a speech before a Communist-front organization, the dictator argued that "so far as our nutrition is concerned, we are already consuming too much."

2. To finance his grandiose plan for transforming the center of Bucharest at a cost of untold billions. Thousands of workmen labored day and night to tear down scores of historic buildings and to raise in their place an enormous neo-Classical Palace of the Republic, sitting on an artificial hill, which was to house the Communist Party headquarters and the official residence of the Ceausescus. There was also a spectacular new Boulevard of the Victory of Socialism, 3.5 kilometers long and 110 meters wide, bordered by large white structures whose function remained unknown. The nearby Piazza of National Unity was the site for acre upon acre of towering apartment blocks. More than forty thousand people who used to live in the gutted center of the Romanian capital were displaced. "There isn't anything this big going on in the world," said a proud official spokesman. "It's not simply a question of architectural change; it's about remodeling a whole culture." This was urban redevelopment on a monstrous scale, the kind of thing that Adolf Hitler had in mind for Berlin before his death in the Fuehrerbunker. Ceausescu lived to see *his* dream fulfilled, regardless of cost, a memorial to himself as the master builder of what passed for socialism in Romania.

3. To speed completion of Ceausescu's plan to tear down thousands of villages and to move their inhabitants into

some six hundred "agro-industrial centers." Each of the new centers was to have its own hospital, school, pharmacy, and a community center known as Hymn to Romania. The peasant population, its traditional gaily painted homesteads destroyed, would be moved into identical prefabricated apartment blocks, there presumably to lead identical prefabricated lives. Romania's most efficient farmers, mainly ethnic Germans and Hungarians, feared for the survival of their culture and language when their centuries-old villages fell to the bulldozer and the inhabitants were dispersed. The Magyar minority, almost two million strong, bitterly resented the demolitions. Many thousands fled across the border into Hungary, complaining of official persecution and forced assimilation.

But Ceausescu was unrepentant. He contended that the "systematization" scheme would erase the differences between town and countryside and make possible a more efficient use of arable land. "We start from the fact," he said, "that socialism must create the best conditions of life for all inhabitants without distinction, that we cannot divide the country in two, with one part in modern, developed housing and the other part in shabby, unhealthful housing." His disbelieving critics, on the other hand, argued that the plan was designed to appropriate the last remaining plots of privately cultivated farmland and to rob the ethnic minorities of their separate identities.

The heavy hand of Ceausescu's Securitate reinforced the inbred caution of most Romanians, expressed in a folk saying: "The bowed head avoids the sword." However, even in the Era of Light, the official designation of Ceausescu's quarter-century in power, occasional voices were raised in protest. On November 15, 1987, hundreds of workers from the huge Red Flag truck and tractor factories in Brasov stormed the local headquarters of the Communist Party, seized personnel records, and looted a special food shop reserved for privileged party officials.

Angry over wage cuts and food shortages, the workers built a bonfire in the central marketplace of Brasov, feeding the flames with stacks of party documents and a portrait of Ceausescu. The Securitate closed in with overwhelming force, arresting dozens of the riotous strikers. This was the first act of working-class defiance in Romania since a coal miners' strike ten years earlier. Almost three weeks passed before the regimented Bucharest newspapers were allowed to report that an unspecified number of workers had, in some unspecified manner, "provoked disorder" in Brasov and assuring the readers that the guilty would be "brought to account in accordance with the law." As in the case of the open letter to Ceausescu from the six Communist veterans, the Romanian media left the story to be told by Radio Free Europe, the overseas service of the British Broadcasting Corporation, and the Voice of America. Truth was an orphan in Ceausescu's Romania.

Bulgaria's human rights record also bears careful watching. In 1984 the government launched a mailed-fist campaign against its Turkish-speaking Islamic minority of more than one million citizens. It assigned to the army and paramilitary forces the task of imposing a uniform Bulgar ethnicity on the whole of the population. Official spokesmen put out an implausible tale that the minority were voluntarily giving up their Turkish names in favor of Slavic names. The government repeatedly denied that force was being used to compel the assimilation of the ethnic Turks. Besides, the government argued, "there are no Turks in Bulgaria" and never had been. Citing academic studies of ancient skulls exhumed in Turkish areas of the country, the party press claimed to possess proof that the Turks were not Turks at all but "pure Bulgarians," who had been forced to embrace Islam during five centuries of rule by Ottoman Turkey.

This ostensibly scientific finding failed to explain, however, why Bulgarian citizens whose ancestors had been free to speak Turkish and worship in mosques for countless generations must now be stripped of these basic rights. The campaign did not stop with enforced name changing. The regime also closed mosques and banned Turkish-language newspapers, schools, broadcasts, even conversation in public places. Islamic rituals like male circumcision were forbidden. The official press denounced the practice, not alone on hygienic grounds but as an "ideological diversion of imperialism" designed to separate Bulgarian workers along religious lines.

When I visited Bulgaria in the late summer of 1988, many Turks were trying to emigrate, but the regime, which was facing a labor shortage, refused to let them go. A wave of protest demonstrations, hunger strikes, and other displays of civil disobedience flared up the following spring, touching off violent clashes with the police. These led to a sudden policy reversal. In an extraordinary broadcast, Zhivkov announced that "all Bulgarian Moslems" were free to leave the country. He asked Turkey to "keep its borders open." Turgut Ozal, Turkey's prime minister, replied, "Our borders are always open. They have never been closed to our brethren." The first group of two hundred ethnic Turks to reach Istanbul turned out to have been expelled for protest activity. Many were forced to leave behind their property and families. One of them, Nasif Bilaloglu, had spent sixteen months in jail for refusing to accept the Slavic name Nadir Slakovski. He was deported, Bilaloglu said, with nothing but "the clothes on my back."

Before long the systematic expulsion of protesters turned into a mass exodus, which had reached 310,000 when Turkey shut off the flow. The new arrivals were temporarily

housed in tent cities, school dormitories, hospitals, and police stations at the start. But Prime Minister Ozal, who had
pledged to receive every one of the ethnic Turks being expelled or otherwise encouraged to leave, was forced to concede that Turkey could not keep accepting all who wanted
to come.

Under Zhivkov's leadership since 1954, Bulgaria had been
the most pliant of satellites. When Gorbachev came to power
in Moscow, Zhivkov appeared to follow his example loy-
ally. Bulgarian newspapers reported Gorbachev's reformist
speeches in considerable detail, opening their pages to unprecedented debate. Zhivkov also proposed measures to
overhaul the lagging economy through market-oriented reforms. But not much came of the promised reforms, owing
in part to the determined resistance of some thirty thousand
bureaucrats whose secure jobs were suddenly threatened.

*Glasnost,* Bulgarian style, fared even less well than Zhivkov's stalled version of *perestroika.* When the ruling party
agreed to allow the formation of independent associations,
it stipulated that they must not engage in "anarchy, chaos,
and demagoguery." The few groups that did form were soon
repressed. For example, activists founded the Independent
Association for the Defense of Human Rights in Bulgaria,
dedicated to monitoring abuses and campaigning for the re-
peal of laws that restricted civil liberties. The regime at first
appeared to hesitate, but after several months it cracked
down, sending several of the new association's founders into
internal exile without trial. The association's secretary, Tzeko
Krustev Tzekov, condemned the suppression of Turkish-
speaking citizens in a telephone interview with Radio Free
Europe. He claimed there were 140 political prisoners in
Bulgaria, a number that did not include people imprisoned
for attempting to leave the country illegally.

The regime also cracked down on the Club for the Support of Perestroika and Glasnost, formed in November 1988

by a group of about one hundred prominent intellectuals. Its leaders were promptly arrested and expelled from the Bulgarian Communist Party. About a dozen members of the club, writers and academics, met with President François Mitterrand of France, in January 1989, at breakfast in the French embassy. Mitterrand, who had spoken out for human rights in Eastern Europe at an official banquet the previous evening, listened closely to complaints that members of the club were being persecuted in spite of Zhivkov's acknowledgment that it was a legal organization. Contradictions between official word and official deed have been commonplace in Bulgaria.

A striking example involved grassroots demands for a more open press. The Politburo responded in 1988 with a resolution coupling a guarantee that investigative reporting would be allowed with an ambiguous commitment to what it called "socialist pluralism of opinion." In a matter of months, three Bulgarian editors lost their jobs for taking the Politburo at its word. Damyan Obreshkov, editor of the trade union daily *Trud,* was replaced after publishing a series of reports on corrupt practices in the Communist Party. The editors of two weeklies were dismissed for publishing articles on controversial historical and cultural topics. Their sin, according to Zhivkov, was that the articles promoted a "negative view" of Communism.

Foreign ambassadors in Bulgaria, as in other bloc countries, learned to watch for subtle signs of dissent wherever they might appear. A recent play, *Balkan Syndrome,* caught their attention as a veiled comment on the rigors of life under Communism. Compared with many plays and motion pictures recently produced in Moscow, this was rather pale stuff: a play within a play, focusing on a theatrical director who is fired in midrehearsal for — in the words of a Western ambassador — "letting people ask too many questions." Discussing the contrast between Moscow and Sofia, a Bul-

garian intellectual offered this explanation: "What makes
the Soviet cultural scene so much more lively than ours is
that journalists, historians, playwrights, and filmmakers are
free to expose the dark side of the Stalin and Brezhnev years.
In our case, unfortunately, Zhivkov is the past, the present,
and possibly also the future. He alone can be blamed for the
state of the country after more than thirty-five years in power,
and that is strictly forbidden."

Zhivkov's long and rigidly Stalinist rule ended abruptly on
November 10, 1989. He was overthrown in a palace revolt
encouraged and engineered, according to several reports,
from the Kremlin. The new party chief, Petar Mladenov,
promptly started a purge of Zhivkov's closest associates in
the Politburo with the full support of the defense minister,
Dobri Dzhurov.

Although there was no evidence that the overthrow came
in response to pressure from the people, Mladenov soon
faced demands for far-reaching economic and political reforms, reinforced by mass demonstrations that would have
been unthinkable in Zhivkov's time. A newly established
Union of Democratic Forces, speaking in the name of ten
little-known independent groups, published a set of demands remarkably similar to those raised in Czechoslovakia
and East Germany: free elections, the rule of law, a free and
independent press, unions free of party control, and multiparty politics. The union also called for more liberal treatment of Bulgaria's ethnic and religious minorities, including
the Turkish population, which had suffered systematic persecution in the latter years of the Zhivkov regime.

Yielding to the demand of 50,000 citizens at a pro-democ-
racy rally in Sofia on December 10, the new leader promised
to abolish the Communist Party's political monopoly and hold
free parliamentary elections by the spring of 1990. This would
be done by abolishing Article 1 of the Bulgarian constitution. "The position of the party cannot be declared admin-

istratively," Mladenov said. "It must come from the trust of the people. We need to adopt the principle of a multiparty system."

It is time, he added, for the party to separate itself from the government. The rubber-stamp National Assembly would then be free to operate like a real legislature. In adopting these radical reforms, Bulgaria was falling into step with other East European countries, all except Romania. It was an extraordinary departure from Bulgaria's past under Zhivkov, all the more remarkable in light of the country's historic relationship with Russia.

Bulgaria and Romania, like East Germany, can be expected to encounter serious difficulties in moving from authoritarian rule to some form of democracy. The East Germans have lived under totalitarian regimes for fifty-six years — twelve years under the Nazis and forty-four years under the Communists. Only the aged among them have any recollection of the Weimar Republic or the political parties that played a leading role in German politics before Hitler came to power in 1933. As for Romania, it is not a country in which the Communists suppressed the democratic tradition: it never had a democratic tradition. The outlook for democracy in Bulgaria is only slightly more hopeful. In both Balkan countries, dissent has been so rigorously suppressed that it is difficult to imagine where new democratic leadership would come from.

# 7

## *Yugoslavia*

### Graveyard of Reform

DOBRICA COSIC, a renowned Serb novelist, fondly recalls his youthful years, when Yugoslavia broke free of Stalinism to become a model of sorts for reform in other Communist-ruled countries. He continues to speak of his country with love ("This miracle called Yugoslavia, the most complex, contradictory society in all of Europe"). But he is anxious about his homeland, describing it as "a gravely ill Balkan patient with an uncertain future." In a free-flowing conversation on the terrace of his spacious Belgrade villa, Cosic talked of his disappointment. "The Yugoslav crisis," he said, "is a double crisis. It is the crisis of socialism, and the crisis of an alternative to socialism. Unlike the countries of the Soviet bloc, we have no excuse for this state of affairs. We tried reform long before the others, but we failed to produce a fundamental change." Today's Yugoslavia, he seemed to be saying, has become irrelevant to the yearnings of other East Europeans for national independence and personal liberty.

A member of the Central Committee of the Yugoslav League of Communists in the 1960s, Cosic frequently engaged President Josip Broz Tito in long political discussions.

He quit the party more than twenty years ago, thoroughly disenchanted with Tito and with what he called the political religion of Bolshevism. "Tito," he said, "was a 'consumer Stalinist,' who ruled by corruption, a tyranny of lies, and of demagogy. His was a regime in which all the evils of nationalism came to the surface. It will take decades to emancipate ourselves from all that. Tito had great political talent and a genius for seizing power. But in 1966 I wrote him a letter, saying that I could not follow him any longer. I had realized that he was an autocrat who would never reject Bolshevism. We parted, and in 1968 I left the party."

Cast out of the Soviet bloc in 1948, Tito's Yugoslavia became the first Communist-ruled state to chart its own road. Long before Hungary, Poland, or the Soviet Union itself under Nikita Khrushchev and later under Mikhail Gorbachev, the Yugoslavs embarked on a reform program. They virtually abandoned collective agriculture, restored much of the land to private cultivation, established a novel system of workers' councils to participate in management, proclaimed a nonaligned foreign policy, and received substantial economic assistance from the West. The Communist Party, however, held on to its political monopoly.

Since Tito's death in 1980, Yugoslavia has floundered like a ship moving through angry seas without a compass in working order or a captain on the bridge. Its constitution, devised six years earlier by Tito and his chief lieutenant, Edvard Kardelj, is widely blamed for the country's loss of direction and momentum. Once a working federation of six republics and two autonomous provinces, the nation has degenerated into a loose and fragile confederation of quarrelsome local bureaucracies. Yugoslavia today is said to have "nine of everything" — nine Communist parties and nine governments, all separate and supposedly equal, one set for each republic and autonomous province plus, of course, the federal establishment.

The central government, not surprisingly, has lost much of its authority. A revolving-door system of collective leadership rotates the federal presidency year by year in predetermined order among the republics and provinces. Tito took pride in this arrangement, his own handiwork. He designed it, his many critics say, to make certain that no successor would emulate his command of the country and its institutions. For the most part, his successors have turned out to be a succession of gray bureaucrats who would pass unnoticed in a street crowd.

A Belgrade friend of thirty years past told me over cups of Turkish coffee that his dreams of a better life for his children had been blasted by rude reality. "The party is a hollow shell," he said. "The federal leadership has lost much of its power. Socialism, as we have known it, is of course a dismal failure. The ordinary peasant has known that all along. Now even high officials of the party and state know it. I doubt that real reform will be possible until — and unless — we dismantle what is left of our bankrupt forty-year-old system. Even Tito, as you see, is no longer immune to criticism. The myths come crashing down. Everybody talks about moving toward democracy, but you can't call it democracy as long as one party has a permanent hold on power."

He did not need to mention the chaotic state of the Yugoslav economy, which tended to dominate most of my Belgrade conversations. Every literate citizen knows the awful numbers by heart: the officially estimated inflation rate, 251 percent at the end of 1988; unemployment, at least 15 percent and rising; external debt, $22 billion; and a battered currency, the dinar, that falls day by day. It's not Weimar Germany, but even here it takes a thick wad of bills to pay for dinner at a less than grand restaurant. Real living standards fell back in 1989 to the levels of 1965.

Prime Minister Ante Markovic, appointed in March 1989, promised a sharp turn toward capitalism. New laws were enacted, allowing foreign investors to buy up Yugoslav companies and easing the restrictions on the number of workers a private enterprise can employ. Although few of the knowledgeable Yugoslavs I met quarreled with the need for radical changes in economic policy, many doubted that Markovic's once-heretical ideas would meet with success. There are too many obstacles, and the most serious of them are embedded in the minds of middle-aged to elderly party officials, according to Lenart Setinc, a Central Committee secretary in Slovenia.

"It's a hangover from the Bolshevik days," he said. "You see it in the way so many Yugoslav Communists load the concepts of property, capital, and profit with negative implications." Professor Ljubisa S. Adamovic, chairman of the department of international economics at the University of Belgrade, put the issue even more bluntly. "We are simply not allowed to have prosperity in this country," he said. "There are too many barriers, there is too much dogma, and too much unjustified fear of the private sector. People keep asking where the limits are. Why talk of limits? Why is there so little talk of opportunities? It's not as if capitalism were about to sweep the country. Our major industries, the schools, the hospitals, will remain in the public sector, no matter what happens."

The residue of dogmatism, Adamovic added, has prevented Yugoslavia from taking advantage of new opportunities. He pointed out that tens of thousands of Yugoslav workers had taken jobs in West Germany and Sweden during the 1960s and 1970s, learning something in the process about how business is done in Western Europe. "A lot of them are potential managers and businessmen, with money in German banks," he said. "All we need to do is create conditions that would encourage these people to invest their skills and their savings in starting businesses here at home. What a beautiful opportunity! But we're not doing anything about it. That's the price we pay for all those years of the Big Guy, who surrounded himself with yes men, not with creative people. Nowadays, of course, they all say they want a modern economy, but they want to keep political control. The effect of this thinking is that we wind up with more and more control over less and less."

I hesitated to interrupt the flow of the professor's indignation, but when I asked him about the effects of the legal and constitutional changes of the 1970s, he was off and running again. One proviso of the Associated Labor Act of 1976, he said, specifies that "communities" are responsible for ensuring prosperity on their territory. The result has been to erect barriers between republics and even within them. "This is a self-inflicted wound," he said. "In the age of the European Community, which seeks to lower trade barriers between countries, this is a counterhistorical move. Instead of encouraging what you Americans call interstate commerce, we are impeding the flow of labor and materials across republican boundaries. It gives us ethnic bureaucracy at the expense of Yugoslav efficiency. For too many years now we have been subsidizing inefficiency on the mistaken notion that this serves to increase security."

Remarkably, in view of the country's virtual bankruptcy, shop windows along Marshal Tito Street in Belgrade are filled with consumer goods, not of high quality, admittedly, but business appears to be brisk. When I worked in Yugoslavia three decades past, there was little automobile traffic to clog the narrow downtown streets, except for the black Mercedes 300 limousines, mostly chauffeur-driven, favored by the Communist hierarchy, and an assortment of American, German, and Italian cars bearing diplomatic plates. All that and a great deal more has changed since the 1950s. The traffic is heavy today, and exhaust fumes hang over the city streets. Most of the smog is generated by Yugoslav-owned vehicles. One hears talk of people in grinding poverty, of gray loaves baked especially for the poor, who can't afford ordinary bread. But apart from Gypsies selling trinkets or begging along the Terazije, the poor are somehow invisible.

Government statistics show that Yugoslavia's per capita "social product" in 1985 was "only 25 percent of the average national products of eight developed European countries." Average annual growth rates plummeted from 8.9 percent in the peak period, 1953–60, to 0.6 percent in the 1981–85 period. *The Handbook on Yugoslavia,* published by the federal government, acknowledges that a "relatively large influx of foreign money encouraged consumption expenditure beyond what the country could afford, led to high dependence of investment projects on imports, and brought about balance-of-payments difficulties."

I asked Dr. Ljubomir Madzar, an economist at the University of Belgrade, to put some flesh on the bare-bones account published by the government. He explained that from 1950 to 1964 fully one third of Yugoslavia's capital formation came from abroad (including credits and grants from the United States and other Western countries). After 1965 the Yugoslav *gastarbeiter* (guest workers), who flocked to well-paid jobs in Western Europe, sent home remittances valued at $3 to $4 billion a year. "This was a rare, possibly unique, case of a country that was able to rely for about three decades on a steady stream of foreign money," Madzar said. Why, then, did Yugoslavia do less well than other countries in building a productive economy? Madzar cited three main reasons:

1. The system of workers' self-management, long touted as the most original Yugoslav contribution to Marxist theory, has operated badly. Workers tend to be unduly generous when they determine their own wages, driving up the cost of their product. Workers' councils also tend to favor short-term investment at the expense of

badly needed longer-term investment. In short, it's a queer system that produces queer results, not all of them intentional. Even though labor is abundant in Yugoslavia, it keeps growing more expensive without accompanying gains in productivity. Capital, being scarce, should be expensive, and labor, being abundant, should be cheap. Instead, what should be cheap is expensive, and the other way around.

2. In Yugoslavia's "irrational system" of setting prices, authority is divided among federal, republican, and local bodies, an arrangement that places an impossible burden on the bureaucracies at all levels.

3. The 1974 constitution and the Associated Labor Act, passed in 1976, have broken many of the natural links within the Yugoslav economy. With each of the six republics and the two autonomous provinces trying to build its own self-sufficient economy, it becomes impossible for the federal government to carry out a consistent national policy.

"In some respects," Madzar acknowledged, "the East European systems are more logical than ours. In theory, at least, a strong totalitarian state can do a good job of extracting resources from the population. We pushed the Yugoslav state out of the process — on ideological grounds. It was supposed to wither away, in any case. Thus we denied ourselves the benefits of either a command economy or a true market economy."

For all the politicians' glib talk about a transition to what they call market socialism, progress is painfully slow. As in Poland and Hungary, reformers in Yugoslavia recognize that free markets cannot prosper as long as the ruling party, whether at the republican or federal level, continues to interfere in the economy. They agree that the party must not be allowed to go on appointing or approving company man-

agers, directing investment, and bailing out failed enterprises, almost invariably for political reasons. The federal
Economics Ministry concedes that more than half of Yugoslavia's industrial enterprises are insolvent, with aggregate
debts of some $15 billion. Closing them necessarily means
increased unemployment.

"All the politicians support reform in words but not in
deeds," said Kosta Cavoski, a Belgrade legal scholar. "They
all say, 'Sure, close down unprofitable firms — but not in my
republic.'" Cavoski estimated that in Slovenia, the most advanced of the republics, perhaps 10 percent of the existing
companies would go bankrupt, while in Montenegro, one of
the poorest, something like 80 percent would be out of business. "No Montenegrin politician, not even the most reform-minded, would accept that sacrifice," Cavoski said.

The halting reform and austerity measures taken till now
by the weakened federal government satisfy neither the advocates nor the opponents of radical change. In the wes-
ternmost republics, Slovenia and Croatia, there is widespread disappointment over the sluggish pace of reform.
But in the poorer republics — Montenegro, Macedonia,
Bosnia, and even in Serbia, the largest of them — opposition to an expanded role for market forces is powerful, driven
by fears that more unemployment is too high a price to pay
for the hypothetical gains promised by reformers. Having
failed to put the country on the road to recovery, the unpopular federal prime minister, Branko Mikulic, resigned
at the end of 1988 after serving little more than half of his
four-year term. That was too short a time, Mikulic told the
Federal Assembly, to resolve the economic crisis his administration had inherited from (as he gently put it) "past decades." Refusing to accept responsibility for the mistakes of
his unnamed predecessors, Mikulic made the valid point that,
owing to the constitutional changes dating from Tito's time,
it was not the federal government that set economic policies

but officials in some seven thousand to eight thousand local communities. He added that "it is more honorable to resign than to be blamed for all the country's ills."

Restless Yugoslavs do blame the government. Strikes and protest marches proliferated over the summer months preceding the Mikulic resignation. Tens of thousands of workers converged on the Federal Assembly building in Belgrade to protest across-the-board pay cuts of up to 40 percent and rising prices. Some carried framed photographs of Tito as if they were sacred icons, and as if he bore no responsibility for the current crisis. One group, apparently unaware that the assembly was not in session, burst into the building with shouts of "thieves and traitors" directed at a handful of bewildered clerks. They might have done better to march on the Central Committee of the Communist Party, a Belgrade friend remarked, although several groups of strikers did win wage concessions as a result of their excursion to the capital.

An equally peaceful protest march in the autumn by Montenegrin workers ended less happily. They were forcibly dispersed with tear gas and clubs by federal militiamen and police. In recent years the number of strikes, officially tolerated though not strictly legal, has risen dramatically. In 1987, for example, some 365,000 Yugoslav workers took part in 1570 strikes, eight and a half times as many as in 1982. Labor unrest was literally unheard of in Tito's Yugoslavia until January 1958, when coal miners at Trbovlje in Slovenia went underground and stayed there for two days to protest a pay cut. It was an old, virtually exhausted mine, which had been worked since the distant days when Slovenia was part of the Austro-Hungarian Empire. The miners were having their pay docked because Trbovlje had failed to meet its production quota as compared with newer mines that benefited from modern machinery.

I reported the few known facts at the time to the *New York Times*. Angry government officials promptly accused me of having invented the story. "You should know that strikes are impossible in socialist Yugoslavia," a woman official thundered. "How can Yugoslav miners, who own the mine, go on strike against themselves? Our own press does not publish these malicious fairy tales." The fairy tale was, of course, the simple truth, which the controlled Yugoslav press had been forbidden to publish. Marshal Tito joined in the denunciation of the foreign press. "Whatever is positive in our country is not mentioned," he complained a few days afterward in a speech before a youth congress. "But whenever there is something negative, a big noise is made." His indirect acknowledgment that "something negative" had occurred at Trbovlje, however, broke the official silence. That first strike turned out to be a benchmark. Thirty years later, strikes were an everyday occurrence.

I heard an uncommonly sympathetic rationale for the continuing labor unrest from a Slovenian government spokesman named Marjan Sifter in Ljubljana, the republican capital. "Strikes," he said, "are a legitimate form of pressure and a warning to the authorities that something must be done. They draw attention to important issues. We used to behave like ostriches. As recently as three years ago, our newspapers did not report strikes on the theory, I suppose, that they would disappear if we ignored them. All that has changed now. Strikes tell us that people have had enough of poverty, the poverty of socialism."

The statement was not altogether surprising in view of its source. Slovenia, the smallest of Yugoslav republics, is also the most prosperous, the most advanced industrially, and in recent years the most hospitable to democratic ideas. Slovenia's leaders, though tried-and-true party members, sound less like committed Communists than their counterparts elsewhere. Only in this predominantly Roman Catholic region framed by alpine scenery would the president of the Socialist Alliance, a former newspaper editor named Joze

Smole, appear on television every year, with the bishop of Ljubljana at his side, to wish the people a happy Christmas.

The passion for democratic reform, while not unique to Slovenia, is more openly expressed here. Janez Stanovnik, president of the Slovene republic, told a Washington audience in 1988 that it was time for "the Communist Party to step down from directly interfering in governmental affairs" and become one of several parties competing for votes in free and direct elections. His views would be condemned as heresy in other regions, but they are popular in Slovenia, which borders on Italy and Austria. In the same Washington press conference, Stanovnik spoke out bluntly against resurgent Serbian nationalism, personified by Slobodan Milosevic, the dynamic party chief in Serbia. He charged Milosevic with fanning the flames of ethnic antagonism.

Yugoslavia, home of the South Slavs, is an implausible country of six republics, five nationalities, four languages, three religions, two alphabets, and (so the flippant catechism went in his lifetime) one Tito. The "national question" had torn prewar Yugoslavia apart. It plunged the country into bloody civil war between Croats and Serbs under cover of the larger war against the Axis powers. It also bedeviled Tito's Communist regime time and again before his death and remains unresolved into the final decade of the century.

The Yugoslav state, in fact, ceased to exist during World War II. It was dismembered by the invading Germans and Italians. They carved out an "independent state of Croatia" under a dedicated fascist named Ante Pavelic, extending its borders to include Bosnia and Herzegovina. Much of Dalmatia and the Adriatic islands went to Mussolini. Slovenia was simply erased from the map of Europe, the southern two thirds annexed by Italy and the northern, industrial third by Hitler's Third Reich. Montenegro, once an independent kingdom, had its crown restored in theory, but in fact it was attached to the Italian royal house. The Kossovo region, home to many ethnic Albanians, was awarded to Albania, which itself had been under direct Italian rule since 1939. Bulgaria helped itself to Yugoslav Macedonia. Hungary, then an Axis ally, was rewarded with parts of the Vojvodina. The remainder was administered by *Volksdeutsche*, ethnic Germans native to the area. Serbia, now greatly diminished, suffered under German military occupation though it was administered by local collaborators. It defied conventional wisdom at the time to predict that Yugoslavia would ever be made whole again.

Pavelic's Croat fascist gangs, known as Ustase, set out in the name of Catholicism to purge their enlarged domain of infidels — Orthodox Serbs, Moslems, and, of course, Jews. It was a crude inquisition, offering the minorities a choice between instantaneous conversion to the Church of Rome at the point of a knife — or death. Before the agony ended, the Ustase had massacred one third of the population of Bosnia-Herzegovina and 15 percent of Croatia's entire population, inviting countermassacres by enraged Serbs. Relations between Croats and Serbs, seldom cordial even in the years between the two world wars, never fully overcame the memories of that terrible time.

That mutual antagonism, hardening into hatred, survived the struggle against foreign invaders and the civil war for control of postwar Yugoslavia between Tito's Communist-led Partisans and the Chetniks, commanded by General Draza Mihajlovic, loyal to King Peter II and his exile government in London. It was a shaky foundation on which to erect a new Yugoslav state once the Communists came to power. Tito preached conciliation among warring nationalities under the slogan of "brotherhood and unity." He promised a new order based on federalism, respect for national rights, and socialism. Tito himself was of mixed Croat-Slovene ancestry. His closest collaborators during and after the war represented a mix of nationalities: Edvard Kardelj, a Slovene schoolteacher; Milovan Djilas, a gifted Montenegrin who had successfully recruited dozens of university students to the Communist cause; and Aleksandar Rankovic, once a tailor's apprentice in Sumadija, the heartland of Serbia.

Other prominent figures of the early period were Vladimir Bakaric, a Yugoslav statesman as well as a Croat leader; the wise and witty Mosa Pijade, a Serbian Jew who had instructed Tito in Marxism and translated *Das Kapital* while both were in prison; and an appreciable number who lost their lives in the war. More than three hundred veterans of the Spanish Civil War held Partisan commands, among them Koca Popovic, a surrealist poet and the son of a Belgrade millionaire.

As the memories of war faded in the 1950s, the idea of a united Yugoslavia whose independence was no longer threatened by the Soviet Union appeared to gain ground. The enormous task of postwar reconstruction, lubricated by generous credits and grants in aid from the West, stimulated economic growth. It was considered a welcome sign of material progress (though not by nutritionists) that the peasants, now substantially freed of the pressure to collectivize, were eating a lot more sugar and white bread. But certain stubborn features of the discredited past had not, after all, disappeared. In the new Yugoslavia, as in the prewar years, the Serbs were once again wielding disproportionate power in the highly centralized state and party apparatus. The Croats were not alone in grumbling that federal power had become synonymous with Serbian power.

The grumbling was not limited to politicians. Driving one spring day in Croatia, I offered a ride to a young hitchhiker. She looked faintly foreign, possibly German, so I asked her whether she spoke Serbian. "Only Croatian," she replied with a touch of indignation. That was, of course, a political statement. Croats and Serbs speak much the same language, although they write it differently. Serbs use the Cyrillic alphabet; Croats use the Roman alphabet.

One source of envy and resentment among Yugoslavs of other nationalities was the large number of government jobs held by Serbs in Belgrade, the capital of Serbia and the seat of the federal government. Another, more significant source of complaint was the preponderance of Serbs in the army and the federal security apparatus, known in those days as the UDBa. Bakaric, the widely respected Croatian leader, once estimated that Serbs accounted for 70 percent of the army's officer corps.

The most powerful Serb and, after Tito, the most important Yugoslav was Aleksandar Rankovic, minister of the interior and vice president. An intimidating figure by reputation if not in person, he created and controlled the ubiquitous and all-powerful UDBa. Rankovic had agents everywhere. On constant alert for suspected subversion, they busied themselves tapping telephones, intercepting mail, watching and listening in coffee houses, browbeating uncooperative citizens, and worse. Their boss stood for party discipline, strong-arm tactics whenever necessary, and Serb nationalism. His legion of critics called it "Serbian hegemonialism." As organizational secretary of the party, he also had the last word on important appointments. No less a founder of the new Yugoslavia than Tito, Rankovic inspired fear more than respect. Even as Tito settled comfortably into the role of world-class statesman, father figure, and the embodiment of Yugoslav self-confidence, Rankovic continued to be viewed as a sinister character, the central focus of anti-Serb resentment, and the scourge of premature reformers.

As a foreign correspondent of the *Times*, based in Belgrade at the height of the Cold War, I soon realized that Yugoslavia was not, and could never become, a nation-state like France or Poland. The people made that clear to me in their fashion. They spoke of Rankovic as a Serb, first and last; Kardelj was forever a Slovene; Bakaric, a Croat; Djilas, a Montenegrin. Tito alone seemed to be identified in the public mind as somehow a Yugoslav.

I discovered another feature of life that seemed unique to Yugoslavia. Issues of politics or economics could never be discussed on their merits. They were always linked to ethnicity or, as Yugoslavs preferred to describe it, nationality. It was easy enough to discern the differences between so-called liberals and conservatives, although both terms seemed to me wildly inappropriate in the Yugoslav context. The liberals, I found, tended to be Slovenes or Croats whose ideas fell short of Jeffersonian democracy but who were suspicious of federal power. The conservatives, on the other hand, whether Serbs, Bosnians, or Macedonians, insisted on strict Leninist orthodoxy, with all significant decisions made at the federal level in Belgrade.

The divisive issues were chiefly economic: differences over investment policy, income distribution, the role and power of workers' councils, and the extent of continued reform. Through the 1960s, the most important single issue was investment policy: Who would rule on the competing claims of the federal government, the republics, local communes, and individual enterprises? But economic decisions in Yugoslavia could not be insulated from the powerful pull of ethnic rivalry. Slovenia and Croatia, the most prosperous and industrially advanced republics, nursed a grievance over money. Federal law demanded that they make what seemed to them excessive contributions to a fund for the economic development of the poorer republics in the south. This was a classic north-south issue, one that has bedeviled many other countries, including the United States as recently as the New Deal era. Croats and Slovenes, not all of them liberals, complained bitterly that many of these forced investments in distant regions were politically motivated. Everyone knew that "political factories" were being built in unlikely places, wasting a great deal of hard-earned northern money in the process.

Serbia, Rankovic's power base, argued for continued federal control of investment in the underdeveloped south. It made economic sense, the Serbs contended, to go on subsidizing new industries in the poorest regions of the country in order to make them more self-sufficient. Until that happy day, justice demanded that the richer northern republics should pay more than their fair share to the federal government, which in turn would distribute resources to the south. This struggle between the have and have-not republics has not yet been resolved. Then as now, Serbia was the center of the storm.

The Serbian conservatives, led by Rankovic, fought a series of battles within the party to preserve federal power in allocating resources and to stave off reform. They were defeated with the passage in 1963 of a new constitution that weakened central control. It greatly increased the powers·of local communes, enterprises, and other self-management bodies at Belgrade's expense. Two years later, again over the opposition of Rankovic and his conservative allies, a major reform program was enacted, stipulating that the market should be the chief mechanism governing the country's economic life. Taxes were cut, reducing the state's share of the net income of enterprises from 50 percent to 30 percent. Federal control of investment policy was rolled back, if not wholly abolished, and subsidies for failing industries were eliminated.

For Rankovic the 1965 reform was a crushing defeat. Tito had come down in favor of economic reform, and that would ordinarily have settled the matter. But the opposition continued to agitate the issue. Tito's response was to demand party unity in support of the agreed reform policy. He spoke of dark machinations by the "class enemy" within the party, a plain warning that heads would roll. Rather than fight Rankovic on arcane issues of economic policy, Tito shrewdly launched a secret investigation of the UDBa. In July 1966 he broke Rankovic in a single dramatic stroke. The country was shocked to learn that Rankovic had been stripped of his high positions and expelled from the party. A sweeping purge of his henchmen followed, amid disclosures that the UDBa had been rife with corruption, that it had brutally repressed the Albanian majority in Kossovo, that it had been used to frustrate reform and to build up Rankovic as a possible successor to Tito. Among other revelations of high-handed UDBa actions, the Yugoslav press reported that Rankovic had bugged Tito's private quarters.

Abuses of secret police power had been exposed a decade earlier in the Soviet Union and the rest of Eastern Europe. Now millions of Yugoslavs were pained to discover that their independent country had been infected with the same disease.

The banishment of Rankovic and the victory of reform changed the climate radically, though briefly. The central government's authority was seriously undermined. Local party organizations, long subservient, now dared to challenge decisions imposed from on high. The Yugoslav press developed a new liveliness, and the federal parliament showed signs of challenging traditional taboos. But the ethnic tensions and antagonisms, which had been expected to subside when the reform battle was won, soon reappeared in alarming forms. The most alarming of these was an unexpected crisis in the republic of Croatia.

The Croatian crisis of 1971 made instant nonsense of Tito's boast a few years earlier that "we have solved the national problem." Money was again at the heart of the dispute. Following the 1965 reform, federal banks had replaced the state as the main source of investment funds. When the banks turned out to be no more responsive to Croatian requests for credit than the federal government had been, many Croats found a ready explanation: the banks, after all, were in Belgrade, the Serbian capital. Even more galling was the fact that Croatia was required to hand over to the federal treasury a large part of the hard-currency income earned by the popularity of its long and beautiful Dalmatian coast among free-spending Western tourists. The Croats promptly demanded a new right for each of the republics to keep a much larger share of the foreign currencies it earned.

Emotions still ran high over the amount of investment funds Croatia had to provide for the less developed southern republics. This accumulation of grievances created a climate in which traditional Croatian nationalism reasserted itself, a trend the republican leadership felt powerless to overcome. Instead, it pressed for more constitutional changes designed further to dilute federal authority. Tito allowed matters to drift for many months as the nationalist passions soared to the point where, many Yugoslavs felt, the federal system was threatened. Only then, at the age of almost eighty, did Tito crack down. On December 1 he told the Croatian party leaders that his patience was at an end, and the following day, in a nationwide broadcast, he charged them with having pandered to nationalists and separatists. He even threatened to use armed force, and later disclosed that the Soviet Union had offered "help" in solving the Croatian problem. A purge of the Croatian leadership followed; more than four hundred nationalists were arrested, and Matica Hrvatska, a traditional cultural organization that had exploited the nationalist movement, was banned.

Throughout the Croatian crisis, Serbia had remained quiet and at peace under new leadership. Marko Nikezic, president of the Serbian party, and its secretary, Latinka Perovic, had scrupulously avoided any speech or action that might aggravate the age-old Serb-Croat antagonism. Nikezic, once Yugoslavia's foreign minister and earlier a highly regarded ambassador to the United States, showed promise of rising to the top one day. He had skillfully neutralized Rankovic's conservative and nationalist supporters by rejuvenating the party's Central Committee. He and Perovic were comparatively young, liberal in economic and political outlook, and were on speaking terms with alienated intellectuals and students. A Serb who could not be accused of seeking hegemony over other nationalities, Nikezic was already being mentioned as a thoroughly modern man who might well, in the fullness of time, move up to larger responsibilities.

For reasons that remain obscure, Tito decided otherwise. It has been suggested that he wanted to eliminate a potential liberal successor. Another theory is that, having cracked down on the Croatian leadership, he felt a need to even the score by purging the Serbian leadership as well. The case against Nikezic and Perovic, in any case, was less than compelling. They were accused of exaggerating the dangers of federal bureaucracy and the "firm hand" policy it exercised at Tito's behest; of encouraging too much freedom for "technocrats"; of encouraging the wrong sort of self-management; and of harboring unduly passive notions about the proper role of the Yugoslav party.

More solid reasons for Tito's desire to get rid of Nikezic have been suggested. As foreign minister, Nikezic was said to have questioned Tito's Middle Eastern policies, arguing that it was more important for Yugoslavia to establish close relations with the European Economic Community than to curry favor with Third World countries, and cautioning against closer ties with the Soviet Union. In Moscow he appears to have been viewed as anti-Soviet, a consideration that may have influenced Tito's decision.

In any event, Nikezic and Perovic were forced to resign, although Tito's purge ran into unexpected resistance from other Serb leaders whose obedience he had taken for granted. Tito had to press his demand a second time before the republican party heads reluctantly agreed that Nikezic must go. He retired prematurely to spend his days carving wood sculptures. There were other victims. Aleksandar Nenadovic, editor in chief of the respected Belgrade daily *Politika,* was eased out of his position in 1972 and expelled from the party. He was charged with being under "bourgeois influence" and a member of the "Nikezic faction." For these offenses, Nenadovic was to spend the next eight years as an anonymous employee of the paper he had once headed with uncommon distinction. Publication of his name in its columns was expressly forbidden. The whole episode demonstrated that, although Stalin was long dead and Yugoslavia free to go its own way, the disorder known as Stalinism was not extinct in Yugoslavia. In style if not always in substance, it lingered on.

So also does the nationality problem, notably in Slovenia, the smallest republic, and once again in Serbia, the largest. The new element is the charismatic leader of Serbia's Communist Party, Slobodan Milosevic. A former American ambassador who knew him well described Milosevic as the most popular Serbian leader since Nikezic. "I believe his ambitions go well beyond Serbia to national leadership," the diplomat told me. "When Milosevic talks to Westerners, he sounds like Adam Smith's best friend. He talks democracy, openness, no more backroom deals." But outside the diplomatic circle and beyond the borders of Serbia, Milosevic is more often described as an ambitious, bullying, rabble-rousing demagogue whose populist tactics may further fracture the divided country he seeks to dominate. "He has the makings of a dictator," an old friend remarked. "And the last thing this poor country needs is one more dictator."

A close aide said it was his own clear impression that Milosevic harbored a vaulting ambition, nothing less than to assume Tito's mantle. "I admit it's a high-risk policy," the aide added. The thought of Slobodan Milosevic coveting Marshal Tito's power and prestige is enough to chill the blood of millions in Croatia and Slovenia. The Milosevic phenomenon suggests to them a sinister design to turn the country — with its several languages, cultures, and religions — into a new Greater Serbia. Fear of Serbian domination has haunted many Yugoslavs since the state was founded in 1918 as the Kingdom of Serbs, Croats, and Slovenes.

But to the swelling crowds that have turned out for him in the streets and squares of Serbian cities and elsewhere, Milosevic is part savior, part avenger. They look to him to restore Serbia's primacy in Yugoslav affairs, blaming Tito for the Serbs' having been denied the power, after World War II, to which their numbers entitled them. Mobilizing vast street crowds, and igniting their Serb patriotism through flaming oratory, Milosevic has already managed to wrest constitutional changes from the federal establishment that returned the two autonomous provinces, Kossovo and Vojvodina, to Serbian control. Few Yugoslavs I met believed that Milosevic would be satisfied with these meager gains.

Milosevic has come a long way in very few years. He was born in 1941, four months after Hitler's armies invaded Yugoslavia. He studied law at the University of Belgrade and, in a spectacular display of upward mobility, raced through a succession of director-level positions to become the president of Beobank, the Bank of Belgrade. Joining the Serbian party hierarchy in 1982, he advanced swiftly and surefootedly. Within four years he became the party secretary for Belgrade, thanks in large part to the influence of his mentor and patron, Ivan Stambolic. When the two quarreled over the nationality issue, Milosevic staged a coup of sorts to oust Stambolic from the presidency of the Serbian republic. In 1987, Milosevic took over as head of the Serbian party.

In his speeches before adoring crowds, Milosevic plays variations on two highly emotional themes: the depressed state of the Serbian economy and the indignities that Kossovo's shrinking Serb minority claims to have suffered at the hands of the Albanian Moslem majority. In theory a province of Serbia but to all intents a mini-republic in its own right since the 1974 constitution was proclaimed, Kossovo reminds every Serb of ancient triumphs and tragedies. It was here, in what is now a poor southwestern enclave bordering on Albania, that Serbia's kings were crowned in the Middle Ages. Here also the kingdom lost its independence to the Turks in the notoriously bloody battle of Kossovo Polje in 1389. It was not until 1912 that Serbia reclaimed the Kossovo region and started to recolonize it. By that time Kossovo had a substantial population of Albanian Moslems, who were multiplying rapidly. According to the last Yugoslav census, in 1981, Serbs constituted barely 13 percent of Kossovo's population and were emigrating in large numbers to Serbia proper. The birthrate of Kossovo Albanians is the highest in Europe, nearly three times the Yugoslav average.

None of the Serbs I interviewed was able to explain how those demographic facts could be reversed by what Milosevic proudly calls his "policy of the hard hand." The Albanians, who constitute 77.5 percent of the Kossovo population, are angry and rebellious. They deeply resent accusations that the Serb emigration is being forced by Albanian knife attacks, rapes, and desecration of graveyards. The truth, they insist, is that Serbs are leaving because jobs are so scarce. Unemployment in Kossovo has risen to a level approaching 60 percent.

Milosevic has alarmed much of Yugoslavia by his tough talk and by the power he has mobilized in the streets, an extraordinarily populist approach to politics in a Communist-ruled state. But he enjoys idolatrous support in Serbia and to a considerable extent also in Macedonia and Montenegro. People talk admiringly of his remarkable presence of mind when, during a party meeting, a crowd of thousands pressing forward to listen was held back with police truncheons. "They are beating us," a voice in the crowd called out. Milosevic grabbed a microphone and stepped to a second-floor window, where he told the suddenly hushed crowd, "Nobody has a right to beat you. You will never again be beaten." The crowd below cheered. There is reason to doubt that it had ever heard a Communist leader defend the people from the police. That incident, which occurred in 1987, is already legend.

So also was a remarkable Belgrade rally, the following year, of 600,000 cheering, chanting Serbs, the biggest in Yugoslav history. "We will win the battle for Kossovo," Milosevic assured them. "We are not afraid of anything. The leaders will listen to the people — or time will sweep them away." This was the voice of a leader, not a cipher, people said afterward. A well-rehearsed group within the vast throng chanted, "With Slobodan to unity and freedom."

On issues other than Kossovo, however, Milosevic's views remain opaque. He talks frequently about "the market" as the cure for Yugoslavia's economic ills, but so does almost everyone else in the leadership. Yugoslavs have paid lip service to the idea of the market since the 1965 reform without doing much to encourage it. He has talked of abolishing barriers to trade among the six republics in order to create a single unified market. That would please economists like Professors Adamovic and Madzar, but few outside Serbia trust Milosevic to respect the autonomy of other republics. It is not difficult to find inherent contradictions between one Milosevic position and another. He promises, for example, to re-create a strong central party, and at the same time he advocates free-market economics. What useful role can a strong central party play, his critics ask, in a truly free market? Although many fear his unbridled ambition, and some

predict it will be his undoing, the need for radical change is
so apparent that an impressive number of intelligent citizens
have been slow to condemn him. Even Milovan Djilas, the
eternal dissident, and other Yugoslav intellectuals half-ad-
mire his effrontery.

I asked Djilas, who had spent nine years in Tito's jails, whether
he was troubled by the resurgence of narrow nationalism.
Yes and no, he replied. "The nationalism of party bureaucrats is bad, of course, but nationalism can also produce the
most dynamic form of liberalization, as in the case of Slovenia," he said. "One simply must differentiate." Djilas left
no doubt of his admiration for Milan Kucan, the Slovene
party leader, who advocates local autonomy, more pluralism
in politics, and more private enterprise in the economy. Under his leadership the Slovene party has encouraged considerable press freedom and "alternative movements," including a popular and growing group of environmentalists who,
as in Germany, call themselves Greens. Kucan also favors
official recognition of separate factions within the ruling
party. "Kucan and Milosevic," Djilas said, "are the most remarkable Yugoslav leaders today. The rest are gray creatures."

Dobrica Cosic also bracketed Milosevic and Kucan together in spite of their apparent differences on fundamental issues. "I'm not a supporter of Milosevic," Cosic said. "But
I must admit that he is more democratic than his predecessors; only he and Kucan warrant that description." Cosic,
nevertheless, acknowledged some reservations. He could not,
for example, condone the Milosevic crackdown in the summer of 1988 on *Politika,* the leading Serb daily, and on *NIN,*
a weekly news magazine published by *Politika,* which turned
both of these respected and widely read publications into
house organs for the Serbian party. A *Politika* editor told me
that, although the paper's international coverage has not been

affected, its domestic coverage is essentially a propaganda outlet for Milosevic.

There is evidence that Milosevic's alienation of many leading journalists does not extend to Serb intellectuals. He seems, in fact, to be cultivating their favor. Svetozar Stojanovic, a philosopher who lost his job at the University of Belgrade in 1975 for advocating what he calls Marxist humanism, told me that Milosevic has talked of seeking reinstatement for all eight of the professors then fired. "He wants the intelligentsia on his side," Stojanovic said. Another member of the Belgrade Eight, Mihajlo Markovic, said he was troubled by the turmoil over Serb nationalism, though he did not feel unfriendly toward Milosevic. The need exists, he said, to reverse an old Comintern policy, dating from Stalin's time, which had influenced Tito to build up the smaller republics as a way of containing Serbia. Professor Markovic was anything but hopeful. "Either each group will go its own way to solve its problems, or Yugoslavia will disintegrate," he said. "In the current climate, it is hard to imagine achieving the necessary unanimity for reforms that would make Yugoslavia viable again."

Disintegration is not the preferred option of any Yugoslav I met, but in present conditions it is no longer unthinkable. If the political process should collapse, the armed forces would almost certainly intervene. Their leaders have already warned the politicians that the army will not stand by idly if the party should tear itself and the country apart. At a meeting of the federal Central Committee in January 1989, Admiral Petar Simic said it bluntly: "The military will confront with all its power and means anyone who wants to play dangerous games with the achievements of our liberation struggle and our socialist revolution. If someone has declared a battle for Yugoslavia, it will not be fought without the Yugoslav Liberation Army and millions of working people who have Yugoslavia more at heart than certain blinded and bureaucratically numbed groups of individuals hungry for power . . ."

That kind of talk from a military leader has not been heard before in Yugoslavia. The admiral doubtless had one or more specific targets in mind, but he left the Central Committee guessing.

# PART II

# 8

## *History's Heavy Burden*

Mieczyslaw Rakowski, prime minister of Poland for less than a year and more recently chief of its Communist Party, knew nothing about Marxism when he joined the party in 1945 at the age of eighteen. "What attracted me," he said in a published interview, "were the slogans about equality and land reform . . . I had no idea that we were an ideological minority." That the Marxists remain a despised minority to this day was demonstrated emphatically in June 1989, when Rakowski, along with dozens of others, lost his seat in the parliament, even though he ran unopposed.

"Naturally, we Marxists or leftists are the minority," he said. "Poland is Catholic, though I cannot equate its Catholicism with the [popular] revulsion against the system." Asked by the interviewer to explain Poland's crisis-dogged postwar history, Rakowski said it would have been unrealistic to expect smooth, straight-line progress in a poor country that for more than forty years had been trying to transform its social, political, and economic structure. "We were a peasant people," he said, "by nature conservative, technically underdeveloped, destroyed by war; and beyond all that there was the ancient tradition that Poles govern themselves badly."

That tradition was not uniquely Polish. Enlightened self-government had not been the hallmark of Eastern European societies between the world wars or earlier. Romania and Bulgaria were something less than islands of democracy in the Balkans. East Germany, an integral part of Hitler's Third Reich, had its brief and rather unhappy experience of democracy during the Weimar Republic. Hungary under Admiral Nicholas Horthy had endured a succession of more or less oppressive right-wing regimes. Czechoslovakia alone prospered in freedom for two decades, only to be crushed and dismembered on Hitler's orders while Great Britain and France looked the other way.

The Communist parties of Eastern Europe, each a small minority at the time, owed their installation in power to the historical fact that Stalin's armies had overrun their countries in pursuit of the retreating German armies, rather than to their own revolutionary successes. There was no revolution worthy of the name in Poland, Hungary, Czechoslovakia, Romania, Bulgaria, or Germany. Although the conditions were not identical, Soviet military power and shrewdly manipulated political pressures were sufficiently persuasive to allow trusted Communists to be put in control of key government ministries. That was the indispensable first step toward the eventual consolidation of state power in Communist hands. Only in Yugoslavia, under the leadership of Tito, and in Albania did Communists succeed in taking over a country largely through their own efforts.

The Yugoslavs paid a cruel price for their national liberation. More than two million lost their lives, close to half of them in a civil war between Tito's Partisans and the rival guerrilla force, the Chetniks, led by General Mihajlovic. For Tito it was a war within a war, more precisely two concurrent wars with separate goals: to discredit and defeat Mihajlovic, who supported King Peter, and to harry and attack the occupation forces of Nazi Germany and Fascist Italy. Tito won the civil war, thanks in no small part to Winston

Churchill's determination that Mihajlovic, who had been receiving Allied support, was making local accommodations with the Germans and saving his strength for the climactic struggle against the Communist-led Partisans. At the Teheran conference in November 1943, Churchill, Roosevelt, and Stalin agreed to shift Allied support to Tito on the ground that his Partisans were more actively fighting the Germans. By the summer of 1944, the Partisans were receiving as much as six thousand tons of military equipment a month from the West, much of it by parachute.

Tito was exceptional in another crucial respect. Although he had spent several years in Moscow during the mid-1930s, working for the Comintern and living at the Hotel Lux with other Communist exiles, he returned to Yugoslavia in time to organize and eventually command the armed Partisan resistance to the hated German and Italian invaders. That bloody struggle won him control of the country, worldwide recognition as a war leader, and new credentials, rare among Communist functionaries, as a patriot. No such claim could be advanced in behalf of the "Muscovites" elsewhere in Eastern Europe — Matyas Rakosi and Erno Gero, for example, in Hungary, Ana Pauker in Romania, Walter Ulbricht in Germany, or Boleslaw Bierut and Jakub Berman in Poland — who returned under the protection of the Red Army as Stalin's surrogates. Installed in power by their Soviet patrons and schooled in the tenets of Marxism-Leninism-Stalinism, they set about creating replicas in miniature of the harsh system Stalin had imposed on the Soviet Union. Their first order of business was to intimidate, divide, and destroy the last remnants of prewar non-Communist parties. That process was completed by 1948. In the case of Poland, a tiny minority of Communists who had somehow survived Stalin's liquidation of the prewar party, in which five thousand activists were executed, soon found themselves subordinated to an assortment of real and counterfeit Poles, many of them Soviet citizens and all operating under Moscow's discipline.

The party's ranks swelled rapidly in the early postwar years, reaching one million in 1948 and approaching three million by 1980, some 12 percent of the adult population. Many, like the young Rakowski, were drawn by the promise of a new, classless society; others, by ambition to get ahead, that is, by opportunism. Overwhelmingly, they were ambitious sons and daughters of peasants, who saw in the party the chance of education and social advancement.

Much the same pattern could be observed in other East European countries. Party membership had become the indispensable key to a better life: a job with a future, an apartment, admission to a university, ultimate access to the powers and privileges reserved for the Communist hierarchy. The fact that 12 percent of adult Poles joined the party at its peak strikes me as less remarkable than the other side of the coin — that 88 percent did not respond to these seductions.

Ancient nations like Poland, repeatedly partitioned at the hands of Russians, Germans, and Austrians, or Magyars, Czechs, Slovaks, and others long ruled by Ottoman Turkey or imperial Austria, once again became subject peoples of a foreign empire. In the West they were known as "satellites" of the Soviet Union or, less delicately, as "captive nations." Insulting terms, protested the new leaders hoisted into power by the Soviets. But their behavior over the decades left no doubt that their first allegiance was to the Soviet Union, the "socialist motherland," in the name of the doctrine of "proletarian internationalism."

At the heart of that doctrine was the implied threat of armed force to compel ideological conformity. Leonid Brezhnev, third in the line of Stalin's successors, plainly invoked that threat in browbeating the Communist leaders of

Czechoslovakia before the tanks rolled into Prague on August 21, 1968. "Your country is in the region occupied by Soviet soldiers in World War II," he said. "We paid for this great sacrifice and we will never leave. Your borders are our borders. You do not follow our suggestions and we feel threatened . . . We are completely justified in sending our soldiers to your country to be secure within our borders." Send them he did, without shame or embarrassment.

A few months after the invasion, Brezhnev laid down a retroactive justification in a speech before the congress of the Polish Communist Party: it was the duty of the Soviet Union and its Warsaw Pact allies to intervene, with whatever means they deemed necessary, whenever and wherever a ruling Communist Party was in danger of being overthrown by its own people. The rule of any Communist Party, in short, was irreversible. *Pravda* explained that neither considerations of state sovereignty or international law nor the principle of self-determination of peoples could stand in the way of armed suppression once a Communist-ruled country dared to depart from "socialism" as defined by the Kremlin.

No such doctrine had been proclaimed in 1956, when Hungarians revolted against Stalinism, and Prime Minister Imre Nagy announced that his country was quitting the Warsaw Pact. In justification of its resort to armed force, the Soviet Union later branded the uprising a counterrevolution, adding that Nagy had lost control of events and that "honest Communists" were being murdered in the streets of Budapest. This tortured rationale was based on the Leninist dogma that Communist rule, once established, could never be reversed. The legitimacy of such a regime rested on the revolution that brought it to power. The awkward fact that no such revolution had taken place in Hungary, or elsewhere in Eastern Europe, with the exception of Yugoslavia and Albania, did not embarrass the party ideologues. In country after country, they had taken the precaution of fabricating revolutionary myths to satisfy the ideological requirement.

None of Moscow's criteria for armed intervention in Hungary was in any sense relevant to Czechoslovakia in 1968. Alexander Dubcek's regime of Communist reformers had not lost control of events. Communists were not being murdered in the streets of Prague or Bratislava. Dubcek had no intention of quitting the Warsaw Pact, and there was no threat of power being captured by anti-Communist parties.

In search of a more persuasive rationalization, Moscow floated a number of vague, unsubstantiated charges: the Communist Party under Dubcek had degenerated into a "discussion club"; "antisocialist and revisionist forces" were in control of the Czechoslovak media; and Prague had been "flirting" with West Germany. Called to Moscow after the invasion, Dubcek refuted these accusations. He pleaded with the Kremlin leaders to understand that the changes his regime had introduced were transforming Communism for the benefit of the Soviet Union as well as his own country. On the contrary, Brezhnev replied; Dubcek must understand that what the Communist Party had done in Czechoslovakia was to threaten the very existence of socialism, and this the Soviet Union would not tolerate.

The Brezhnev doctrine can be seen in retrospect as an effort to codify an all-purpose justification for armed Soviet intervention against any Communist-ruled country that allowed its people freedoms the Kremlin might find excessive or repugnant. Mikhail Gorbachev, who did not shrink from blaming Brezhnev for the stagnant state of the Soviet economy, the spread of corrupt practices, and unspecified abuses of power, hesitated to repudiate the doctrine bearing his name. To have done so would almost certainly have strengthened his opponents by inviting bitter accusations that he was abandoning the European empire, a highly emotional issue for many Soviet citizens. Unrepudiated, however, the Brezhnev doctrine could only be an embarrassment for Gorbachev in his relations with Eastern Europe. On the one hand, he was urging the party leadership of each country in the bloc to institute reforms. On the other hand, the doctrine remained a stern warning against letting reform and innovation go too far. How far was too far? Nobody I met in Eastern Europe during the summer of 1988 had the answer.

The weather map of Europe, as a general rule, shows storm systems beating across the continent from west to east. In the same way, lines of political influence have tended to follow an eastward track. Like a good many other recipes for change, the idea of social revolution was born in the West, primarily in France and Germany, not in the Russia of the tsars. It was two Germans, Karl Marx and Friedrich Engels, who in 1848 issued their *Communist Manifesto,* summoning the working class to revolutionary action: "The proletarians have nothing to lose but their chains. They have a world to win. Workingmen of all countries, unite!" They could not have foreseen that the first Communist revolution would take place in Russia, a vast feudal country of peasants and landlords, with little modern industry and only a small middle class.

Marx and Engels had another part of Europe in mind. They prophesied that social revolutions would erupt in highly developed capitalist countries like Germany and Britain. Only in these countries did the necessary conditions for revolution exist, Marx argued, and the most important of these was the presence of a large working class that would be capable of seizing power. He believed that socialist revolution, once launched, would quickly spread through the capitalist world and that it would be an international revolution. If not, the capitalist powers would throttle it.

Born in Trier on the Moselle River, Marx had studied law in Bonn and philosophy at the University of Berlin soon after the death of Georg Wilhelm Friedrich Hegel, the great German philosopher. While sharply critical of Hegel's ideas for the most part, Marx adapted some of them in line with his own thinking about the role of the working class in changing society. He came to believe that just as the rising middle class had broken the grip of feudalism, so the proletariat, in turn, under the leadership of dedicated revolutionaries, would triumph over the bourgeoisie.

But because the proletariat (as Marx recognized) was not yet prepared to lead a communist society, the revolutionaries would have to use the coercive powers of the state to establish and defend the new order through a dictatorship. Ultimately, Marx wrote, the last remnants of bourgeois rule and property would be eliminated. The state would then wither away, leaving the people happy and content in a truly free, truly communist society, where the exploitation of the poor by the rich and powerful had been forever abolished. Wisely, Marx did not specify the year, or the century, in which his prophecy would find fulfillment.

Across Western Europe, his messianic vision fired the imagination of millions. Intellectuals wrote feverish tracts about the new heaven on earth foretold by Marx and Engels. Militant workers marched behind red banners, organized strikes, and clashed with police during the late nineteenth and early twentieth centuries in the cause of Marxist revolution. But they failed to capture and hold power anywhere — except, improbably, in Russia. In that unhappy country, Lenin's Bolsheviks triumphed over the ramshackle tsarist system through three bloody years of revolution and civil war. The new Soviet state, far from withering away, armed itself with totalitarian powers and, after defeating Hitler's invading armies in World War II, imposed virtually identical dictatorships on the countries of Central and Eastern Europe as the Red Army advanced westward to the line of the Elbe River in Germany. Marx, who died in 1883, would not have been pleased by that outcome. He detested imperialism, above all the imperial Russia of the tsars. His dictum that "no nation can be free so long as it oppresses other nations" was shrugged off in the Soviet Union as applying only to Western imperialism.

After the breaks with Yugoslavia in 1948 and Albania in 1961, Stalin's European empire remained intact. But the monolith showed signs of erosion. Nationalistic fervor, long insulted by the Kremlin's heavy-handed insistence that the subject nations must emulate the Soviet model regardless of local needs and conditions, expressed itself throughout the region.

"History is alive and well in the area," a United States official remarked. Communist regimes in Eastern Europe were always aware that nations need heroes, but until recently they tended to stress those aspects of their national traditions which could be depicted as safely "progressive." Then several of them bent the rule to rehabilitate, or to assess more favorably, the reputations of historic figures long officially execrated or ignored. As we have seen, the East Germans restored Frederick the Great and Martin Luther, even Otto von Bismarck, to their niches in the national pantheon. In Czechoslovakia, the Communist press rediscovered the patriotic virtues of Thomas Masaryk, founder and first president of the republic, after some four decades of silence. In Poland, thanks in large part to Solidarity's efforts, several chapters of national history were reopened — among them the Katyn massacre, the Warsaw Uprising, and the role of Jozef Pilsudski, who was chief of state from 1919 to 1922 and the virtual dictator of Poland from 1926 until his death in 1935. Few Poles I met could resist the satisfaction of recalling that Pilsudski, a general as well as a politician, had defeated the Red Army at the gates of Warsaw in 1920, forcing Lenin (who had expected the people to welcome his troops) to sue for peace.

History is also at the root of disputes, no longer secret, among several countries of the bloc. A cold war flared between Hungary and Romania over the fate of the large Magyar minority in Transylvania, a region that changed hands three times since the end of World War I. When the United Nations Commission on Human Rights took up the case in 1989, it condemned Romania's government for "serious violations of human rights and fundamental freedoms" by a vote of twenty-one to seven, with ten abstentions. The Soviet Union, preferring not to be seen as taking sides between two Communist-ruled countries, was among the abstainers. Hungary, which joined with several Western countries in sponsoring the resolution, naturally voted for it. The voting in Geneva broke two precedents. For the first time, one Communist government voted to condemn another. It was also the first time that the Soviet Union failed to vote against a resolution censuring another East bloc country.

Poland and the Soviet Union are at odds over what both call the "blank spots" in their relations dating back to World War II. The Soviets have yet to accept responsibility for the mass killing in 1940 of Polish officers in the Katyn Forest, and the government in Warsaw now agrees with the rest of the population that the evidence of Soviet guilt is overwhelming. Another blank spot dates from the Warsaw Uprising in the summer of 1944, when the Red Army sat passively in the suburb of Praga on the far bank of the Vistula River while Polish insurgents, heavily outnumbered and outgunned by the Germans, fought a doomed sixty-two-day battle to liberate their capital.

Bulgaria shocked many East Europeans by forcing its Turkish minority to adopt Slavic names in a campaign of compulsory assimilation. Its age-old dispute with Yugoslavia over Macedonia remains unresolved. Poland and East Germany, meanwhile, are caught up in a squabble over maritime boundaries.

The emergence of long-repressed nationalist issues became a significant divisive element in the relations among members of the "socialist camp," not a state of affairs that Stalin would likely have tolerated for very long. Gorbachev's silence on these matters could doubtless be traced to his preoccupation with nationality issues at home — in Soviet Armenia, Azerbaijan, Georgia, the Baltic states, and the Ukraine. It could also be read as a sign of indecision about how harshly he could afford to deal with problems of this sort. As various Soviet commentators have written, the time for giving "fraternal advice" is past.

Another category of change, also rooted in history, concerns marked disparities in the levels of economic and social development within the bloc. These disparities existed long before Communist regimes were installed in Eastern Europe, and they have widened in recent years. The Czech lands of Bohemia and Moravia, for example, were far more advanced in industry and agriculture than prewar or postwar Bulgaria. Western Poland, which belonged to Germany until 1945, was a long way ahead of Romania then, and remains ahead today. Charles Gati of Columbia University and Union College estimates that the roughly equivalent living standards of East Germany and Hungary are twice those of Bulgaria and Romania. He puts the average living standard for Eastern Europe as a whole at no less than a third higher than the Soviet standard.

Although the countries of Eastern Europe started with more or less identical political systems after 1948, they remained distinctly different in language, culture, and tradition, and different also in terms of job skills, industrial development, and natural resources. All the countries of the region were on a rapid-growth curve in the 1950s and 1960s. World markets were less competitive then, and the Soviet Union was still willing to deliver scarce raw materials in exchange for frequently shoddy industrial goods. But economic growth slowed in the 1980s, and life became more difficult for most people as governments started to raise rents and the prices of basic foods by canceling or reducing state subsidies.

In the realm of ideology, the Soviet bloc witnessed a strange reversal of roles. Moscow, for decades past the guardian and enforcer of ideological purity, was carrying the banner of reform while four of its Warsaw Pact allies clung to the old, discredited orthodoxies. The leaders of Czechoslovakia, Bulgaria, Romania, and East Germany wanted no part of the reform process under way in the Soviet Union, Hungary, and Poland.

Toward the end of 1988, Erich Honecker's old-guard regime in East Berlin, which used to make a state secret of its occasional differences with the Kremlin, was provoked into open criticism. The immediate cause, though not perhaps the only one, was the publication in *Sputnik,* a Soviet press review, of several historical articles accusing Stalin of collusion with Hitler in the 1930s. One article carried the headline WOULD HITLER HAVE BEEN POSSIBLE WITHOUT STALIN? It depicted the prewar policies of Stalin — and of the German Communist Party, acting on his orders — as a series of tragic blunders that helped Hitler capture power in 1933. That struck at the heart of the official East German myth that the Communist Party of then-undivided Germany bore no responsibility for Hitler's rise. *Sputnik* exposed that myth by recalling that the obedient German party had rejected cooperation with the Social Democrats to overcome the looming Nazi danger, in line with Stalin's theory of "social fascism." According to that dictum, the Social Democrats, not the Nazis, were the main enemy of the German working class.

For Honecker, who had spent ten years as a prisoner of the Nazis, that was too much. He promptly banned the German-language edition of *Sputnik,* along with five Soviet films, and publicly berated Moscow for propagating an unseemly revision of history (as it was taught in the GDR) by "bourgeois types gone wild." The German Democratic Republic, he insisted, was not about to change course at Moscow's bidding and join a "march to anarchy." His reference to anarchy suggested a warning against the reforms under way in the Soviet Union, Poland, and Hungary.

After that turning point, East German party officials and publications did not hesitate to attack the reformist parties for abandoning the true principles of socialism. The attacks concentrated on the meager results of economic reform in all three countries, their efforts to redefine socialism and to experiment with limited political pluralism, all ideas that bordered on heresy.

Otto Reinhold, director of the East German Central Committee's Academy of Social Sciences, scoffed at the leaderships in Poland and Hungary for allowing talk about power sharing. The term "political pluralism," Reinhold said in 1989, had long been used by bourgeois politicians to signify "the existence of antisocialist, oppositional ideas and organizations," and that kind of thing would not be allowed in East Germany.

Reinhold made the case against political and economic reforms on the Gorbachev model rather bluntly in a speech before an audience of teachers. His tone was boastful, contrasting East Germany's "dynamic development of both economy and society" over the past decade with the acknowledged stagnation in the Soviet Union. His plain implication was that East Germans had nothing to learn from Russians or Hungarians about how to manage a modern economy. Reinhold also attacked the Hungarian argument that restructuring the economy would necessarily involve transitional unemployment. "Socialism and unemployment are not compatible," he said.

As for *glasnost,* which Reinhold translated crudely as openness to Western influences, East Germany had lived with it from the beginning, he said, owing to its location "directly on the dividing line between the two social systems, the two military alliances, on the most sensitive border in the world." According to Reinhold, that meant resisting the seductions of the rich Federal Republic on the far side of the wall and the daily output of foreign radio and television stations. "There is no other socialist country," he said, "that had to create a socialist society under such open conditions." Published accounts of Reinhold's speech made no mention of openness in the domestic context, that is, freedom for East German citizens to voice dissenting opinions.

The Hungarians, disheartened by the stubborn hard line of the East Germans against far-reaching reforms, answered back. Reszo Nyers, head of the Hungarian party presidium and the guiding spirit of its New Economic Mechanism (NEM) in 1968, complained in an interview that the stalling tactics of East Germany and Romania were making it impossible for the bloc's Council of Mutual Economic Assistance (CMEA, or COMECON, as it is better known in the West) to move forward with agreed-upon changes in the way it conducted business. The Hungarian government newspaper, *Magyar Nemzet,* followed up with an editorial criticizing unnamed Soviet bloc countries that continued to resist or reject reforms.

Lest any reader remain in doubt about the identity of its target, the newspaper mentioned a country where "they are dissociating themselves from *perestroika* and standing up in defense of the symbol of European division" — an unmistakable reference to Erich Honecker's Berlin Wall.

The erosion of ideological unity did not at first shatter the Soviet bloc. The command structure of the Warsaw Pact was intact, and the Soviet Union continued to exert its powerful controls over the national military establishments of Eastern Europe. In a matter of hours after Moscow announced that it would withdraw six tank divisions from East Germany, Czechoslovakia, and Hungary, all the bloc countries except Romania announced their own marginal reductions in troop levels and military spending.

The mutual fear of war that, in the words of John Foster Dulles a generation ago, is "the cement that holds [an] alliance together" has receded on both sides of the East-West fault line. The fact that it was Gorbachev who initiated these symbolic reductions was bound to undercut the time-worn Communist propaganda line that, over four decades, justified the severity of life among the subject peoples by repeatedly raising fears of an imminent NATO attack. I talked with scores of East Europeans in six countries over a three-month period, and the fear of war was mentioned exactly twice, each time by an East German party official.

Thomas W. Simons, Jr., a perceptive American diplomat, said: "This lifting consciousness of imminent danger may be a management problem for both alliance systems, but it certainly provides more margin for maneuver for East European countries . . . The benefits of orthodoxy and centralization are just not self-explanatory when the Cold War lifts . . . Lifting the black cloud of the Cold War produces political debate in Communist countries, which starts with details and sometimes goes on to fundamentals."

One such fundamental institution is COMECON, whose grandiose plan to create an East European common market is wallowing in heavy seas. Its prospect of success appears remote as long as the decision makers remain divided over the need to reform its ramshackle structures and procedures. COMECON's efforts to promote joint ventures within the bloc and to develop a rational division of labor among its member states have done little to make East European products more marketable in the rest of the world. As a result, Hungary, Poland, and Czechoslovakia, which need to increase their hard-currency earnings in order to pay for imported technology, see more advantage in joint ventures with Western companies.

Other basic premises of Communism — the "leading role" of a single party, central planning, and state ownership of the means of production — were being questioned in the present crisis. The theoreticians of reform in Moscow, Budapest, and Warsaw tried to confine change within strict limits. They sought to adapt the system so that it could survive changing conditions, and they did not see themselves as the gravediggers of Communism.

In late 1988, then Vice President George Bush asked Gorbachev to assess the prospects for the success of *perestroika*. The Soviet leader replied, "Even Jesus Christ couldn't answer that question." Here was a statesman who had stood up to the Red Army marshals by cutting the military budget, allowed Soviet voters a degree of choice in electing a new legislature, canceled the special privileges of millions of bureaucrats and managers, and repudiated the failed agricultural system over which he used to preside. He also promised *"demokratizatziya"* and vowed to make the leadership more accountable to the people. Yet he has continued to speak of the Communist Party's "irreplaceable role," as if nothing had changed or could change. Looking back on the experience of restructuring, he concluded that the Soviet Union was now "in even greater need of a theoretically, ideologically, and organizationally strong party." These inherent contradictions recalled the famous dictum of the first Henry Ford that car buyers could have any color they wanted as long as it was black.

The choices are somewhat wider in Poland, though again within prescribed limits. Three months in advance of their June 1989 election, Polish voters were told that, regardless of the actual numbers, Solidarity candidates could win no more than 35 percent of the seats. The Communists were assuring themselves of a majority no matter what the voters decided. In Hungary, the party leader used more subtle methods. They sounded positively eager to share power with non-Communist parties. "We're getting rid of the model we have used up to now," said Janos Berecz, then a Politburo member in charge of ideology. "We're not the only ones with brains or answers." A new constitution was drafted, providing for competing parties and civil rights.

New opposition groups, such as the Democratic Forum, are expected to run candidate slates, offering an alternative to the Communists for the first time in forty-five years. Thus, in Hungary as in Poland, opposition parties look forward to a transition from one-party rule to some semblance of political pluralism — assuming, of course, that there is no political upheaval to set back the clock of reform and national reconciliation. Free multiparty elections in 1990 were also in prospect for East Germany and Czechoslovakia after the peaceful revolutions that toppled Honecker in East Berlin and Jakes in Czechoslovakia the previous autumn.

There is also open discussion in Budapest of Hungary's seeking membership in the European Economic Community and some hopeful talk that observer status in the European Parliament at Strasbourg can be negotiated. More than one Soviet official has made it known that Moscow would not take a tragic view of a Hungarian move toward closer relations with Western Europe. Oleg Bogomolov, a Gorbachev adviser, is said to have passed the word that even "a neutral Hungary would constitute no threat to the Soviet

Union." Bearing in mind the tragic fate of Imre Nagy, Hungarian leaders are not eager to test that assurance. Some have argued that even if Hungary should contemplate neutrality in the uncertain future, that would not imply leaving the Warsaw Pact. "There is no question of leaving the system of alliances to which we belong," said the vice minister for foreign affairs. But neutrality on the model accepted by neighboring Austria strongly appeals to many, perhaps most, Hungarians, even if it defies conventional logic to suppose that any country can be neutral and at the same time belong to a military alliance.

In the Soviet Union, meanwhile, Gorbachev engineered a general election that, for the first time in seven decades, allowed most voters a choice among competing candidates. One third of the 2250 seats in the newly formed Congress of People's Deputies were prudently reserved for nominees of official organizations. The general public had a choice among almost 2900 candidates to fill the remaining 1500 seats, certainly an extraordinary event by Soviet standards — if hardly revolutionary. The political monopoly of the Communist Party, nevertheless, did not come into question. Nine of every ten candidates turned out to be members of the party or the Communist Youth League. Although the multiplicity of candidates attracted worldwide attention, the reformist leaders of the Soviet Union evidently were not prepared in 1989 to follow the Hungarian and Polish examples in contemplating multiparty politics.

Yugoslavia, in fact, was the first Communist-ruled country to experiment with multicandidate elections; it did so as far back as 1958. The outcome was somewhat farcical, although it seemed newsworthy at the time that more than one candidate had been nominated in six of 301 electoral districts. I visited one such district in Eastern Slavonia to meet the candidates. There were two of them, both in their early thirties and both endorsed by the Socialist Alliance, the transmission-belt organization controlled by Tito's Communist Party. One wore a sober blue business suit, the other a chocolate-brown zipper jacket. In other respects it was impossible to tell them apart.

Mirko Lackovic, the man in the blue suit, did most of the talking. His rival, Bosko Vuletin in brown, seemed content to nod approval. "We are both children of the revolution," Lackovic explained. Vuletin nodded. "We go together to all the political meetings in the district and we agree beforehand what each of us will talk about," Lackovic continued. Again, Vuletin nodded approval. "The voters are free to decide whether Bosko or I will be more effective in carrying out our common program," Lackovic said. This time Vuletin found his tongue. "I agree with Comrade Lackovic," he said, and so it went. Lackovic won.

If that naïve Yugoslav experiment with bogus pluralism came to nought, Gorbachev's carefully managed election in the Soviet Union pushed to the surface a number of issues that would have been regarded as seditious just a few years earlier. The campaign brought forth demands seldom if ever heard in public — for expanded political and economic freedoms, less central control by the Moscow bureaucracy, drastic legal reforms, improved food supply, more and better housing, and in one case veto power for local authorities over state industries that are ecologically harmful. There was even a campaign proposal that would have explicitly subordinated the Communist Party to the Soviet constitution, thus striking at the party's "leading role" in society. The more startling fact was that, given a choice between reform advocates and local party potentates, the citizens voted for the reformers in dozens of districts, turning away among others the party boss of Leningrad and an impressive number of military commanders. Clearly, the election tapped a vast pool of citizen anger over existing conditions that was directed

against certain identifiably conservative members of the ruling *apparat.*

The outcome had its inevitable effect in the Soviet empire. It heartened and emboldened reformers to go on
pressing for further change, not only in Hungary and Poland, where the process was under way, but also in Czechoslovakia and East Germany, where hard-line leaders were
making few concessions to the new climate. The entrenched
leaders in these countries doubtless congratulated themselves on their wisdom in having denied even a limited choice
to their people. But they could take no lasting comfort from
the election results in the Soviet Union. Sooner or later, they
should have realized, their time would come.

# 9

## *The Troubled Command Economy*

JAN WINIECKI, a Polish economist, remembers standing in a crowded ice cream parlor in Warsaw with an American guest. The American, impressed by the size of the crowd, remarked that he could imagine how much more crowded the place would be after working hours. Wrong, said Winiecki. The place would be half empty after hours as the crowd drifted off to go home or to join a queue elsewhere. The visitor's natural though mistaken assumption was that in Poland, as in the United States, people worked during working hours. Not necessarily, Winiecki said. In a centrally planned economy plagued by perpetual shortages, he explained, there is little incentive for serious work. Shopping for goods in short supply takes priority in and out of working hours. It's a situation characteristic of command economies, whether in Poland, Czechoslovakia, or the Soviet Union.

In the command economy the state owns all natural resources and virtually all forms of capital — land, buildings, machinery, equipment, and most factories or workshops. The state also owns and operates all branches of industry — mining, construction, media, transportation, wholesale trade, most retail trade, the educational system, hospitals, and clinics. It is a system in deep trouble. I recall the embarrassment of a Yugoslav friend who lives in a shabby high-rise apart-

ment block fifteen minutes from downtown Belgrade. "You
see how we live," he said, pointing to the bare ground surrounding his building, the dying trees that someone had
planted, then forgotten, and the unsightly gouges in the walls
of the unswept lobby. "When the state owns everything," he
said, "nobody is responsible for keeping things in repair."
True, I agreed, though equally true of public housing projects in the United States. "Of course," my friend replied,
"but here it is not only the underclass that lives in public
housing. We all do."

The command economy, an all-embracing system of control and management modeled on Stalin's Russia, was imposed throughout Eastern Europe at the end of World War
II. The fact that it works badly, and is deeply resented by
the people, has been common knowledge for many years. It
is a system based on "illogic," according to Winiecki, a professor at the Institute for Labor Research in Warsaw. In a
recent book, *The Distorted World of Soviet-Type Economies,* he
argues that enormous waste is an inescapable characteristic
of centrally planned economies — a system in which most
statistics are false, cheating is endemic, and there is little incentive for managers to make rational decisions.

Behavior that would seem irrational in a market economy
is regarded as entirely rational in a system of central planning. A factory manager, for example, is being rational when
he disregards the poor quality of its output if that serves to
fulfill his assigned production quota. He can earn a bonus
by meeting or exceeding the quota, not by turning out products of higher quality. It is also advantageous for a manager
to hoard unused resources (labor, materials, even plant capacity). Because the central authorities are willing to subsidize losses more or less indefinitely, there is no incentive for
managers to practice financial responsibility.

Another characteristic of the Stalinist model, most visible
in East Germany, Poland, Hungary, and Czechoslovakia, is

the vast amount of scarce capital invested in heavy industry. The Czechoslovak economist Valtr Komarek estimated that heavy industry in his country "swallows up half and more [of the] productive resources of industry as a whole," including capital, energy, and imports. "The difference in the productivity of labor and in aggregate efficiency between the developed capitalist countries and Czechoslovakia," he said, "continues to widen to our disadvantage."

The obligatory emphasis on heavy industry has inevitably increased Eastern Europe's dependence on the Soviet Union, the region's main supplier of oil, natural gas, and iron ore. The region, generally speaking, lacks many of the natural resources that are essential to industrialization, except for Polish coal and Romania's dwindling petroleum reserves. It also lags far behind Western Europe in technological development, with an industrial plant that is to a large extent obsolete or obsolescent. Even more than the Soviet Union, Eastern Europe needs and wants closer economic ties with the West in order to acquire the modern technologies without which its products have no real prospect of competing in world markets. To reduce waste and strengthen their competitive position, many economists acknowledge, the East bloc countries must begin to dismantle their command economies.

Much the same prospect confronts the Soviet Union in the age of Gorbachev. His senior economic adviser, Abel Aganbegyan, has disclosed the long-hidden fact that Soviet national income did not grow at all between 1981 and 1985. Other Soviet economists, emboldened by the new climate of openness, revealed that per capita output in the mid-1980s fell slightly below the level of ten years earlier. It is also no longer a secret, though strenuously denied in the past, that the Soviet Union has been running huge budget deficits for a good many years and that inflation is not, after all, a plague peculiar to capitalist economies. In short, the command economy is in trouble not only in Eastern Europe but in the Soviet Union itself.

Although the peoples of Eastern Europe do a lot of complaining about their lot, they live better on the average than citizens of the Soviet Union. One index of the disparity is the impressive number of Soviet day-trippers who arrive by the busload every day in neighboring Hungary and Czechoslovakia to load up on food, clothing, shoes, kitchen utensils, and other consumer items that are less available or more expensive at home. The Soviet poet Yevgeny Yevtushenko has described the ordeal of the Soviet shopper as an endless series of humiliations. In a brief, bitter essay published in *Literaturnaya Gazeta,* Yevtushenko excoriated his countrymen for their "servile patience": "We humiliate ourselves in stores, beauty parlors, tailor shops, dry cleaners, car repair garages, restaurants, hotels, box offices, and [airline] counters, repair shops for TVs, refrigerators, and sewing machines . . . We spend all our time trying to get something. It's humiliating that we still can't feed ourselves, having to buy bread and butter and meat and fruit and vegetables abroad." He added: "It is time to stop blaming everything on the bureaucracy. If we put up with it, then we deserve it."

The shipyard workers of Gdansk and Szczecin, the coal miners of Polish Silesia, and their counterparts in other parts of the empire are less servile, also less patient. They keep pressing the leadership "from below" for better economic conditions, more housing, more freedom, and political reforms. In the Soviet Union, by contrast, the pressure for change came "from the top" of the power pyramid — from Nikita Khrushchev in the 1950s and 1960s, from Mikhail Gorbachev in the 1980s. It was a significant difference.

The distortions wrought by the command economy, Stalin's enduring monument, have been accepted passively by Soviet citizens as if ordained by God. Not so in much of

Eastern Europe, where Communist leaders had to face popular revolts in Hungary and Czechoslovakia, as well as food riots in Poland in 1956, 1970, and 1976 that were followed in the 1980s by waves of illegal strikes. East Germany had its own uprising in 1953, quickly suppressed when workers, squeezed by miserable wages and constant pressures to increase production, took to the streets in protest. East bloc living standards rose in the 1970s, thanks in large part to easy credits from Western banks and governments, but dropped sharply in the mid-1980s as repayment schedules began to bite. Czechoslovakia managed to maintain tolerable conditions by postponing investment in the modernization of its antiquated industrial plant to increase supplies of consumer goods in the shops. That was the price Prague paid for its post-1968 policy of "normalization," which amounted to buying off a population still embittered by the memory of Soviet tanks roaring into the city more than twenty years earlier.

Although the many shortcomings of the Stalin model are universally acknowledged today, real change has been slow in coming. There has been much discussion of far-reaching economic reforms, but in 1989 the systems in place, Hungary's apart, still closely resembled the blueprints for development drawn in the 1940s and 1950s. These remained command economies, subject in good years and bad to recurrent shortages and bottlenecks. That's why prudent industrial managers hoarded and concealed their available resources. They couldn't afford to fall short of meeting their often-unrealistic production targets.

Since prices, moreover, were fixed without regard to demand or supply, it was extremely difficult in East European countries to gauge the efficiency of any enterprise or industry. The almighty plan continued to be based on the number of units (say, X million tons of steel or brown coal) produced in a quarter or a year, rather than the monetary values created. Heavy industry — meaning the metallurgical, engineering, machine tool, and petrochemical industries — had come to symbolize socialist economic development. This led East European countries lacking many of the resources that make for success in these fields to invest huge sums in heavy industrial complexes that cannot survive without subsidies. The Nowa Huta complex near Krakow, Poland, is a striking example. There are others in Hungary, Bulgaria, and Romania, monuments to inefficiency in the name of socialism.

The search for economic salvation through radical reform in the Soviet Union did not begin with Gorbachev's *perestroika*. It dates from 1921, less than four years after the revolution, when Lenin proclaimed his New Economic Policy (NEP). Faced with economic collapse after years of civil war and general disruption, he turned to a market solution. The NEP legalized small-scale private enterprises, allowed peasants to accumulate wealth, and freed some industries to operate on the basis of market demand instead of government directives. These abrupt departures from Marxist orthodoxy resulted in a fairly vigorous recovery of agriculture and industrial production. In spite of Lenin's personal assurance that the NEP was a serious policy and that he meant it to last a considerable time, many Communists of the period looked on it as a temporary tactical retreat. After Lenin's death in 1924, and Stalin's accession to power, the NEP was replaced by a hard-fisted policy of collectivizing the land and ruthlessly centralizing economic decisions in Moscow.

Remarkably, the NEP period is being depicted today in Moscow as a golden age in Soviet history, at once both precedent for, and validation of, Gorbachev's "new thinking." When Tatyana Zaslavskaya, a prominent theorist of *perestroika,* was asked where the Soviet economy had gone wrong, she replied, "Lenin's NEP was cut off before it should have been and we were put on the path of centralized, administratively controlled development." The resulting Stalinist model of the command economy has survived without major modifications for more than sixty years — a success in mobilizing resources for the powerful military machine, but a dismal failure in providing a more abundant life for most Soviet citizens. Among the people of the empire, the command economy is looked on as a recipe for permanent poverty imposed by a foreign power.

In this part of the world, reformist ideas sprouted earlier and more profusely than in the Soviet Union. As early as the mid-1950s, economists and a few politicians (notably in Hungary, Czechoslovakia, and Poland) set about analyzing the weaknesses of the Soviet system and looking for alternatives. Almost without exception, these reform-minded economists wanted to see a comparatively decentralized system put in place. They differed on the scope to be allowed market forces. Wlodzimierz Brus in Warsaw favored "a regulated market economy" or what he called an "indirectly centralized system"; to some that sounded like a mixed economy in which the state sector would be forever paramount. Ota Sik and his colleagues in Prague countered that it was unrealistic to expect harmonious coexistence between a market sector and a centrally planned economy. They argued that prices should be determined by the market, not the state. Sik also stressed the need of linking economic with political reforms. Unless there was some degree of political pluralism, Sik argued, the inherent flaws of the centralized system would be nakedly exposed. Brus, on the other hand, held that democratizing the economy would be enough to ensure its success without concurrent political reforms. Both wound up as exiles in the West.

The Hungarian school of economic reformers tended to chart a pragmatic course. Janos Kornai, one of Hungary's most influential economists, called many of his colleagues in East bloc countries "naïve reformers" — a label he attached, incidentally, to Brus and Sik as well as to Yevsei Liberman in the Soviet Union (and to his own early writings). It was the height of naïveté, he wrote in 1986, to believe that simply by decentralizing the command economy one could cause everything else to fall into place, with the central plan and the market at peace.

In his book *Economics of Shortage,* Kornai offered a penetrating analysis and indictment of central planning. The fundamental difference between Soviet-type and Western capitalist enterprises, he wrote, is that the former go on producing whatever they are programmed to produce, regardless of demand, as long as the state provides sufficient labor, materials, and other necessities. A capitalist company, by contrast, is seldom constrained by scarcity of resources, only by lack of demand. In Eastern Europe, where resources are almost always in short supply, Kornai found that a smart manager will demand more resources than he needs on the shrewd assumption that his full request is not likely to be approved. The inevitable result is an aggravation of existing shortages. Kornai also developed a parallel concept that helps to explain the poor quality, low technical standard, and unattractiveness of many products. He pointed out that a socialist enterprise, unlike its capitalist counterpart, is in effect immune to the laws of the market; no matter how inefficient it may be, no matter how great the losses, it can always count on a bailout by the state. Kornai called this operating under a "soft budget constraint." Given the prevalence of chronic shortages, he added, socialist managers enjoy a permanent seller's market. They need not trouble their heads about improving the quality or salability of their products.

One direct outcome, apparent among window shoppers throughout the region, is a raging East European passion for products from the West: Japanese high-fidelity and television equipment, Italian sweaters, athletic shoes from West

Germany. Many imported products can be bought only in state stores for hard currency, but local shoppers are determined and resourceful. A foreign tourist must be made of stern stuff to ward off the swarms of unauthorized money-changers offering many times the official exchange rate for deutschemarks and dollars.

The American dollar reigns supreme in Warsaw even when it sinks in Frankfurt and Tokyo. On the black market, which the state makes no great effort to police, $1.00 brought 3500 zlotys in early 1989, seven times the official rate of exchange, and still rising. Poland is so desperate for hard currency that the government has turned a blind eye to these transactions, asking no questions about where the dollars come from. Import restrictions have been abolished, to all intents. Poles who can lay hands on hard currency are free to travel abroad and to bring back such high-demand items as computers, videorecorders and cassettes, even automobiles, without paying customs duties. Most promptly resell the imported merchandise, helping themselves to a handsome profit. Smuggling, in short, has been decriminalized. An assistant professor at a provincial university told me that he traveled to West Germany several times each summer to buy high-technology items with borrowed money and resell them on his return. "It's simply impossible to survive on my academic salary," he said. "After one more summer, I hope to be in a position to marry my girlfriend — if we can find a place to live."

Inflation is soaring in Poland and real incomes are declining also in Hungary as the government raises prices on basic foodstuffs. In Czechoslovakia, where living standards are less precarious, the economy stagnates. The public mood swings between sullen resignation and anger born of frustrated hope. Hungarian leaders predict a rise in labor unrest as the government moves to shut down unprofitable factories and mines, idling many thousands of workers at least temporarily. Like Poland and Yugoslavia, Hungary borrowed heavily in the 1970s and is hard pressed to repay its external debts.

The substantial economic failure of unreformed Communism is all but universally acknowledged among the people of the external empire. They are less willing than ethnic Russians to accept endless privation as they see their living standards lag farther and farther behind the prosperous countries of Western Europe. Members of the under-forty generation in particular say they cannot understand or justify the acquiescence of their elders in a system that perpetuates what many of them described as "the poverty of socialism."

Economists throughout the region make no secret of their anxiety that unless the pace of reform is accelerated the East bloc countries will forfeit their opportunities for increased trade with the West. They worry about 1992, the year in which the European Economic Community plans to establish a single market, assuring its members free movement of people, goods, and capital across national frontiers. "The train is about to leave the station," an unhappy Pole told me, "and we are likely to be left behind."

Eastern Europe, moreover, has become an economic burden for the Soviet Union, whose leaders complain that it is being shortchanged in its trade relations with the rest of the bloc. The Stalin era, when Russians felt free to loot the machinery and industrial raw materials of such countries as East Germany and Romania, is long past, though not forgotten. Today there are grievances on both sides. The Soviets supply their resource-poor allies with vast quantities of petroleum, natural gas, iron ore, and other commodities, some of which would command higher prices on the world market. The East Europeans, in exchange, supply machinery, grains, and other foodstuffs, mostly products they cannot readily sell to the West.

It has not been an easy or pleasant relationship; each side claims that it is exploited by the other. The Soviets at various times have complained that the Warsaw Pact allies hold back their best products for sale in Western markets, where they can earn hard currency to pay for the modern technology they need. They also have chided some East European countries for buying more Soviet oil than they need in order to resell the surplus in the West for dollars or deutschemarks. Back in 1982, the Soviets cut oil deliveries to the bloc countries by an average of 10 percent. In East Germany's case, however, the cut was 24.7 percent, motivated to some extent by its profitable diversion of Soviet oil to Western markets. According to the Institute for Economic Research in West Berlin, East Germany nevertheless imported 23.9 million tons of crude oil in 1984. It used only ten million tons at home and exported the rest. In 1983, more than 60 percent of Bulgaria's exports to the West took the form of crude or refined petroleum products; four fifths of this trade was in petroleum from the Soviet Union. There are no producing oil wells in either East Germany or Bulgaria, but their state trading organizations apparently recognize a good deal at first sight.

Who, then, is exploiting whom? The question cannot be answered categorically. At times the East European countries have paid less than the OPEC price for Soviet oil, at other times more. The reason is that the price Moscow charges its allies for oil is based on a five-year moving average of world prices. When OPEC prices rose steeply in 1973–74, Eastern Europe paid less than the world price; when the OPEC price dropped sharply, as in the late 1980s, they paid more than the world price. The Soviets doubtless could have driven harder bargains, but the losses they incurred were part of the price they paid for continued stability in the empire.

The costs of empire are difficult to disentangle from other accounts in the Soviet budget, but a RAND Corporation study in 1986 found that they had risen steadily and fairly steeply throughout the 1970s. [1] By 1983, according to the RAND study, these costs had dropped about 33 percent, as measured in 1981 dollars, from a peak of about $44 billion in 1980 to $29 billion. Because these calculations include Soviet subsidies to Communist-ruled countries outside Europe — Cuba, Vietnam, and Outer Mongolia, for example — the figures need to be adjusted. It is clear, nonetheless, that the greater part of the decline in support costs for imperial purposes can be attributed to reduced subsidies for Eastern Europe. When world oil prices dropped by 15 to 20 percent between 1980 and 1983, the moving average delayed the passing on of benefits to the bloc countries, which complained bitterly though discreetly that they were paying more than the rest of the world for oil.

Another and more compelling reason for the overall decline in the costs of empire has been the worsening performance of a stagnating Soviet economy. Estimates of real Soviet economic growth through the end of the 1980s run at 2 percent or less a year, some 40 percent below the estimated growth rate for the 1970s. The reduced costs of empire may thus be attributed not alone to falling oil prices but, perhaps decisively, to the severe economic problems besetting the Soviet economy. The gravity of these problems is now openly discussed by Gorbachev and his supporters, a striking departure from traditional Kremlin secrecy.

It has been an unquestioned article of faith throughout the Soviet bloc that unemployment, inflation, and sharp wage

1. Cited by Charles Wolf, Jr., in *The Costs and Benefits of the Soviet Empire,* in Henry S. Rowen and Charles Wolf, Jr., eds., *The Future of the Soviet Empire* (New York: Institute for Contemporary Studies / St. Martin's Press, 1987).

disparities are unavoidable in capitalist systems but unthinkable in a socialist society. That belief has taken some hard knocks in the age of *perestroika*. The fact that some Soviets have responded to changing times by working harder than their neighbors in order to live better goes against the grain with many in the population who have looked to the state for decades past as the ultimate provider of all the necessities of life.

After forty years of much the same system in the rest of the bloc, personal initiative is not wholly extinct. But one hears a great deal of grumbling and occasional loud complaints that the principle of egalitarian wages is being abandoned. In the sooty Hungarian city of Miskolc, a newspaper editor told me of his regret that equality in wages had become a fundamental issue for many workers: "If we are going to climb out of the present stagnation, the wage gap must be widened. We'll never make it as long as the lazy and the hard-working draw the same pay. We simply must overcome the popular opposition and find a way to reward good work. In this city, the competent worker, like the intellectual, is not paid enough to provide his children with a decent education."

Job security is an even more highly charged issue. The right to a job is enshrined in the constitutions of several countries. But the notion that every citizen has been guaranteed a lifelong job is no longer sacrosanct. Government and party officials concede that with the closing of failed enterprises there will be layoffs, and workers will have to move or acquire new skills.

The historic commitment to full employment at all costs has given way to a new concept: jobs must be "rationally justified." The commitment to stable prices is also being abandoned, most markedly in Poland and Hungary, as the governments decree increased prices for commodities in daily use by phasing out traditional consumer subsidies. There is unusually candid and heated discussion about slack labor discipline, overmanning, and the subsidizing of inefficient factories — all recognized for what they are: a form of hidden unemployment.

In Poland, several dozen factories and shipyards have been cited as bankrupt and marked for closing. Jozef Kaleta, rector of the Oskar Lange Academy of Economics in Wroclaw, disputed official claims that there was no unemployment in Poland. He estimated that at least 5 to 10 percent of the twelve million workers employed in the state sector faced a loss of jobs, a case of what he called "latent unemployment."

The Hungarian authorities have been more forthright. Hidden unemployment, according to recent studies, may account for 20 to 25 percent of the payrolls in state-owned industries, and in some branches of industry less than 50 percent of the capacity is being utilized. Official estimates forecast the loss of more than 200,000 jobs by 1990. It is a sign of the Hungarian government's serious intent to carry out restructuring that unemployment benefits have been introduced to ease the pain of transition. The Soviet Union, with its vastly larger population and industrial plant, appears to be heading in the same direction. In a speech to the Supreme Soviet, Prime Minister Nikolai Ryzhkov said that some 13 percent of all state-run enterprises were unprofitable and might have to be shut down.

None of these negative developments in individual countries of the bloc bodes well for the grandiosely titled Collective Concept for the Socialist International Division of Labor for the Period 1991–2005, adopted in 1988 and touted in the Communist press as the cornerstone of a new framework for integrating the economies of Eastern Europe and the Soviet Union. This formidably complicated blueprint, four years in the making, was first disclosed at a meeting in

Prague of COMECON. Its purpose, according to the Prague communiqué, was the "gradual formation of conditions for the free movement of goods, services, and other production factors among them, with a view to forming a unified market in the long term."

That language invites comparison with the prior decision of the European Economic Community in Brussels to create a "Europe without frontiers" by 1992. In fact the two are no more alike than chalk and cheese. The EEC intends to abolish all remaining barriers to the movement of goods, services, labor, and capital among its members. There is even discussion, over British objections, of creating a common currency for Western Europe, establishing a European central bank, and harmonizing the monetary policies of all member states. The Soviet bloc project is a tentative first step toward establishing conditions that could make possible a common market for Eastern Europe in the more distant future.

There are, of course, no market economies in the bloc. Prices are set not by the play of market forces but by administrative action. Currencies are not convertible, and COMECON is still a long way from permitting the free movement of goods, capital, and labor within the bloc. Bringing the Collective Concept to fruition will mean even more wrenching changes.

The impeccably capitalist principle of "comparative advantage" is to be applied in determining the "Socialist international division of labor." This means that the COMECON country with the highest production costs in a particular branch of industry should get out of that business and concentrate instead on product lines where its costs are among the lowest. Efficiency is to be the yardstick. It takes no wild leap of the imagination to foresee sharp disputes between COMECON countries as one or another of them is required to phase out its high-cost producers and, in the process, impose new hardships on its own population for the greater good of its neighbors. Romania has already chosen to stay out of the unified market instead of running that risk. Considerations of prestige will almost certainly stand in the way as well.

As the senior partner in this collective enterprise, the Soviet Union has the main responsibility for redirecting the flow of trade within the bloc. The plan, accepted by all COMECON members except Romania, calls for increased specialization of output in such areas as electronics, engineering, construction materials, energy, industrial raw materials, food, and consumer goods. There is early evidence that not all governments are ready to yield pride of place to their more efficient neighbors by abandoning comparatively wasteful branches of their domestic industries. There are signs also of developing competition for primacy in modern industries such as electronics and robotics. Czechoslovakia, for example, has made known its ambition to become "an exporter of a narrow range of high-technology products" and to phase down more traditional but energy-wasting industries. Bulgaria wants to move in the same direction, and the Soviet Union has declared its intention of exporting more manufactured goods to other COMECON countries. It is no longer content to serve as the bloc's main supplier of energy and raw materials — a role that in empires of the past was played by the colonial countries.

Mikhail Gorbachev once called COMECON "a garbage can" for obsolete products that could not be sold outside the bloc. The system is in crisis. Hungary and Czechoslovakia are determined to cut back their exports to the Soviet Union and build up their trade instead with hard-currency markets. Each country ran up a surplus of one billion dollars with the Soviets in 1989. Trying to control the situation, Hungary has now imposed stiff financial penalties on companies that increase their exports beyond the previous year's level.

In discussions with economists, bankers, and government officials, I encountered considerable skepticism about the survival of the system. "Doing business through COMECON is an incredibly complicated, highly frustrating business," according to Vladimir Dlouhy, the youthful new head of Czechoslovakia's planning commission. "The deep reforms we must make in our country over the next ten to fifteen years are not likely to be facilitated by our membership in COMECON. We have a desperate need — so do the Russians, by the way — for modern technology of the sort that only the West can supply. We'll have to pay for it through increased exports to hard currency countries, and that, as I see it, will require determined actions outside the COMECON framework."

The large unanswered question that confronts the Soviet Union and the East European region is whether limited economic reforms, including some concessions to market forces, can possibly lift these countries out of their chronic stagnation. On this point as well there is reason to be skeptical. Pawel Bozyk, a Polish economist, put it this way: "I no longer believe in the possibilities of a mixed economy. Either the state or the private sector will necessarily predominate."

In Yugoslavia, long the pace setter in economic reform because, after 1948, it owed no allegiance to Moscow or Muscovite methods, I found deep disillusionment. Ljubomir Madzar, a Belgrade economist, told me that Yugoslavia's experience with a mix of command and market approaches had left the country without the benefits of one or the other. Madzar added: "The system of workers' self-management, which was to have been our unique contribution to socialism, simply doesn't work. It's a case of authority divorced from responsibility. The truth is that we share the common problems of the region and we have not been able to come up with better answers than our neighbors."

The central dilemma of Communist leadership in Eastern

Europe remains unresolved: how to reshape and reinvigorate national economies that have lost their forward thrust without jeopardizing the parties' grip on state power. It's a false dilemma, many East Europeans are saying; both the command economy and single-party rule will have to go. They contend that economic salvation won't come through patchwork on the failed system. That view strikes many others as utopian. They believe that the Soviet Union won't hold still for a return to capitalism and the establishment of untrammeled democracy.

Although the limits on what the Kremlin would tolerate have been widened to a significant degree, the specter of Soviet tanks rolling into Budapest or Prague again has not vanished from people's minds. It seems to me an improbable scenario if Mikhail Gorbachev stays in power, though not altogether inconceivable.

# 10

## *The Punishing Price of Reform*

THE EXILED POLISH PHILOSOPHER Leszek Kolakowski once wrote that "democratic Communism" was
like "fried snowballs," an utter impossibility. It was an illu-
sion, he argued, to believe that any Communist Party in power
could or would democratize the system from above. That
proposition is being tested today in the Soviet Union, where
the pressure for change was initiated by Mikhail Gorbachev
and may now be slipping out of his control. In East Germany and Czechoslovakia, hard-line Communist regimes
collapsed under the pressure of determined citizens, numbered in the hundreds of thousands, marching in the streets
to demand peaceful revolutionary change. In Poland, the
Communists were forced to relinquish much of their power
in favor of Solidarity following an election defeat. Only in
Hungary has the progress toward political pluralism been
guided by reform-minded Communists, leading to a split in
the ruling party.

Real reform of their bankrupt economies, however, car-
ries an intimidating price tag, and blue-collar workers have
reason to fear that they will be presented with a large portion of the bill. That is the down side of Solidarity's famous
victory at the polls in 1989. A broad social movement as well
as a trade union, Solidarity had no realistic choice but to

support, in partnership with the Communist Party, the imposition of painful sacrifices on a reluctant people: higher prices, fewer jobs, reduced consumer subsidies, and a further reduction in depressed living standards.

The Lenin Shipyard in Gdansk, birthplace of Solidarity, may yet be spared the fate of other insolvent state enterprises, thanks to a rescue effort by Barbara Piasecka Johnson, the Polish-born widow of a New Jersey multimillionaire. But dozens of less fortunate state-owned industries face the prospect of early shutdown or cutback because, like the Gdansk yard, they have been losing money steadily. In a capitalist society, shutting them down would seem a rational management decision. For Polish workers, who have never known the bitter taste of unemployment, it would be a cruel travesty of socialism.

The workers know all about other failures of Polish socialism: long lines at food stores, empty shelves in many of them, punishing prices, milk unfit for babies to drink, fouled air and water. Having to give up their jobs, too, strikes many of them as an exorbitant price to pay for industrial efficiency and representation in the parliament. But that is the shape of the future being planned in Poland and Hungary. For blue-collar workers in particular, the market-oriented reforms under way necessarily mean that life will be harder and more precarious before it gets appreciably better. The architects of reform, on the other hand, argue that sacrifice is unavoidable because the system imposed on these countries in the 1940s by the Soviet Union and its surrogates has collapsed. Their aim, they say, is to build solvent economies, not to tinker with the failed system of centrally directed, state-owned industry under the monopolistic and heavy-handed rule of a single party. They seek to replace it over time with modern mixed economies, driven to a large extent by market forces.

"The time has come," a Hungarian Foreign Ministry official told me, "to replace the dictatorship of the proletariat with a new dictatorship of economic efficiency. We realize now that 'heavenly socialism' is not attainable. Reality demands that we redefine the concept of socialism if we are going to end the present disastrous stagnation. Our citizens have been passive for too long. We need to share power with other groups in society."

The preferred model of many East European reformers is neither the Soviet Union nor the United States. They want to go the way of such prosperous, democratic, and neutral states as Sweden, Finland, and Austria. They also hope to regain the national sovereignty that was denied them, or was deeply compromised, with the arrival of the Red Army in the closing stage of World War II.

Professor Seweryn Bialer of Columbia University recalls that after Stalin the Soviet Union started to allow East European leaders some leeway in following "different roads to socialism." In the Gorbachev era, he suggests, East Europeans are searching for "different roads *from* socialism." It looks like a hazardous journey, never before attempted, along a route not marked on any existing map.

In the remarkable case of Poland, the first steps toward a new order were taken by Solidarity, the independent trade union that turned into a peaceful resistance movement, a political alternative, and a rallying point for opponents of the system. It is important to remember that the round-table accord of 1989 was not the first of its kind. The regime had shredded an earlier agreement, signed on the last day of August 1980, when it imposed martial law in December 1981 and imprisoned hundreds of Solidarity militants. One of those political prisoners, the historian Adam Michnik, analyzed the significance of the original accord in a brief essay written in his cell: "For the first time in the history of Communist rule in Poland, the 'civil society' was being restored, and it was reaching a compromise with the state. For both sides this compromise was a marriage of convenience, not love."[1]

Seven years later, when the round-table talks were convened, it was again need, not love, that brought the negotiators together, but some things had changed. The government's chief negotiator, General Czeslaw Kiszczak, acknowledged that Poland's "reformed sociopolitical system is to rest on the idea of civil society." In adopting Solidarity's vocabulary, the regime was symbolically abandoning its timeworn claim to speak for Polish society as a whole. It was entering into partnership with an organized group of citizens — ten million strong at Solidarity's peak — that it had labored and failed to eradicate. The election that followed, on June 4, 1989, was a triumph for Poland's civil society, an all-but-total rejection of Communist leadership.

The seed from which Solidarity sprouted was a liberating idea, attributed to the Italian Communist theoretician Antonio Gramsci and later adapted to Polish circumstances by Leszek Kolakowski, Jacek Kuron, and Michnik. Frontal attack was out of the question. The regime held all the face cards — the army and the police; if those failed, the Soviet Union could send in the tanks, as it had in Budapest and Prague. Yet the idea that Poles could build what they called a civil society outside the rigid, oppressive structures of the party and state was a ray of light. In his essay *On Hope and Hopelessness*, published from exile in 1971, Kolakowski had conceded that "bureaucratic despotic socialism" could not transform itself. He argued, however, that the reformist cause was not hopeless "if it is understood as an idea of active resistance exploiting the inherent contradictions of the system." The pressure would have to come from below as aggrieved citizens organized groups with common interests and

1. Adam Michnik, *Letters from Prison and Other Essays* (Berkeley: University of California Press, 1985), pp. 124–125.

built new social movements aimed at creating a more open, more democratic Polish society. The secret was for Poles to behave as if they were living in a free society. It sounded quixotic, but somehow the prescription worked.

By 1979, a tacit alliance had emerged that claimed to represent "the society" against what many Poles call "the power." It was, and remains, a strange convergence: industrial workers led by Lech Walesa, intellectuals like Michnik, Kuron, and Bronislaw Geremek, Catholic laymen (and priests like Father Jozef Tischner of Krakow), all taking shelter under the wing of the church. Nothing remotely resembling this alliance of diverse groups had existed in Poland or anywhere else. It was a coalition of Polish nationalists, fallen-away Marxists, democratic socialists, a so-called loyal opposition that accepted basic Communist principles while demanding structural reforms within the party, and tens of thousands of ordinary citizens unattached to any ideology. This was the remarkable alliance that, after ten years of storm and stress, took its place in parliament alongside the disgraced Communist Party.

Solidarity had no counterpart in Hungary or in any other country, East or West. But the Hungarian Communist Party, now renamed the Socialist Party, decided to move in a similar direction, allowing the re-emergence of long-suppressed old parties and the founding of new "political associations" that were to form the nucleus of a loose, unprecedented democratic opposition. There was also hopeful talk of creating independent judicial systems, allowing the opposition to publish its own newspapers, and assuring it free air time on the state's television and radio networks.

The orderly and dignified people's revolt that toppled the old regime in Czechoslovakia, a movement led by a dissident playwright from the basement of a decrepit Prague theater, may have looked like a political improvisation. But Vaclav Havel's Civic Forum was soon negotiating the surrender of the long-entrenched Communist Party. Here, as in East Germany a month earlier, the party started to crumble as soon as the people filled Wenceslas Square to demand democratic reforms and basic human rights. Once Mikhail Gorbachev had made it clear that he would not intervene to save his Stalinist allies, the outcome was inevitable.

East Germany's "revolution from below" burst upon the world even more spontaneously, forcing the ouster of Erich Honecker, the long-time party chief and head of state, on October 18. The long-silent people of Leipzig, Dresden, and East Berlin were carrying out their own revolution. Honecker's successor, Egon Krenz, followed his mentor into political oblivion in less than seven weeks. On December 3, a Sunday, the East German Politburo and the entire Communist Central Committee resigned in a body. But the opposition, leaderless and divided, was operating without a plan or program.

As in Poland, Hungary, and to a lesser extent Czechoslovakia, the new leaders of East Germany would inherit the extremely awkward task of turning around a near-bankrupt economy. Poland and Hungary, both deeply in debt to foreign lenders, face the more difficult turnaround. Both have a desperate need to modernize their industries with new technology from the West if they are to compete successfully in world markets. The trouble is that they can't afford the new technology without further assistance from Western Europe, the United States, and Japan. In any event, the International Monetary Fund will first have to be satisfied that wasteful subsidies to inefficient industries are being cut and that the regimes are serious about promoting private enterprise.

Blue-collar workers, who earn far less in Eastern Europe than their counterparts in Western countries, have a great deal to lose by local standards. Assembly workers at the Polonez automobile plant in Warsaw, for example, still earn three to four times the salary of young physicians. These premium wages, seldom reflected in high quality or productivity, are supplemented by perquisites not available to most Poles: comparatively generous benefits, social services, and subsidized meals on the job. The workers owe their favored position not only to the Communist value system but to their demonstrated power to roll back consumer price increases, even to topple governments, through strike action.

The transition is bound to be painful as the least efficient state industries in Hungary and Poland close down or curtail operations. Hundreds of thousands of jobs will be at stake, even as real wages are reduced by inflation and cuts in consumer subsidies. Solidarity has been saddled with the precarious assignment of negotiating factory closings, price increases, and new wage structures on terms the workers can be persuaded to accept.

Bronislaw Geremek, Solidarity's parliamentary leader and by vocation a medieval historian, harbors few illusions about the difficult days ahead. "We need to convince people," he said, "that if they accept hardships now they will be rewarded with a dignified and decent life in the future. Our greatest problem is that so many people now, after all the failures of recent years in our country, have no hope. We have to find a way to give it to them."

Finding a way to give hope to the hopeless will be a daunting task. The fact that nearly 40 percent of the Polish electorate failed to vote in the 1989 election, in spite of the novelty and excitement over Solidarity's rebirth, suggests that millions of Poles remain apathetic or deeply pessimistic about their future. Many of these nonvoters, moreover, are uncomfortable with Solidarity's new role as the principal partner of the Communist Party, which they do not trust and continue to blame for the country's sad state. Workers under the age of thirty-five, who account for one fourth of Poland's population, are more militant than their elders, according to government opinion surveys. Their response to a regime of forced austerity could be a new wave of strikes that would deepen the country's economic crisis.

No Communist regime has yet discovered a way out of the box in which Poland and Hungary find themselves. The economic gains they have promised to deliver by instituting market reforms and performance incentives will demand of their people a willingness to sacrifice and to accept risk as an inescapable condition of life. There can be no guarantees of success. Nothing in the life experience of working-class Poles or Hungarians has prepared them for the risk inherent in a world of winners and losers, where there are few certainties, not even the assurance of a job. In addition to some degree of transitional unemployment (the degree is never specified), they will have to accept wage differentials designed to reward diligence and enterprise. Among people long conditioned to think of profit making as synonymous with black market cheating, that is not a popular doctrine.

Envy of more successful neighbors, a traditional peasant trait, runs deep in these societies. The Chinese call it "the red-eye disease." Mikhail Gorbachev calls it "leveling," in the sense of wanting to hold others down to one's own level. Vassili Selyunin, a prominent economic journalist, has written that seventy years of Soviet socialism produced an overly dependent citizen who keeps shouting, "Give me a free house, give me cheap meat, give me this, give me that, and at the same time get rid of my neighbor, who has started working on his own and now lives — the son of a bitch — better than I do." Chinese workers have gone on strike to block the introduction of incentive bonuses for the diligent among them. In the Soviet Union, jealous farmers set fire to buildings at a comparatively prosperous collective that, in their view, was altogether too successful at raising pigs. In another Soviet case, villagers destroyed a greenhouse built by an ambitious neighbor who wanted to grow tomatoes in and out of season. As Flora Lewis of the *New York Times* has suggested, it is hard for many people to give up the idea of egalitarianism, because it is all that remains of the early vision of Communist society.

I encountered less violent objections in Hungary, where privatization had a head start. A Marxist professor, who readily acknowledged that "the old socialist ideology" was a proven failure, nevertheless complained that the government was too lenient with private operators of food stores, restaurants, and workshops leased from the state. "The individualism that goes with free markets is too egocentric, an invitation to corruption," he said with undisguised bitterness. "Most of these private enterprises don't give receipts to their customers. They want to avoid taxes." Not all the Hungarians I met shared the professor's righteous indignation. In Miskolc, a smoky steel town not renowned for fine cuisine, Communist functionaries steered me away from a state-owned restaurant to a private place where the food and service were said to be better. "You will be pleased," one of them said. He was right. The food was unexpectedly delicious and I did not think to ask for a receipt. The proprietor, incidentally, drove a Mercedes.

Hungary, in spite of its heavy external debt and unchecked inflation, strikes many observers as a better prospect for successful reform than Poland, in large part because at the top and middle ranks of the party and state one encounters less residual hostility to freer markets and private enterprise. Elemer Hankiss, the Hungarian sociologist, has paid particular attention to this phenomenon. In his small office on Castle Hill in Budapest, Hankiss talked with me about his vision of an emerging coalition, drawn together by a shared concern that unless the economy improves, the country will see increasing poverty, which could spark potentially dangerous unrest. The coalition's members, he said, are drawn from the ruling elite — middle- and upper-level party officials, their counterparts in the state bureaucracy, managers of large state enterprises (including state farms and industrial cooperatives), and private entrepreneurs. In short, an alliance of elites.

Hankiss believes this group is opposed to the dogma of the caretaker state and that it tends to look with favor on risk-taking. Seven out of ten fashionable Budapest boutiques he studied are owned by people with a direct or indirect connection to highly placed functionaries of the party or state. "[Important] members of the state and party bureaucracies," Hankiss has written, "are moving in growing numbers into the managerial sphere, in smaller numbers into the entrepreneurial class, and into the new market-oriented structures; and they have changed their bureaucratic power into managerial power." To illustrate the close ties between these elites, Hankiss described a fictitious but plausible family reunion, which brought together the father, a leading member of the party; his daughter, who owned a small shop; his son, the head of a Western joint venture in Hungary; his brother-in-law, the director of a new stock company; and his mother-in-law, who owned a small pension on Lake Balaton. In Budapest it is not difficult to put names to certain characters in the Hankiss scenario.

There is half-serious talk in Poland as well that members of the *nomenklatura* have started to move into, or build profitable alliances with, the emerging private sector, where they can use their influence and connections to make things hum. The old joke that socialism is the shortest road from capitalism to capitalism has been modified by Warsaw comedians. The current version comes in the form of a question: What better way is there to speed the transition from Communism to capitalism than to convert Communist bosses into capitalist bosses? A bizarre idea, but Solidarity's leadership was sufficiently concerned to write into its election program a specific provision that bars *nomenklatura* members from becoming owners.

The Warsaw and Budapest elites did not, in fact, suffer unbearable hardships under the old, unreformed system, because they knew how to manipulate it for their own advantage. That is the unique strength of elites anywhere. But there is a much larger class in both countries that, although it has never shared the spoils of the Communist order, finds talk of change threatening. These are the poor — unskilled workers, the elderly, Gypsies — people far removed from the levers of power. For them, reform has already meant hardship: inflated prices for food and other necessities, less job security, increased awareness of corrupt practices, and a sense that further change can only make their miserable situation worse. In Hungary the real income of people in this category has declined more than 40 percent over the past decade.

Economists in both Hungary and Poland attribute their slow progress to a timidity in high places about scrapping and burying the system of centralized controls that has been in place for more than forty years. That the system has been a colossal economic failure is not seriously disputed in either country. Yet neither regime has been prepared to push reform to its logical conclusion; that is, to dismantle the swollen bureaucracy to which the party long ago assigned the impossible task of fixing all prices, all wages, and rates of production for every branch of industry, in addition to allocating labor, materials, and capital to individual enterprises. Year by year, and industry by industry, with some exceptions, this system has produced a succession of operating deficits, which are made up through subsidies at the expense of the average citizen's living standard.

Janos Berecz, former chief of ideology for the Hungarian Communist Party, who was dropped from the Politburo in

1989, has conceded: "Our policies were both practically and theoretically hasty. Our central planning policies established monopolies instead of the competition that would have helped develop the economy. As a result, the people . . . started to lose interest in production. We reached a stage where we could not progress, and so we became underdeveloped."[2] That shorthand explanation of where the party went wrong will not satisfy many knowledgeable Hungarians. Ivan Berend, the economist who is president of the Hungarian Academy of Sciences, has labored over the years to teach the political leadership that ideological purity is a poor guide to economic progress. "I believe," he told me, "that if our ideology stands in the way of reform, then we need to reform the ideology."

Reforms that encourage private initiative are still viewed with suspicion by many party members as possibly dangerous departures from socialism. In Warsaw, the chief ideologist of the Polish party was asked, "What guarantees do people have that the party is not going to give up, one by one, the values and goals implicit in socialism?" Marian Orzechowski replied bluntly, "There are no guarantees, because some of the things said by Marx, Engels, and Lenin are no longer true in [today's] world."

Even if Marx, Engels, and Lenin could be consigned to history's famous dustbin, the task of dismantling a system of near-total state ownership and transforming it into a modern mixed economy, sparked by an underdeveloped free market, would recall the ancient conundrum about how to cook an omelette without breaking eggs. Eggs will in fact be broken, and other questions bristling with difficulty remain to be answered.

Will the party bureaucrats, in fact, stop interfering in every detail of economic management, a task at which they have

2. Interview in *New Perspectives Quarterly*, Winter 1988–89, p. 12.

proven themselves to be grossly incompetent? Is it realistic to expect massive new credits from the West when Poland and Hungary together have unpaid external debts amounting to more than $55 billion? It is no less critical that neither the ruling Communist parties nor the opposition have given much thought to the question of how failing state industries can, as a practical matter, be transferred to private ownership.

Selling Hungarian companies to foreign interests is now legally permissible. But any foreign buyer will expect to repatriate his hypothetical profits one day, and that, in turn, depends on Hungary's making its storm-battered currency convertible. Although members of the Budapest leadership have mentioned the idea from time to time, convertibility is at best a long-term hope, not a certainty. Hungary's minister of foreign trade, Tamas Beck, has been traveling the West European circuit in search of buyers for fifty large Hungarian companies. The results have been sparse so far, although General Electric did buy a 50.1 percent interest in Tungstrom, a light bulb manufacturer that enjoyed a better business reputation than most Hungarian industrial companies. An official of the Hungarian Credit Bank, which handled the Tungstrom sale, said it was often impossible to determine the value of a Hungarian company because its managers have no understanding of the concept of net worth. The bank has contracted with Price Waterhouse and other Western accounting firms to help educate the managers of companies marked for sale to foreign investors.

Another alternative, discussed more often in Hungary than in Poland, would be to privatize selected state-owned industries by "going public" in the Western sense of the term; that is, selling shares to the public. That was the idea behind the opening of a rudimentary stock market in Budapest. Prime Minister Margaret Thatcher took just this course when she sold off such nationalized enterprises as British Telecom and

British Airways. The British example, however, does not fit
the Hungarian facts. The companies placed on the block by
Mrs. Thatcher's government were solvent. Moreover, the
London stock exchange had no difficulty selling the shares,
thanks to the confidence of investors that the corporations
would do even better under private management. In Hungary, after forty years of pauperization, there cannot be many
potential investors with the cash and the confidence to invest
in chronic money-losing enterprises.

Communist officials such as Jerzy Urban, the chief
spokesman for the Polish government, told me in 1988 that
the spirit of enterprise was all but dead in his country. After
forty years of looking to the state for all the necessities of
life, he said, Poles were no longer capable of looking out for
themselves. Urban's was the most profoundly pessimistic assessment I heard anywhere in Eastern Europe. Stefan Nowak, one of Poland's most respected sociologists, disagreed.

Professor Nowak, who has directed careful studies of Polish opinion trends over a span of many years, gave me a
copy of a summary analysis he had prepared at the request
of the governing board of the Polish Sociological Society.
The document included this finding: "There has been a clear
increase over the past few years in the acceptance of the
private sector in the economy . . . Almost one third of all
Poles today are in favor of the new introduction of private
ownership of business — small and medium-sized manufactures and wholesale and foreign trade. The acceptance of
existing private ownership is nearly unanimous."

Although a large majority still rejected privatization of
heavy industry, Nowak suggested that public attitudes even
on this point might be changing. "These changes," he wrote,
"exemplify both the negative view of the efficiency of the
socialized economy and the conviction that limiting private
production and services will have serious negative consequences for standards of living . . . One can clearly say that

the model of the mixed economy has overwhelming support in Polish society."

The truth seems to be that it was not the people but the regime that continued to discourage private enterprise in spite of all its protestations to the contrary. Professor Nowak cited the example of an enterprising young couple who had started a small private shop in his own apartment building to supply such household necessities as brooms, mops, brushes, paints, and cleaning materials. Their little business prospered for a couple of years, offering a service the state stores did not try to match. The Nowaks were astonished one morning to find a sign posted on the front door to the effect that the shop was closing. They asked the owners what had gone wrong. It was the tax bill, they replied. The government was demanding some 90 percent of all they had earned from the day they opened for business. They saw no point in running the little enterprise if the government, in effect, was going to confiscate their meager earnings.

Nowak's story is no more than an anecdote, but I heard dozens of similar accounts from would-be entrepreneurs. Taken together, they raised serious questions in my mind about the sincerity of East European regimes when they claim to be promoting market-driven economies.

# 11

## *Challenge to the West*

N OT SINCE 1848, the Springtime of Nations, has Europe
lived through a year that was remotely comparable to
1989. A wave of revolution, driven by long-suppressed national feelings and demands for liberal democracy, swept
across the continent in 1848, threatening the breakup of the
Habsburg empire and forcing the last Bourbon king of
France to abdicate his throne. Tsar Nicholas I saved monarchical rule by sending the armies of imperial Russia to crush
the insurrections and snuff out the hopes they had raised.

In the profoundly different conditions of 1989, another
wave of national revolutions swept Central and Eastern Europe, toppling oppressive Russian-imposed regimes from East
Germany to Bulgaria. This time the old regimes, Romania
excepted, surrendered without a fight, and the Kremlin did
nothing to prevent their fall from power. A vast transformation was under way. For more than four decades, the
continent had been torn in two by an Iron Curtain bristling
with watch towers, death strips, and border guards armed
with machine pistols. Now, in swift succession, Hungary, East
Germany, and Czechoslovakia opened their borders on the
West. The Brandenburg Gate in Berlin, for twenty-eight years
the symbol of Germany's partition, became a peaceful pedestrian passageway, and the Berlin Wall was no longer a

barrier between the two German states. Hungary, in a commercial decision equally ripe with symbolism, was hawking strips of the barbed wire fence that used to mark its border with Austria to foreign tourists.

The push to make Europe whole again was proving infectious. In his 1988 speech before the United Nations General Assembly, Mikhail Gorbachev had signaled a historic change: the subject peoples of Stalin's empire were free to go their own ways. "Freedom of choice," Gorbachev said, "is a universal principle which allows no exceptions." Poland and Hungary were the first East bloc nations to take the Soviet president at his word. They abandoned the Leninist principle that Communist parties must forever play the "leading role" in society. Both ruling parties made history by allowing citizens to register their rejection of Communism at the ballot box. When Moscow raised no objection, East Germany and Czechoslovakia also terminated the Communists' power monopoly.

Gorbachev certainly would have preferred to have change move at a more deliberate pace, but he did not question its direction. He had inherited a nation in crisis. Supplies of food and consumer goods were scarcer than they had been in twenty years. The Stalinist system of centralized planning, artificial prices, production quotas, and a nonconvertible currency was in deep trouble, not only in the Soviet Union but throughout Eastern Europe. The system had served the needs of the military remarkably well, but it was out of date in the new era of high technology and rising consumer demands.

The subject nations of Stalin's external empire, moreover, were becoming a drain on Soviet economic and military resources. Although Gorbachev was not disposed to dismantle the Warsaw Pact on short notice, he acknowledged that change was inevitable even in the sphere of military arrangements. "Life changes, and this alliance, too, will be transformed," he said at a Warsaw Pact summit conference in July 1988. "Alliances are not forever."

These were not cosmetic changes designed, as some American conservatives believed, to hoodwink the West into dropping its guard and agreeing to subsidize the failures of Soviet-style economics. The changes cut too deep to be dismissed out of hand. Nor is it realistic, as former Secretary of State Henry Kissinger has remarked, to ascribe all the changes in Eastern Europe to Gorbachev's influence or example. Solidarity was born five years before he came to power in the Kremlin, and Hungary's first economic reform was launched long before that, in 1968. Gorbachev's contribution has not been to initiate these reforms but, as it turned out, to protect the reformers. In fact, he has taken no steps to slow or halt the retreat from Communism in either country. On the historical evidence, it seems clear that Nikita Khrushchev and Leonid Brezhnev would have shown less forbearance.

It must be apparent to Gorbachev, and to any potential successor in the Kremlin, that the United States (its huge arsenal of high-technology weapons notwithstanding) poses no actual military threat to the Soviet empire in decay. Intentions in this case are more decisive than capabilities, and the American record over the past several decades does not suggest a country determined to destroy Communism by military means. A superpower that accepted defeat in Vietnam, that tolerates Fidel Castro's regime ninety miles off the Florida coast, and has been all thumbs dealing with tiny Nicaragua is not likely to plunge into military adventures in Eastern Europe. That region's assigned role as a buffer against attack from the West looks more like a waste of scarce resources. Even the Red Army's political role as the ultimate enforcer of bloc unity is becoming obsolete in the Gorbachev era. Eastern Europe in the 1980s and 1990s, moreover, has become a heavy burden to the overtaxed Soviet economy rather than a source of strength. Moscow's legitimate interest in stability must eventually outweigh the importance of coerced ideological conformity. Forty years of imperial rule have yielded the Soviet Union neither political stability nor material gain in recent years.

Gorbachev has hinted at a possible solution. The Soviet Union is prepared, he said, to accept further political changes in Eastern Europe on condition that the West does not seek to exploit change for military advantage. The precise meaning of his words needs to be explored through diplomatic channels. What limits does Gorbachev have in mind? Would he accept neutralization on the Austrian or Finnish models for the countries of Eastern Europe? Hungary and Czechoslovakia are obvious candidates. They have watched their immediate neighbor, Austria, prosper in freedom and neutrality since the Soviets withdrew their occupying forces in 1955. In exchange for the end of occupation, the Austrians accepted strict limits on armaments and a bar against their joining NATO.

In the case of Finland, a historical adversary of Russia, the results have been no less satisfactory to Moscow. The Finns were forced to make territorial concessions and pay reparations to the Soviets in compensation for the two wars they fought against the Red Army. Today they enjoy unlimited freedom to manage their own affairs, debarred only from making war against their powerful neighbor. Finland was not occupied by Soviet forces, and its Communist Party never came to power. It has maintained its rugged individuality in a state of disarmed neutrality. By any common-sense measure, Finland has proven a far less troublesome neighbor of the Soviet Union than has Poland or Hungary.

Although "Finlandization" entered the language at the peak of the Cold War as a term of opprobrium in some circles, its negative implications have faded over the years. Many East Europeans told me that they would happily change places with the Finns. In 1989 Henry Kissinger, more surprisingly, also cited Finland as a possible model for the countries of Eastern Europe. In a dialogue with the editorial board of the *Christian Science Monitor,* Kissinger called for quiet negotiations with the Soviet Union to determine "whether it is possible to create a political framework in Eastern Europe which separates the security issues from the political issues." What he had in mind, Kissinger added, was "something like Finland in which the peoples of Eastern Europe are free to choose their own governments and there are clearly defined limitations on military capabilities."

According to other observers, the outlook for eventual agreement in the Vienna negotiations on conventional force reductions is far from hopeless. President Bush has proposed that both the United States and the Soviet Union reduce their troop strength in Europe to the identical level of 275,000. Cuts on this scale would fall far more heavily on the Soviet side, which has roughly 600,000 troops in the region, than on the United States, with about half that number committed to Western Europe. Gorbachev, who has conceded the principle that troop reductions need not be symmetrical, raised no objection to the Bush benchmark. In fact, he has argued for more drastic reductions on both sides. Whatever else they may accomplish, Soviet troop reductions of more than half, possibly as much as two-thirds, would expand the possibilities for accelerated political and economic reforms.

The stakes are high for both superpowers. A breakthrough in Vienna, and in the strategic arms negotiations at Geneva, could finally break the action-reaction cycle that has driven the United States and the Soviet Union to go on stockpiling new and ever more expensive weapons systems that strain their economic and scientific resources, crowding out many needs of their own citizens. The pinch is far more acute in the Soviet Union than in the United States. But

Americans have their own critical domestic needs that cry out for attention and investment: the plague of drugs, deteriorating schools, homelessness, and a large and growing underclass, urban crime, and industries that have lost their competitive edge, among others.

Neither side is talking about complete disarmament. Even if all the manpower and weapons reductions were settled and faithfully carried out, both the United States and the Soviet Union would remain major powers with interests that reach far beyond their own borders. Moscow would be left with more than enough trained soldiers, tanks, and guns to crush an unexpected uprising in Eastern Europe. But Gorbachev, who is anything but stupid in his dealings with the West, certainly understands that a fresh resort to armed force would undermine all the achievements of his "new thinking," including the hope of transforming an empire based on compulsion into a commonwealth of neighboring states joined in voluntary association.

The superpowers apparently have arrived at a tacit understanding about the course of reform in Eastern Europe. Washington has undertaken not to exploit the loosening of Moscow's hold on the region. The United States is prepared to help the reformist regimes in Eastern Europe without, in the unfortunate words of President Bush, poking a stick in Gorbachev's eye. Moscow, for its part, has sent word that as long as the process of change does not jeopardize the security of the Soviet Union or the integrity of its alliance, it will not interfere with the liberalizing reforms under way in these countries or raise objections to their receipt of economic assistance from the West. Bush and Gorbachev agree that, for the sake of peace and further progress in East-West relations, instability in the region must be avoided. No such understanding was possible or conceivable a year or two earlier.

Secretary of State James A. Baker 3rd, upholding the aspirations of East Europeans for wider freedoms, said, "I think there is a way to speak to that without . . . inciting rebellion and . . . creating instability, which would have significant adverse results in terms of our relationship with the countries of Eastern Europe and, for that matter, our relationship with the Soviet Union." Baker's opposite number, Soviet Foreign Minister Eduard A. Shevardnadze, signaled Moscow's acceptance of change in a speech before the United Nations in September 1989. "It is no secret," he said, "that we were not enthusiastic about the election setback of the Polish Communists . . . Nevertheless, we see nothing threatening in the fact that, in accordance with the will of the Polish people, a coalition government has been formed. We wish it every success and are ready to cooperate with it most actively. Tolerance is the norm of civilized behavior." The Cold War antagonists, in short, were learning to use a new vocabulary to define their changing relationship.

The Warsaw Pact and NATO remain intact, although both face severe tests at the dawning of the postimperial stage in Central and Eastern Europe. Military alliances seldom prosper as fears of war recede. In these rapidly changing circumstances, the old assumption that Europe's division can be overcome by dissolving both alliances is widely questioned. Alliance leaders now speak of transforming them into essentially political organizations, acting together to supervise arms reductions, build a framework for stability in Central Europe, and attempt to guide eventual steps toward German unity. The looming prospect of unification has persuaded many Europeans, in the East as well as the West, that the United States must not withdraw from, or substantially reduce, its NATO commitment. Secretary of State Baker has warned that an enlarged Germany could become a loose cannon if it is not securely anchored in NATO and the European Community.

The Warsaw Pact faces its own problems. Military professionals in the West are inclined to doubt that the Soviet Union can place much confidence in its allies now that Communist parties are losing control throughout the bloc. The new government of Czechoslovakia, still headed by a Communist prime minister though without a majority, has requested the withdrawal of Soviet troops from its territory. Jiri Dienstbier, the foreign minister, has said that there is no basis for 70,000 Soviet soldiers to remain in the country since the Kremlin's admission that the 1968 invasion was illegal. Poland's Solidarity-led government also is requesting Soviet troop reductions.

Like the Warsaw Pact, other institutional links are weakening. In spite of all the solemn resolutions calling for the creation of a new "socialist division of labor" to be guided by COMECON, few sophisticated officials in Prague, Budapest, or Warsaw look for economic salvation from that quarter. The East Germans look westward to the European Economic Community and above all to the Federal Republic in Bonn for subsidies, credits, and access to modern technologies. Czechoslovakia's wisest economists have long since concluded that COMECON is a clumsy instrument, in fact an obstacle to the country's acquisition of advanced technologies that only the West and Japan can supply. Without exception, the East bloc countries are eager to expand their trade with the West, a supremely difficult task as long as their export products fall short of international quality standards.

As the countries of the Soviet bloc continue to assert their own identities, long-forgotten issues rise to the surface, and the most important of these is the future of divided Germany. For decades, unification was discussed only in murmurs as a dreaded though distant possibility. The idea that two Germanys were better than one, even if divided by a wall, appealed strongly to Europeans who had suffered under Nazi occupation in World War II. The French and above all the Russians were dead set against any talk of putting the German states together again. The "German question" was seldom raised even in West Germany, except by small ultranationalist fringe groups, and was not raised at all in the East. Now the decades-old assumption that the unification issue was dead or dormant has been called into question.

The reasons are obvious in the current climate. If Europe is to be made whole again, reconciling East and West, how can the Germanys be excluded? The collapse of authority in East Germany has placed the future of Germany on the international agenda again for the first time since the destruction of Adolf Hitler's Third Reich.

Inside West Germany, leaders of the Bavarian Christian Social Union, which is associated with Chancellor Helmut Kohl's Christian Democratic Party, say they will make reunification a key issue in the 1990 federal election. Even if the chancellor should succeed in dissuading his Bavarian partners, the new, nationalistic Republican Party will certainly campaign on the unity issue, which has been written into its election platform.

Already there is agitated talk and press comment in the Federal Republic on the theme that more than fifty years after the start of World War II, whose main political consequence was Germany's partition, the time has come to consider unification. The idea is unthinkable, a West German writer argued, only for people who lack imagination, not for the visionaries who make history. "Where is it written," he added, "that both Germanys have to maintain armies?" The clear thrust of his question was that the two German states, once free of the alliances into which they have been locked, could come together in one neutralized state.

Western strategists are troubled by the thought that a united Germany, withdrawing into neutrality, would unhinge NATO. The Federal Republic, with some 500,000 men under arms, maintains the largest army in NATO. It is also the host country, staging area, and potential battleground for almost as many more foreign troops committed to the Western alliance. East Germany, moreover, is one of the most heavily militarized countries in the world, with almost 400,000 Soviet troops stationed on its cramped territory. It is difficult to conceive of either alliance surviving, the strategists say, without the participation of its own Germans.

No German politician who can be regarded as responsible has raised the possibility of leaving NATO. Horst Teltschik, Chancellor Kohl's foreign policy adviser, sees no conflict between Bonn's active interest in building stronger ties with the East and its continued loyalty to the West. "It's absolutely wrong," he said, "to say that West Germany is reorienting itself toward the East. We can't pursue an active Eastern policy if there's not a strong NATO alliance, a close friendship with the United States and France, and an effective and dynamic European integration process." Other knowledgeable Germans discount the idea that their country is drifting from its Western moorings.

Neither the Soviet Union nor the United States appears ready to contemplate a united Germany in the heart of Europe in present circumstances. But the "German question" is not likely to disappear from the international agenda. Some in the West, notably in France, have reconsidered their historical opposition to the idea of a single united Germany, provided that it becomes the stout pillar of a strengthened European Community with a common policy toward the East. Where that would leave the rest of Europe, including the Soviet Union, remains an unanswered question.

Although Mikhail Gorbachev likes to talk about East and West coming together in "a common European home," he has said that the Soviet Union opposes the GDR's absorption into an enlarged Germany. On December 9, 1989, addressing the Soviet Central Committee, Gorbachev said: "It is necessary to proceed from postwar realities — the existence of two sovereign German states . . . Departures from this threaten . . . destabilization of Europe. Naturally, this is not to say that relations between them cannot change. Peaceful cooperation between the GDR and the [Federal Republic] can and must develop. As for the future, it will take shape in the course of history, in the framework of the development of the general European process."

Gorbachev did not appear to rule out unification in any and all conditions. Neither he nor President Bush is in a position to control events in the two Germanys. Both are attempting to cool the enthusiasm of the Germans for a quick plunge into unification. The idea is likely to become more acceptable if the developing "general European process" should produce mutual arms reductions, leading to a further relaxation of East-West tensions, with both German states integrated into a broadened European Community that does not exclude close ties with the United States and the Soviet Union.

That scenario strikes many Cold War veterans as nightmarish because, they say, it could upset the military balance that has kept Europe at peace since 1945. The fact remains, however, that just as the Soviet Union finds it increasingly difficult to hold its allies in line, the countries of Western Europe are becoming more assertive and less ready to follow the lead of the United States in alliance matters. Jacques Delors, president of the European Commission, puts the case bluntly: "Europeans must become more responsible for the other [that is, East] Europeans. It's not just for the Americans and the Russians to decide ex cathedra what we're going to do in Europe. That's over." The West Germans, in particular, have grown far more self-confident. They expect to play a bigger role in NATO and the European Community, one that would be commensurate with their great economic power.

They have taken the lead in cultivating trade, financial, and cultural ties with Eastern Europe, not just with their fellow Germans in the East. Hungary, for example, has concluded ten times more joint ventures with West German companies than with American firms. Bonn also has been generous with credits to Poland, a reassertion of historical German interests in Eastern Europe.

West German business leaders are even more interested in the GDR, whose stagnating economy presents new opportunities for profitable investment. With money and technology from the West, it is not inconceivable that the hardworking East Germans could make a success of *perestroika* long before the Soviets, the Poles, or the Hungarians. Recent polls by West German organizations indicate that a majority of GDR citizens, having learned to march in support of their demands for a better, freer life, would prefer to stay and go on changing the system from within rather than be absorbed into the Federal Republic.

Many of the recent East German refugees, interviewed in the West, say their reasons for leaving were primarily political, not economic. They once hoped that reform in the Soviet Union would spread to their own country. They yearned for a German Gorbachev who would blast open the blocked channels of communication between the state and its alienated citizens. It was long past time, they said, to retire the elderly Stalinists in command positions for whom change was the eternal enemy, to end the persecution of people with their own ideas, and to stop treating everyone who questioned the party's official line as a criminal. East German versions of *glasnost* and *perestroika* would have satisfied them, some said, but they grew tired of waiting.

These frustrated hopes are widely shared in Eastern Europe. Many people told me that they dreamed of living in a "normal" country. That code word meant a country where things work, an open society where the people's needs and wishes are taken into account. Lech Walesa, for example, said the real issue in Poland was "how to get out of this abnormal system that can only produce absurdity." In Hungary the preferred code word is "European." Politicians involved in negotiating terms for the transition to multiparty elections say their goal is a more "European" political system. That is a discreet way of saying that the system imposed by the Soviet Union is neither normal nor European, that they prefer a Western model.

After a fumbling start, the industrial democracies have now overcome their hesitations about helping Poland and Hungary to begin dismantling their failed command economies and to introduce market-driven systems. President Bush started the bidding with an offer of $169 million to Poland and $25 million to Hungary. Congress, in a generous mood, more than doubled the president's request for aid to Poland. It voted to create an "enterprise fund" that would provide loans, grants, insurance, technical assistance, and training. The bill authorized $938 million over three years, most of the money coming from the federal treasury. These amounts were soon overshadowed by the European Community's plan for a $660 million economic assistance program in 1990, more than twice the total pledged the previous year. Poland, with four times the population of Hungary and a more crushing foreign debt, would get the greater share. By far the largest contribution to Polish recovery came from West Germany. On a visit to Warsaw, Chancellor Kohl signed an agreement to provide the Poles with $2.2 billion.

There can be no ironclad guarantees that generous Western assistance will put those vanguard countries on the high road to political freedom and financial solvency. The risk of failure is undeniable. Why, then, should the United States and the European Community send good money after bad — as many have argued — to ease their difficult passage from totalitarian misrule to parliamentary democracy? The answer comes down to what President Bush has called "the vision thing." A succession of American Presidents and secretaries of state have urged the peoples of Eastern Europe to liberate themselves from totalitarian rule, coupling their rhetoric with implicit or explicit promises of help. In 1982, soon after the imposition of martial law in Poland, Secretary of State Alexander Haig promised a major program of economic aid "when the basic rights of the Polish people are restored and their quest for a more decent society resumed."

Now that the Poles have legalized Solidarity, held the nearest thing to a free election in Eastern Europe, restored human rights, and installed a new government led by Solidarity, they have a right to expect that the United States will keep its word. No responsible East European expects a new Marshall Plan. All are aware that the United States, laboring under its own enormous budget and trade deficits, simply can't afford largesse on that scale. But Poland, Czechoslovakia, and Hungary need breathing room. The precarious transition they have undertaken is bound to fail, particularly in Poland, if there is no bread and meat on the nation's dinner tables. The United States and the European Community, which spend billions of dollars a year to pile up and store mountains of surplus food, can and should do more to help the Poles through their immediate emergency; such help will not exhaust their resources.

Hungary's short-term situation is less desperate than Poland's. But both countries will need financial assistance to ease their debt burdens and acquire the Western technologies they need to revive their long-mismanaged industries. Poland's external debt of close to $40 billion has almost doubled since 1981. Inflation is raging, all the more so since state controls on many prices have been removed. Chronic shortages, and the unavoidable austerity both countries face as they shut down or cut back failed state industries, could destroy the fragile hopes raised by recent political changes. As Lech Walesa remarked, "If we fail, we can blame the world, even the United States, that you haven't contributed with cooperation."

A failure of vision in Washington and Brussels might well doom the prospects for democratic change in the whole troubled region. American interests in Eastern Europe are primarily political, not economic. U.S. exports to the region, the Soviet Union included, amount to less than 1 percent of the total. Compared with this negligible stake in commerce, the political stake is enormous. It amounts to helping these nations demonstrate that totalitarian rule is not irreversible, that human liberty has a future even in a region the United States has long conceded to Communism, and that over the long term the artificial division of Europe can be peacefully terminated.

One argument for tightfisted policy in the West — that assistance to Eastern Europe could provide Kremlin conservatives with a pretext for overthrowing Mikhail Gorbachev — strikes me as far-fetched. It seems more plausible to suggest that economic success in those countries would strengthen his hand and encourage similar reforms in the Soviet Union. The more traditional argument that new reformist governments in both countries might allow the foreign aid to be wasted in shoring up bankrupt state industries ignores the fact that new people are in charge. Leszek Balcerowicz, the new Polish finance minister, says his goal is to create "a normal market economy of the Western kind." He has talked of combining free prices with a tightly controlled money supply, of setting up a system of commercial banks and a stock market (Hungary has already taken both steps), together with a safety net that would compensate those whose jobs might be abolished when state industries shut down.

None of these changes will be easy to accomplish, but they

should strike Americans as rational goals worthy of their support. We would do well to remember that it was the Communists, not their successors, who brought the economies of Poland and Hungary to their knees.

There is room for doubt about the long-term success of reform in both countries. They are trying to accomplish what has never been attempted elsewhere; that is, to dismantle totalitarian systems without war or revolution and to convert their failed command economies into market-driven systems of production and distribution. The lack of a time-tested scenario would be a poor excuse for withholding the assistance they need to carry out that historic transformation.

# Author's Note

The *New York Times* sent me to Eastern Europe in 1956, at the height of the Cold War, when I was several years younger than my son and daughter are today. As a teenager in Canada, I had been captivated by the writings of Vincent Sheehan *(Not Peace But a Sword)*, John Gunther *(Inside Europe)*, and Negley Farson *(The Way of a Transgressor)*. Reading those books, with their resonant titles, kindled a thought that nothing could be finer than the life of a foreign correspondent. That romantic ambition drew me back into the ruins of Hitler's Third Reich as a junior-grade correspondent for the North American Newspaper Alliance at the end of World War II, in which I had served with the Royal Canadian Air Force. It brought me also to Poland in 1946, my memorable introduction to Eastern Europe, and into the Soviet occupation zone of Germany, which in time would become the German Democratic Republic.

For the next few years, I worked as a journalist in the United States, in a succession of jobs that took me to Los Angeles, to the United Nations, to New York City as an editor on the foreign desk of the *Times,* to Detroit as the *Times's* bureau chief, and to the newspaper's Washington bureau. The overseas opportunity came at last when the *Times* offered me its bureau in Belgrade, Yugoslavia, with freedom to travel through the borderlands between the Soviet Union and Western Europe.

Autumn 1956 turned out to be a season of spectacular upheaval in Eastern Europe, a false dawning of freedom in Poland and Hungary that commanded my full attention. For the next two years I roamed the region, reporting its many agonies and pathetically brief ecstasies in cooperation with my *Times* colleagues John MacCormac in Vienna and Sydney Gruson in Warsaw. There was never enough time to make up for my lack of systematic preparation. I spoke none of the region's many languages, making do with French and German. I also had to bone up on the tangled histories of countries I was seeing for the first time. But that was the way American newspapers, even the elite newspapers like the *Times,* covered the world. They operated on the assumption that a good reporter would come up with "the story" if he were dropped into Outer Mongolia or on the rocky surface of the moon. I like to think that these matters are handled more intelligently nowadays, though the evidence is thin.

Even when I moved on to fresh assignments — India and Pakistan, then Washington again for the *Detroit News* and later for NBC News — my interest in Eastern Europe did not wane. I continued to travel and read after abandoning daily journalism in 1969 for academic pursuits. Twenty years in Academe have not diminished my fascination with that part of the world, nor my commitment to understanding its dynamics. This book is a modest product of that long commitment in an extraordinary period of change.

In the summer of 1988, I spent three months revisiting the region, looking up old friends and discovering new ones who could help me take the measure of that momentous tide of change. (Of the six Soviet bloc countries, Romania alone refused me a visa, for reasons never explained.) A great number of people elsewhere gave generously of their time and knowledge. Most are identified in the text. Others must remain anonymous for their own protection. I am pleased to record a special debt of gratitude to old friends and former colleagues: to Mirjana Petrovic-Komaretsky of the *New York Times* and Dessa Trevisan of the *Times* of London, in Belgrade; also to my departed friend Edmund Jan Osmanczyk and to Marian Podkowinski in Warsaw; Jozsef Szaszi and Istvan Wisinger in Budapest; Eric Bourne of the *Christian Science Monitor* and Paul Lendvai in Vienna; and Klaus Bolling in West Berlin.

Since my return to California, I have depended primarily on press reports to keep my impressions up to date. The dispatches of John Tagliabue and Henry Kamm of the *New York Times*, who share my old beat, helped mightily; also the excellent reports filed by Jackson Diehl of the *Washington Post* and William Etchikson of the *Christian Science Monitor*. As a long-time admirer of *The Economist*, and once its corporate tenant at 25 St. James's Street in London, I must also credit its corps of correspondents in Eastern Europe, who, alas, are mostly anonymous.

A salute is in order to the editors of *The New York Review of Books* for the extraordinarily illuminating essays they have published in recent years tracing political developments in Central and Eastern Europe. Timothy Garton Ash and Abraham Brumberg, in particular, have deepened my understanding through their brilliant analytical pieces out of Poland and Hungary.

Corinne Prevost Abel, my wife and partner through forty-four sometimes stormy years, made her own indispensable contributions. By her reckoning, we have moved thirteen times since we set up housekeeping on Sven Hedin Strasse in Berlin-Zehlendorf as newlyweds. Through all these disruptions she kept her head while I frequently lost mine, never failed to create a serene and stable home environment for our little family, raised two fine children through a series of strange places and strange schools, and still found time to serve as in-house critic of my writings.

I am no less grateful to our son, Mark, a San Francisco editor, who volunteered to review this manuscript, chapter by chapter, as it rolled from my typewriter. His perceptive comments on the work in progress, and his many useful suggestions for improving it, made a significant difference.

Let me, finally, acknowledge the moral support of Arthur Hepner, a friend of many years' standing, who encouraged me to go ahead with this project when others were doubtful.

*— Elie Abel*
*Palo Alto, California*

# Index